1,001 ASVAB Practice Questions

FOR

DUMMIES

A Wiley Brand

by Rod Powers

FOR

DUMMIES

A Wiley Brand

Contents at a Glance

Table of Contents

Introduction

1 f you're ready to ace the ASVAB, you've come to the right place. The ASVAB, otherwise known as the Armed Services Vocational Aptitude Battery, compiles nine subtests into one very long exam. Four of the subtests (the math and language arts ones) determine if you qualify for military service, and each remaining subtest measures your knowledge of certain information the military has deemed important. How you score on the ASVAB determines what military jobs you may be a match for. Most military jobs require a minimum combination score that you must reach to qualify for that specific job. Therefore, studying for and doing well on the ASVAB is vital to enlisting in the military and landing your desired career.

This workbook gives you 1,001 practice questions similar to the types of questions you'll see on the actual ASVAB. You can start at question 1 and then skip to question 20 or 783 or 999, or you can answer all the questions in order. Or you can concentrate on one or two specific subtests until you feel comfortable with them and then work your way around to the others. Keep in mind that some subtests complement each other, so thoroughly reviewing one subject may set you up for an even better understanding of another. If you feel knowledgeable about math but not English, or vice versa, you may wish to concentrate on those weaker areas until they rise up to an even level.

Overall, completing 1,001 ASVAB practice questions certainly is no small feat, but rest assured (before you're on night watch duty) you will know the ins and outs of the ASVAB and each subtest with confidence after you complete this workbook.

What You'll Find

The 1,001 practice ASVAB questions in this book are divided among nine chapters, each one representing an ASVAB subtest. Each chapter simulates a variety of questions you may face on test day according to that specific subject. The questions in each chapter are then broken into subcategories, where similar topics within the subtest are grouped together. Some questions are accompanied by an image or diagram that you need to refer to in order to answer the question correctly.

After you've answered the questions for one chapter or subcategory, or even answered just one question, you can flip to Chapter 10 in the back of the book and check your answers. There, you find thorough explanations for each problem, often including detailed processes using formulas or definitions to explain the correct answer. In many cases, studying an answer explanation can help you better understand a difficult subject, so spend as much time as you need reviewing the explanations.

Beyond the Book

This book gives you plenty of ASVAB questions to work on. But maybe you want to track your progress as you tackle the questions, or maybe you're having trouble with certain types of questions and wish they were all presented in one place where you could methodically make your way through them. You're in luck. Your book purchase comes with a free one-year subscription to all 1,001 practice questions online. You get on-the-go access any way you want it — from your computer, smartphone, or tablet. Track your progress and view personalized reports that show what you need to study the most. Study what, where, when, and how you want.

What you'll find online

The online practice that comes free with this book offers the same 1,001 questions and answers that are available here. The beauty of the online questions is that you can customize your online practice to focus on the topic areas that give you the most trouble. So if you need help with Electronics Information or Arithmetic Reasoning, just select those question types online and start practicing. Or if you're short on time but want to get a mixed bag of a limited number of questions, you can specify the number of questions you want to practice. Whether you practice a few hundred questions in one sitting or a couple dozen, and whether you focus on a few types of questions or practice every type, the online program keeps track of the questions you get right and wrong so you can monitor your progress and spend time studying exactly what you need.

You can access this online tool using a PIN code, as described in the next section. Keep in mind that you can create only one login with your PIN. After the PIN is used, it's no longer valid and is nontransferable. So you can't share your PIN with other users after you've established your login credentials.

This product also comes with an online Cheat Sheet that helps you up your odds of performing well on the ASVAB. No matter how hard you study for the ASVAB, you'll likely come across a few questions where you don't have a clue. Check out the free Cheat Sheet at www.dummies. com/cheatsheet/1001ASVAB for pointers on setting up a study schedule, advice on boosting your knowledge in weak areas, and ways to memorize information. (No PIN required. You can access this info right now before you've even registered to use the online practice questions.)

How to register

To gain access to the online version of all 1,001 practice questions in this book, all you have to do is register. Just follow these simple steps:

1. **Find your PIN code.**

   - **Print book users:** If you purchased a hard copy of this book, turn to the back of this book to find your PIN.

   - **E-book users:** If you purchased this book as an e-book, you can get your PIN by registering your e-book at dummies.com/go/getaccess. Go to this website, find your book and click it, and answer the security question to verify your purchase. Then you'll receive an e-mail with your PIN.

2. **Go to http://onlinepractice.dummies.com.**

3. **Enter your PIN.**

4. **Follow the instructions to create an account and establish your personal login information.**

That's all there is to it! You can come back to the online program again and again — simply log in with the username and password you choose during your initial login. No need to use the PIN a second time.

If you have trouble with the PIN or can't find it, please contact Wiley Product Technical Support at 800-762-2974 or `http://support.wiley.com`.

Your registration is good for one year from the day you activate your PIN. After that time frame has passed, you can renew your registration for a fee. The website gives you all the important details about how to do so.

Where to Go for Additional Help

It's easy to get overwhelmed when trying to study numerous subjects at once. But don't despair. This book is designed to break everything into less complex categories so you can concentrate on one subject at a time. Practicing in smaller areas within each topic helps you identify your strong points and your weak points.

After you've identified the areas you feel need extra effort, you can start studying on your own and then come back here to answer the questions again to measure your improvement. For example, if your knowledge of engine parts is a little hazy (or nonexistent), try the auto portion of Chapter 6. Check your answers and jot down notes or questions you may have. Then research, say, how pistons work or what is connected to an exhaust. You can look for resources at your local library or online, or ask a friend, coworker, or professor to coach you if he or she seems handy under the hood. You can also check out the *For Dummies* series for books about many of the topics covered on the ASVAB. Head to `www.dummies.com` to see the many books and articles that can help you in your studies.

1,001 ASVAB Practice Questions For Dummies gives you just that — 1,001 practice questions and answers in order for you to simulate the real thing. If you need more in-depth study and direction for the ASVAB and Armed Forces Qualification Test (AFQT), you may wish to pick up the following Dummies products:

- ✔ *ASVAB For Dummies:* This book coaches you on everything ASVAB, from the number of questions and amount of time you have to complete each section to the specific information asked under each subtest.

- ✔ *ASVAB AFQT For Dummies:* This book reviews the core concepts that comprise the AFQT portion of the ASVAB, providing the tools you need to get your best score and become eligible for military enlistment.

- ✔ *ASVAB Practice For Dummies App:* This app provides you a portable electronic ASVAB study tool for your iOS, Android, Kindle Fire, or Nook.

Part I
The Questions

In this part . . .

If you're planning on joining the military, you're going to do a lot of counting (think push-ups, pull-ups, miles, targets, grenades . . . you get the picture) and counting off. You may as well get used to it: One. Two. Three . . .

So it just makes sense to answer 1,001 questions on all sorts of topics when you're preparing to take the ASVAB. Here are the categories of problems you'll face:

- Language arts (Chapters 1 and 2)
- Mathematics (Chapters 3 and 4)
- Science (Chapter 5)
- Technical skills (Chapters 6, 7, and 8)
- Spatial skills (Chapter 9)

Chapter 1

Word Knowledge: Testing Your Vocabulary

The Word Knowledge subtest is one of the most important subtests on the ASVAB. This subtest comprises a significant portion of your Armed Forces Qualification Test (AFQT) score — the score that determines your eligibility for military service. To do well on this subtest, you need to be pretty handy with your lingo — that is, your vocabulary. The purpose of the Word Knowledge subtest is to measure your ability to figure out what most words in the English language mean. When taking this subtest, you may come across words you've never seen before, or you may know the words right away (a hopeful scenario). In any event, continually testing (and developing) your word-knowledge skills gives you the best chance for success. Lucky for you, this chapter gives you plenty of practice to help you do just that.

The Questions You'll Work On

The Word Knowledge questions come in one of three forms:

- **Definition:** This type of question asks you for a straight definition of the word given.
- **Sentence context:** When you see an underlined word in a sentence, your job is to choose the answer closest in meaning to the underlined word.
- **Antonyms:** Choose the answer most opposite in meaning to the word given.

What to Watch Out For

Keep in mind the following points as you work on the Word Knowledge questions in this chapter:

- If you see an unfamiliar word, try to figure out the root of the word (the base) to see whether you recognize it.
- A prefix or suffix can help you figure out the meaning of an unknown word if you know how the given prefix or suffix changes the meaning.
- Some questions ask you to choose the word *closest in meaning* to the underlined word.
- Some sentence questions offer clues to the correct answer choice in their context.
- An *antonym* is a word most opposite in meaning to the given word. Although antonym questions are rare on the Word Knowledge subtest, they show up occasionally, so be on the lookout!

Definition

1. Cognizant most nearly means

  (A)   conscious

  (B)   ignorant

  (C)   fearful

  (D)   snooty

2. Abbreviate most nearly means

  (A)   supply

  (B)   enlighten

  (C)   condense

  (D)   satisfy

3. Clarity most nearly means

  (A)   clearness

  (B)   foggy

  (C)   appearance

  (D)   regretful

4. Culminate most nearly means

  (A)   destroy

  (B)   complete

  (C)   fix

  (D)   accumulate

5. Ardent most nearly means

  (A)   trustworthy

  (B)   passionate

  (C)   diligent

  (D)   lonely

6. Falter most nearly means

  (A)   hesitate

  (B)   encourage

  (C)   fail

  (D)   deny

7. Hamper most nearly means

  (A)   regulate

  (B)   prevent

  (C)   prevail

  (D)   discourage

8. Malicious most nearly means

  (A)   grave

  (B)   large

  (C)   harmful

  (D)   exhausting

9. Obtrude most nearly means

  (A)   large

  (B)   distinct

  (C)   offensive

  (D)   intrude

10. Palpable most nearly means

  (A)   practiced

  (B)   touchable

  (C)   collective

  (D)   harmed

11. Quaff most nearly means

  (A)   ducks

  (B)   embarrassment

  (C)   drink

  (D)   loud

12. Savory most nearly means

  (A)   enjoyment

  (B)   spicy

  (C)   appreciative

  (D)   candid

13. <u>Vagary</u> most nearly means

(A) hardship

(B) valiant

(C) fury

(D) change

14. <u>Wean</u> most nearly means

(A) whisper

(B) halt

(C) care

(D) admit

15. <u>Yen</u> most nearly means

(A) hatred

(B) Chinese

(C) desire

(D) calming

16. <u>Diverse</u> most nearly means

(A) diving

(B) various

(C) prejudice

(D) similar

17. <u>Entrust</u> most nearly means

(A) regain

(B) assign

(C) regard

(D) hope

18. <u>Disregard</u> most nearly means

(A) complicate

(B) esteem

(C) respect

(D) ignore

19. <u>Amenable</u> most nearly means

(A) amended

(B) prepared

(C) guided

(D) cooperative

20. <u>Autonomous</u> most nearly means

(A) barred

(B) enslaved

(C) automatic

(D) independent

21. <u>Orate</u> most nearly means

(A) decorate

(B) speak

(C) hygiene

(D) assign

22. <u>Superlative</u> most nearly means

(A) unfortunate

(B) dilapidated

(C) average

(D) exceptional

23. <u>Except</u> most nearly means

(A) decide

(B) besides

(C) allow

(D) deny

24. <u>Criticize</u> most nearly means

(A) soothe

(B) gratify

(C) disapprove

(D) compliment

25. <u>Empower</u> most nearly means

(A) forbid

(B) reject

(C) fuel

(D) allow

26. <u>Invert</u> most nearly means

(A) hold

(B) keep

(C) flip

(D) avoid

27. <u>Divulge</u> most nearly means

(A) eat

(B) talk

(C) confess

(D) steal

28. <u>Prolific</u> most nearly means

(A) barren

(B) abundant

(C) profound

(D) life

29. <u>Munificent</u> most nearly means

(A) magnificent

(B) generous

(C) glowing

(D) helpful

30. <u>Mirth</u> most nearly means

(A) spice

(B) joy

(C) satisfaction

(D) solemn

31. <u>Ken</u> most nearly means

(A) doll

(B) measurement

(C) ambulatory

(D) perception

32. <u>Momentum</u> most nearly means

(A) running

(B) stabilized

(C) force

(D) pushing

33. <u>Facilitate</u> most nearly means

(A) renew

(B) illuminate

(C) prepare

(D) expedite

34. <u>Attainment</u> most nearly means

(A) party

(B) finish

(C) smart

(D) review

35. <u>Forfeit</u> most nearly means

(A) gain

(B) sacrifice

(C) harm

(D) gift

36. <u>Belie</u> most nearly means

(A) false

(B) believe

(C) between

(D) regain

37. <u>Aplomb</u> most nearly means

(A) devotion

(B) confidence

(C) subordination

(D) reliance

38. <u>Indolence</u> most nearly means

(A) involvement

(B) enthusiasm

(C) laziness

(D) boredom

39. <u>Phrase</u> most nearly means

(A) speech

(B) expression

(C) letters

(D) language

40. <u>Calamity</u> most nearly means

(A) desert

(B) disaster

(C) remorse

(D) overeating

41. <u>Comprehensive</u> most nearly means

(A) understanding

(B) knowledge

(C) inclusive

(D) assuring

42. <u>Remunerate</u> most nearly means

(A) generate

(B) compensate

(C) collect

(D) dissolve

43. <u>Pathos</u> most nearly means

(A) emotion

(B) pathetic

(C) ruins

(D) hardship

44. <u>Oscillate</u> most nearly means

(A) destroy

(B) swing

(C) regulate

(D) spiral

45. <u>Repose</u> most nearly means

(A) approve

(B) peace

(C) qualified

(D) retroactive

46. <u>Cease</u> most nearly means

(A) report

(B) halt

(C) remember

(D) fold

47. <u>Dupe</u> most nearly means

(A) eat

(B) change

(C) react

(D) fool

48. <u>Truncate</u> most nearly means

(A) shorten

(B) fixate

(C) pretend

(D) turn

49. Predator most nearly means

(A) alien

(B) hunter

(C) species

(D) hungry

50. Original most nearly means

(A) earliest

(B) latest

(C) designer

(D) new

51. Abolish most nearly means

(A) preserve

(B) harm

(C) end

(D) enslave

52. Abominable most nearly means

(A) avalanche

(B) crazy

(C) incredible

(D) awful

53. Quell most nearly means

(A) launch

(B) support

(C) enrich

(D) suppress

54. Ironic most nearly means

(A) catastrophic

(B) belittling

(C) unfortunate

(D) sarcastic

55. Sober most nearly means

(A) suppressive

(B) sedated

(C) aware

(D) inebriated

56. Forebode most nearly means

(A) try

(B) warn

(C) realize

(D) connect

Sentence Context

57. After the long, freezing winter, all they wanted to do was bask in the Florida sunshine.

(A) play

(B) run

(C) sleep

(D) relax

58. Brevity is the soul of wit.

(A) beauty

(B) intelligence

(C) terseness

(D) humor

59. Mary decided to defer college for a year to travel with her boyfriend.

(A) attend

(B) postpone

(C) allow

(D) ponder

60. The senator hoped his views on tax breaks would convince the civilians to <u>endorse</u> him.

(A) like

(B) support

(C) destroy

(D) discuss

61. The <u>glimmer</u> of hope he had for their love told him there might be a chance.

(A) satisfaction

(B) reality

(C) loss

(D) glimpse

62. The doctor was aware the man had been consuming <u>illicit</u> drugs.

(A) forbidden

(B) helpful

(C) regular

(D) harmful

63. The party became <u>jovial</u> after the news of a new baby was shared.

(A) disheartening

(B) disappointing

(C) hopeful

(D) joyful

64. The <u>kinetic</u> energy was converted to electricity.

(A) regulated

(B) disbursed

(C) frantic

(D) moving

65. The <u>lascivious</u> acts he committed were punishable to the full extent of the law.

(A) offensive

(B) horrendous

(C) loving

(D) shameful

66. The attendant charged Karen a <u>nominal</u> fee to park in the crowded lot.

(A) expensive

(B) insignificant

(C) large

(D) crazy

67. Janice tried her best to talk to her enemy, but it only seemed to <u>perplex</u> the situation.

(A) complicate

(B) help

(C) deter

(D) pressure

68. My grandfather has always been considered a <u>sage</u> in our family.

(A) herb

(B) problem

(C) wise person

(D) old-timer

69. The young apprentice was convinced her chauvinistic boss had <u>ulterior</u> motives.

(A) malicious

(B) hidden

(C) exciting

(D) confusing

70. The politicians were well-known for their <u>venal</u> actions.

(A) corrupt

(B) encouraging

(C) stellar

(D) apprehensive

71. The <u>yearling</u> started to grow mature colored feathers.

(A) one-year-old

(B) goose

(C) animal

(D) pheasant

72. Katie was <u>ignorant</u> to the fact that she was wrong.

(A) blind

(B) aware

(C) wise

(D) used

73. Please <u>remit</u> the following payment to the bursar's office at your earliest convenience.

(A) deny

(B) keep

(C) send

(D) allow

74. Her <u>obdurate</u> attitude was quite apparent when she slammed the door on the hungry, stray kitten.

(A) gentle

(B) insensitive

(C) submissive

(D) compassionate

75. If you choose to <u>accede</u> to these demands, I'll tell my lawyer to back off.

(A) accept

(B) refuse

(C) recommend

(D) challenge

76. The loving couple celebrated their <u>fidelity</u> over the years on their anniversary.

(A) complications

(B) faithfulness

(C) regrets

(D) treachery

77. There seemed to be a likely story <u>among</u> all the gossipers.

(A) behind

(B) about

(C) between

(D) around

78. My mom's annoying demand to do these dishes has become <u>redundant</u>!

(A) repetitive

(B) ridiculous

(C) belittling

(D) overwhelming

79. The threads of the chair <u>intertwine</u>, making a better quality product.

(A) divide

(B) weave

(C) separate

(D) exclude

80. <u>Peruse</u> the instructions and report any issues to the front desk.

(A) analyze

(B) consider

(C) reject

(D) disregard

81. The preacher had to <u>abstain</u> from offending the transgressor.

(A) encourage

(B) denounce

(C) refrain

(D) think

82. The disappearance of the lawnmower from the shed really <u>stumped</u> the landscaper.

(A) helped

(B) confused

(C) annoyed

(D) hindered

83. The stylist hired a new staff she thought would <u>vivify</u> the salon.

(A) invigorate

(B) destroy

(C) enervate

(D) upgrade

84. The gala included a <u>sumptuous</u> selection of cheese and wine.

(A) overwhelming

(B) splendid

(C) regular

(D) simple

85. The operator struggled to answer the customer's <u>query</u>.

(A) question

(B) complaint

(C) input

(D) critique

86. The teenager was quite <u>provocative</u> in her prom dress.

(A) alluring

(B) distasteful

(C) beautiful

(D) offensive

87. She really didn't want to sit next to Bob and deal with his <u>officious</u> remarks.

(A) offensive

(B) biased

(C) opinionated

(D) silly

88. Fran was <u>listless</u> after her dog was lost in the storm.

(A) inattentive

(B) enthusiastic

(C) scared

(D) hysterical

89. Many times they had hoped the result would be <u>instant</u>.

(A) immediate

(B) delayed

(C) harmful

(D) negative

90. The lawyer was certain the jury would not <u>censure</u> the politician after reviewing the incident.

(A) condemn

(B) arouse

(C) review

(D) pardon

91. Everyone who lived by the live volcano became aware of its <u>peril</u>.

(A) beauty

(B) security

(C) danger

(D) smell

92. Barry thought he could <u>forge</u> the paperwork without getting caught.

(A) trash

(B) destroy

(C) fabricate

(D) forget

93. The wedding designer told the couple the flowers were <u>edible</u>.

(A) digestible

(B) colorful

(C) imported

(D) expensive

94. The realty companies were attempting to <u>contend</u> for the top spot in the county.

(A) debate

(B) compete

(C) wrestle

(D) meddle

95. The witness was happy to <u>corroborate</u> the man's explanation.

(A) exaggerate

(B) destroy

(C) confirm

(D) question

96. The Army commander decided to <u>avert</u> trouble by heading back to headquarters.

(A) help

(B) complicate

(C) prevent

(D) attack

97. The nanny disciplined the toddler with great <u>asperity</u>.

(A) pride

(B) division

(C) irritation

(D) confusion

98. The audience continued the <u>adulation</u> after the show.

(A) applause

(B) silence

(C) resentment

(D) whistling

99. Angie looked on with <u>sorrow</u> as her grandfather's farm was repossessed.

(A) frustration

(B) irritation

(C) carelessness

(D) grief

100. Most of the consumers were satisfied with their insurance <u>coverage</u>.

    (A) rejections

    (B) losses

    (C) protection

    (D) treatment

101. Harold used only <u>premium</u> gasoline for his Corvette.

    (A) good

    (B) better

    (C) superior

    (D) clean

102. The homes in the area were sold at a <u>premium</u>.

    (A) auction

    (B) price

    (C) superior

    (D) downfall

103. Sandra carried on with her <u>pretentious</u> attitude in front of the cheerleading squad.

    (A) snobby

    (B) ignorant

    (C) modest

    (D) humble

104. He gave a <u>malign</u> report about the incident.

    (A) ridiculous

    (B) cancerous

    (C) delayed

    (D) harmful

105. It was a <u>thrill</u> to meet the celebrity at the gala.

    (A) disappointment

    (B) boredom

    (C) excitement

    (D) fun

106. She entered a zone of <u>inertia</u> when she finally returned home after a long day at work.

    (A) excitement

    (B) enchantment

    (C) immobility

    (D) relief

107. The aftermath of the storm brought much <u>turmoil</u>.

    (A) death

    (B) chaos

    (C) destruction

    (D) sadness

108. The general became aware that the lieutenant general desired to <u>supplant</u> him.

    (A) promote

    (B) supply

    (C) replace

    (D) sacrifice

109. She vocalized <u>emphasis</u> on the syllables.

    (A) screaming

    (B) happiness

    (C) insignificance

    (D) importance

110. The girl at the dance wore <u>scanty</u> clothing.

(A) pretty

(B) expensive

(C) little

(D) ugly

111. The troops were prosecuted for <u>sedition</u> after the incident.

(A) secrecy

(B) insurrection

(C) lying

(D) regression

112. The explanation by the operative was more than <u>specious</u>.

(A) erroneous

(B) practical

(C) unclear

(D) derogatory

113. The <u>shard</u> of the sword was stuck in the rock.

(A) front

(B) beginning

(C) piece

(D) handle

114. His <u>unmitigated</u> success was attributed to his mentor from the company.

(A) candid

(B) complete

(C) half-hearted

(D) horrible

115. The gangsters involved themselves in <u>noisome</u> activity.

(A) loud

(B) immoral

(C) humble

(D) criminal

116. Anna possessed a great <u>allure</u> about her.

(A) cheapness

(B) intelligence

(C) attraction

(D) youthfulness

117. Elmer wished his muscles would <u>intimidate</u> the bully.

(A) encourage

(B) threaten

(C) harm

(D) destroy

118. It was essential that the members follow the <u>canon</u>.

(A) law

(B) presentation

(C) exercise

(D) direction

Antonyms

119. The word most opposite in meaning to <u>delay</u> is

(A) rush

(B) curb

(C) defer

(D) restrain

120. The word most opposite in meaning to
<u>reflect</u> is

(A) ponder

(B) consider

(C) ignore

(D) speculate

121. The word most opposite in meaning to
<u>blame</u> is

(A) attribute

(B) reprove

(C) muster

(D) exalt

122. The word most opposite in meaning to
<u>insult</u> is

(A) compliment

(B) sulk

(C) aggravate

(D) abuse

123. The word most opposite in meaning to
<u>forthright</u> is

(A) honest

(B) polite

(C) blunt

(D) outspoken

124. The word most opposite in meaning to
<u>profound</u> is

(A) thorough

(B) mild

(C) absolute

(D) intense

125. The word most opposite in meaning to
<u>keen</u> is

(A) fervent

(B) reluctant

(C) zealous

(D) appetent

Chapter 2

Paragraph Comprehension: Understanding and Analyzing Written Concepts

• •

*T*he Paragraph Comprehension subtest is a very important part of the ASVAB because it accounts for a significant portion of your AFQT score (you know, the Armed Forces Qualification Test — the score that determines your eligibility for military service). To do well on this subtest, you need to have strong reading-comprehension skills. The Paragraph Comprehension subtest measures your ability to understand what you read and then draw conclusions from the material. The questions are based on random excerpts and passages. You read each passage and answer questions about it.

The Questions You'll Work On

The Paragraph Comprehension questions take one of four forms:

- **Finding specific information:** This question type asks you to give specific information found within the passage, such as a number or a month.

- **Recognizing the main idea:** Questions in this category ask you to figure out the topic or main idea of the passage.

- **Determining word meaning in context:** This type of question asks you to figure out how a specified word is being used in the passage and then to choose the appropriate answer based on the context.

- **Drawing an implication from a stated idea:** This question type asks you to draw a conclusion based on what you read.

Note: To streamline the presentation of passages and questions in this chapter, I present each passage with one or more questions from the various categories following it. I put the category each question fits into in italics and parentheses after Choice (D).

What to Watch Out For

Keep in mind the following pointers as you work on the Paragraph Comprehension questions in this chapter:

- When a question asks you for the main idea, focus on what the entire passage — not just one sentence — is about.

- Choose your answers based on the passage, not your opinion of the given subject.

- Vague answer options are usually incorrect, so be wary of picking them.

- Words often have more than one meaning, so make sure you understand how the word in question is being used in the context before you choose your answer.

Joe felt that his greatest accomplishment was helping to organize and create the City Antique Car Club in 1995. When his fellow organizer and president of the club left town five years ago, the acting VP, Al, took over the presidency of the club. Joe and Al were never on good terms. Not long after Al took over the presidency, Joe and Al had a terrible argument. Al was a charter member of the club and has a 1967 Chevy Chevelle muscle car with a big block. Joe has to admit that it is a nice car.

126. How long has Joe been a member of the club?

  (A) since 1995

  (B) since 1967

  (C) since 2005

  (D) since five years ago

  (Finding Specific Information)

127. Based on the information in the passage, which of the following is a reasonable conclusion?

  (A) Al was the founder of the car club.

  (B) Joe and Al used to be friends.

  (C) Joe likes Al's car but doesn't like Al.

  (D) Joe is dating Al's ex-wife.

  (Recognizing the Main Idea)

128. In the passage, what is the meaning of *block?*

  (A) to stop

  (B) the casting that contains the cylinders of an internal combustion engine

  (C) a lightweight wooden or plastic building toy that's usually provided in sets

  (D) a quantity, number, or section of things dealt with as a unit

  (Determining Word Meaning in Context)

In prehistoric times, people hardly ever saw each other and had much less to do with each other. Human interaction was not the chief problem in this society. Their environmental problems had to do with such things as the elements, violent storms, extremes of heat and cold, darkness, and the ever-present menace of wild beasts whose flesh was their food yet who would eat them first unless they were quick in brain and body.

129. Which of the following is not supported by the paragraph?

  (A) Primitive man had to cope with extreme weather conditions.

  (B) Primitive man did not struggle with human relationships.

  (C) Primitive man ate flesh.

  (D) Primitive man had little contact with other humans.

  (Finding Specific Information)

130. What is the main thought of the paragraph?

  (A) Prehistoric people had little human contact.

  (B) Prehistoric man's greatest challenges had to do with their environment.

  (C) Prehistoric man had to be quick and sharp in mind.

  (D) Prehistoric man's chief problem was the weather.

  (Recognizing the Main Idea)

Let me now take you on to the day of the assault. My cousin and I were separated at the outset. I never saw him when we forded the river; when we planted the English flag in the first breach; when we crossed the ditch beyond; and, fighting every inch of our way, entered the town.

It was only at dusk, when the place was ours, and after General Baird himself had found the dead body of Tippoo under a heap of the slain, that Herncastle and I met.

131. What would be a good title of the passage?

(A) "Attacking Japan"

(B) "War without Violence"

(C) "Moving to the Mountains"

(D) "My Account of the War"

(Finding Specific Information)

132. How long was the main character fighting in the area?

(A) two hours

(B) from day to dusk

(C) a few days

(D) none of the above

(Finding Specific Information)

133. In this passage, what is the meaning of the word *heap?*

(A) pile

(B) rubbish

(C) marker

(D) note

(Determining Word Meaning in Context)

134. According to the passage, you can assume the main character is

(A) at a community function.

(B) in a war.

(C) dreaming.

(D) moving to a new town.

(Drawing an Implication from a Stated Idea)

Questions 135 through 137 are based on the following passage.

It is a commonly believed theory that global warming is a result of the decay of the ozone layer of the Earth's atmosphere. The theory concludes that a weak ozone layer allows greater amounts of harmful wavelengths of light to reach the Earth's surface. Recent studies have proposed that the danger produced by the decay of the ozone is not limited to global warming. It has been proposed that permanent eye damage to some animals is being caused by the harmful wavelengths of light that are now reaching the Earth.

135. Which of the following is most strongly supported by the paragraph?

(A) Some wavelengths of light that produce eye damage in certain animals are more likely to hit the Earth due to ozone decay.

(B) The rising temperature of the Earth presents a brutal threat to animals.

(C) Some animals do not experience damage to their eyes when exposed to unfiltered waves of light.

(D) All wavelengths of light from the sun that damage the eyes of animals are blocked by a healthy ozone layer.

(Finding Specific Information)

136. What animals are affected by global warming?

(A) monkeys

(B) terrestrials

(C) frogs

(D) More information is needed.

(Finding Specific Information)

137. In this passage, what does the term *decay* mean?

(A) depletion

(B) rotting

(C) ruin

(D) melting

(Determining Word Meaning in Context)

Questions 138 through 140 are based on the following passage.

One of the first English attempts to settle in the New World was led by Sir Walter Raleigh in 1585. The colony, comprised of about 100 men, was raised on the east coast of North America. Sir Walter Raleigh gave the colony the name of Virginia to honor Queen Elizabeth I, who was known as the "Virgin Queen." Virginia lasted for one year, after which time the settlers returned to England. Raleigh's second attempt to colonize the New World was in Roanoke, Virginia, in the year 1587. The supply ships were delayed and did not arrive until 1590. When the ships arrived there was no longer any evidence of the colony's existence. The Roanoke colony had disappeared except for the word *Croatoan* that was carved into a post.

138. What can be concluded according to the passage?

(A) Sir Walter Raleigh died settling the Roanoke Colony.

(B) Help for the Roanoke Colony was delayed for three years.

(C) The colony left with the Croatoans.

(D) Queen Elizabeth II was the "Virgin Queen."

(Finding Specific Information)

139. How many years have gone by from the beginning to the end of the passage?

(A) 2 years

(B) 3 years

(C) 4 years

(D) 5 years

(Finding Specific Information)

140. What is the author implying when he says that the help found only the word *Croatoan* carved on a post?

(A) that the settlers set up camp with foreigners

(B) that the travelers traded with foreigners

(C) that the Croatoans had something to do with the disappearance of the settlers

(D) that the plan to rescue the settlers was a bad idea

(Drawing an Implication from a Stated Idea)

Questions 141 through 143 are based on the following passage.

The third leading cause of unintentional injury death the world over is drowning. Sad to say, most of these deaths could have been prevented if the simple rules of water safety had been applied. Most drownings are preventable if the victim does not become panicked; therefore, the first and most important safety rule is to remain calm. The ability to swim may save your life, but even an experienced swimmer can panic with fear and stop making rational decisions and begin to flounder. When this happens, the swimmer has taken the first step to drowning. The key to preventing panic is relaxation. When confronted with an emergency, the swimmer must make himself remain calm and in charge, making conscious efforts to escape the situation.

141. According to this passage, what is the first step in drowning?

(A)   going underwater

(B)   giving in to fear

(C)   not wearing a life preserver

(D)   not knowing how to swim

(Finding Specific Information)

142. The word *flounder,* as used in this passage, most nearly means

(A)   a fish.

(B)   a building foundation.

(C)   to splash about helplessly.

(D)   to float.

(Determining Word Meaning in Context)

143. According to the passage, what is the best prevention for drowning?

(A)   staying out of the water

(B)   learning how to swim

(C)   having a buddy nearby

(D)   remaining calm

(Drawing an Implication from a Stated Idea)

Questions 144 through 147 are based on the following passage.

Braille was based on a military code called *night writing,* developed in response to Napoleon's demand for a means for soldiers to communicate silently at night and without light. A soldier invented a tactile system of raised dots. Napoleon rejected it as too complicated, but Louis Braille simplified it for use by the blind. Braille is still used today, consisting of one to six raised dots, representing the alphabet, that a person can feel with his or her fingertips.

144. Why was Napoleon interested in Braille?

(A)   He was blind.

(B)   He wanted to help the blind.

(C)   He couldn't read.

(D)   He wanted a code that could be read at night.

(Finding Specific Information)

145. How many raised dots are used to form each letter of the alphabet in Braille?

(A)   three

(B)   six

(C)   one to six

(D)   none of the above

(Finding Specific Information)

146. What was Louis Braille's contribution to the invention of this reading system?

(A)   He taught blind people how to read.

(B)   He urged Napoleon to have it developed.

(C)   He named it.

(D)   He simplified someone else's complicated idea.

(Recognizing the Main Idea)

147. The word *tactile,* as used in this passage, most nearly means

(A)   a sharp object.

(B)   words on a printed page.

(C)   something that is sticky.

(D)   something that can be felt with the fingers.

(Determining Word Meaning in Context)

Questions 148 through 150 are based on the following passage.

The Fourth Amendment to the Constitution protects citizens against unreasonable seizures and searches. A probable cause must be met in order for a written search warrant to be issued by a judge. No search of a person's home or personal effects may be conducted lawfully without a search warrant. This means a judge must conclude that a legal authorization is necessary upon reviewing factual evidence before a warrant may be issued.

148. According to this paragraph, what do police officers need in order to search a person's home?

   (A) legal authorization

   (B) direct evidence of a crime

   (C) to read the person his or her constitutional rights

   (D) a reasonable belief that a crime has occurred

   (Finding Specific Information)

149. What is the topic of the passage?

   (A) getting approval from a judge

   (B) searching homes

   (C) the Fourth Amendment

   (D) police

   (Recognizing the Main Idea)

150. Which of the following would be considered "probable cause" for a search warrant, according to this paragraph?

   (A) a reasonable belief that a crime has occurred

   (B) sworn testimony of the police

   (C) direct evidence of a crime

   (D) a judge's decision

   (Drawing an Implication from a Stated Idea)

Questions 151 and 152 are based on the following passage.

The modern nominating process of U.S. presidential elections currently consists of two major parts: a series of presidential primary elections and caucuses held in each state and the presidential nominating conventions held by each political party. This process was never included in the United States Constitution and thus evolved over time as the political parties needed to clear the field of candidates.

151. Why are presidential nominating conventions used?

   (A) They're held in each state in order to showcase popular candidates.

   (B) They're used to fulfill mandates set forth in the Constitution.

   (C) They're used to introduce the candidates.

   (D) They're used to reduce the number of individuals running for the office.

   (Finding Specific Information)

152. What can be concluded from the passage?

   (A) Presidential primary elections should be illegal.

   (B) The Republican Party holds a primary election in Florida.

   (C) The Constitution is not necessary to elect a president.

   (D) The presidential nominating process needs to be changed.

   (Drawing an Implication from a Stated Idea)

Questions 153 and 154 are based on the following passage.

As in most fields of occupation, computer scientists have been attempting to make an independent living by creating and running profitable businesses. They have been looking into various ways to run successful businesses for 20 years. For their business to be profitable, it is necessary for them to develop products that produce profit. Because of the profitability motive, computer science has lost its creative aspect.

153. How many years have computer scientists been trying to run successful businesses?

(A) 10

(B) 15

(C) 20

(D) 25

(Finding Specific Information)

154. Which of the following assumptions is most necessary in order for the conclusion in the passage to be drawn from the given argument?

(A) A program cannot be both creative and profitable.

(B) All computer programs must lack creativity in order to be well received.

(C) All computer scientists entirely disregard creativity and choose instead to pursue profit.

(D) Computer scientists are obsessed with the profitability of their work.

(Drawing an Implication from a Stated Idea)

Questions 155 through 157 are based on the following passage.

It is not easy to make a determination of the cause of cancer. There are many factors that are known to put individuals at an increased risk of having the greatly feared disease. Some of the known factors include tobacco use, certain infections, radiation, a lack of physical activity, obesity, and environmental pollutants. Any of these can cause direct damage to genes or combine with preexisting genetic faults to cause cancer. It has been found that approximately 5 to 10 percent of cancers are wholly hereditary.

155. According to the paragraph, which statement is not true?

(A) Tobacco use increases the risk of cancer.

(B) Damaged genes cause cancer.

(C) Radiation will not increase risk of cancer.

(D) Genetic faults are a cause of cancer.

(Finding Specific Information)

156. In this passage, what does the word *faults* mean?

(A) weaknesses

(B) defects

(C) fractures

(D) merits

(Determining Word Meaning in Context)

157. What can be concluded from the passage?

(A) Most cancers are not hereditary.

(B) Most cancers are caused by tobacco use.

(C) Most cancers are easy to detect.

(D) Most cancers kill.

(Drawing an Implication from a Stated Idea)

Questions 158 through 160 are based on the following passage.

Play spaces, such as ice rinks, fields, playgrounds, and skate parks, are great for community members. They provide places where kids and families can gather naturally and enjoy their time with one another outside. When community members have access to these types of quality play spaces within walking distance from their homes, it significantly improves the community's well-being.

158. According to the passage, what is not listed as a play space?

(A) skate park

(B) ice rink

(C) basketball court

(D) field

(Finding Specific Information)

159. What is the main idea of the passage?

(A) Play spaces improve society.

(B) Play spaces are few and far between.

(C) Play spaces are expensive.

(D) Play spaces are fun.

(Recognizing the Main Idea)

160. What can be concluded from the passage?

(A) People like to go play.

(B) Communities with play areas within walking distance are better communities.

(C) Communities can't afford many play spaces.

(D) Kids want to have more play spaces.

(Drawing an Implication from a Stated Idea)

Questions 161 through 164 are based on the following passage.

There seem to be abundant job opportunities for nurses these days. Plus, nurses receive decent salaries and benefits. Nursing jobs are very flexible with work schedules. There is an array of specialties when it comes to nursing positions in a variety of settings. It is true that nursing offers room for advancement and raises. Overall, the biggest advantage to being a nurse must be the satisfaction you get from knowing you are helping others.

161. According to the paragraph, what is the best part about being a nurse?

(A) getting good benefits

(B) helping people

(C) having three days off in a row

(D) having room for advancement

(Finding Specific Information)

162. According to the passage, which of the following is not a benefit of being a nurse?

(A) room for advancement

(B) array of specialties

(C) convenient uniforms

(D) flexible scheduling

(Finding Specific Information)

163. What is the main thought of the paragraph?

(A) There are a lot of nurses.

(B) There are a lot of nursing jobs.

(C) Nursing pays well.

(D) Nursing has many benefits.

(Recognizing the Main Idea)

164. In this paragraph, what is the meaning of the word *abundant*?

(A) excellent

(B) plenty

(C) few

(D) competitive

(Determining Word Meaning in Context)

Questions 165 through 167 are based on the following passage.

Carrying the sand and stone from stock piles to mixing board in shovels should never be practiced. It takes from 100 to 150 shovelfuls of stone to make 1 cu. yd.; it, therefore, costs 50 cts.

per cu. yd. to carry it 100 ft. and return empty handed, for in walking short distances the men travel very slowly — about 150 ft. per minute. It costs more to walk a half dozen paces with stone carried in shovels than to wheel it in barrows.

165. According to the passage, how many feet per minute do the workers walk when carrying stone?

(A)   100 feet

(B)   150 feet

(C)   a half-dozen feet

(D)   50 feet

(Finding Specific Information)

166. In this passage, what is meant by *paces?*

(A)   workers

(B)   mixtures

(C)   animals

(D)   steps

(Determining Word Meaning in Context)

167. According to the passage, what does the author recommend?

(A)   transporting the mixture in a wheelbarrow

(B)   carrying the mixture to the mixing board

(C)   calculating every measurement

(D)   working hard

(Drawing an Implication from a Stated Idea)

Questions 168 through 170 are based on the following passage.

She had spent summers in the country, of course; and she knew and loved nature, but it had been five years since she had been free to get outside the city limits for more than a day, and then not far. It seemed to her now that she had never sensed the beauty of the country as today; perhaps because she had never needed it as now.

168. According to the passage, what did "she" need?

(A)   to spend time in the city

(B)   to spend time in the country

(C)   to go on a vacation

(D)   to take a nap under a tree

(Finding Specific Information)

169. What is the main thought of the paragraph?

(A)   She loves nature.

(B)   She spent the winters in the city.

(C)   She was enjoying being in the country.

(D)   She couldn't wait to get out of the city.

(Recognizing the Main Idea)

170. In the passage, what is meant by *spent?*

(A)   ignored

(B)   purchased

(C)   passed time

(D)   wasted

(Determining Word Meaning in Context)

It is to be regretted that the narrative of the explorer affords no clue to the precise locality of this interesting discovery, but since it is doubtful that the mariner journeyed very far on foot from the head of navigation of the Potomac, it seems highly probable that the first American bison seen by Europeans, other than the Spaniards, was found within 15 miles, or even less, of the capital of the United States, and possibly within the District of Columbia itself.

171. According to the passage, what did the explorer discover?

(A)   new land

(B)   the District of Columbia

(C)   American bison

(D)   the Potomac

(Finding Specific Information)

Questions 172 through 175 are based on the following passage.

In June and July, the thick-set club, studded over with bright berries, becomes conspicuous to attract hungry woodland rovers in the hope that the seeds will be dropped far from the parent plant. The Indians used to boil the berries for food. The farinaceous root they likewise boiled or dried to extract the stinging, blistering juice, leaving an edible little "turnip," however insipid and starchy.

172. According to the passage, what is the author describing?

(A)   seeds

(B)   berries of a plant

(C)   Indians

(D)   how to cook turnips

(Finding Specific Information)

173. According to the passage, how did the Indians prepare the food?

(A)   They juiced the berries.

(B)   They picked them off the tree bare.

(C)   They fried the berries.

(D)   They boiled the berries.

(Finding Specific Information)

174. What is the main point of the paragraph?

(A)   The plant berries appear in the summer and are useful to humans and animals.

(B)   The berry juice has a stinging effect.

(C)   Berries make humans and animals hungry in the woods.

(D)   Indians like berries.

(Recognizing the Main Idea)

175. In this paragraph, what is the meaning of *conspicuous?*

(A)   welted

(B)   obvious

(C)   overwhelming

(D)   targeted

(Determining Word Meaning in Context)

Questions 176 through 178 are based on the following passage.

The groom should have standing orders to take his charge through crowds and to make him familiar with all sorts of sights and noises. If the colt shows signs of apprehension at them, he must teach him — not by cruel, but by gentle handling — that they are not really formidable.

176. According to the excerpt, what is the author explaining?

(A)   how to be nice to others

(B)   how to handle a horse

(C)   how to take orders

(D)   how to walk in public

(Finding Specific Information)

177. What is the best title of the book containing this excerpt?

(A)   *How to Train a Horse*

(B)   *Why You Should Be Afraid of Horses*

(C)   *What to Do When a Horse Charges You in Public*

(D)   *Why You Should Know How to Ride Horses*

(Recognizing the Main Idea)

178. In the excerpt, what is the meaning of the term *formidable?*

   (A)   frightening

   (B)   special

   (C)   important

   (D)   simple

   (Determining Word Meaning in Context)

Questions 179 and 180 are based on the following passage.

Such are the main characteristics of the games which interest a child and aid his or her development at different periods. They are all based upon a natural evolution of physical and psychological powers that can be only hinted at in so brief a sketch. Anyone charged with the education or training of a child should know the results of modern study in these particulars.

179. What studies should a person know about when training or educating a child?

   (A)   playground studies

   (B)   physical and psychological studies

   (C)   how to play games effectively

   (D)   evolution

   (Finding Specific Information)

180. What is the main thought of the passage?

   (A)   Developmental factors of a growing child really have no bearing on education.

   (B)   Adults really shouldn't play games with kids if they haven't done research.

   (C)   Games are great for everyone.

   (D)   The interests of a child can aid in his or her development if the adult is educated on certain developmental studies.

   (Recognizing the Main Idea)

Questions 181 through 183 are based on the following passage.

The partnership between mind and body is very close. Just how it happens that spirit may inhabit matter we may not know. But certain it is that they interact on each other. What will hinder the growth of one will handicap the other, and what favors the development of either will help both. The methods of their cooperation and the laws that govern their relationship will develop as our study goes on.

181. According to the passage, how does the spirit inhabit the body?

   (A)   through partnerships

   (B)   as a glue

   (C)   via DNA

   (D)   It is unknown.

   (Finding Specific Information)

182. What is the topic of the study the author is speaking of?

   (A)   the partnership between mind and body

   (B)   how humans interact with others

   (C)   the development of spiritual gain

   (D)   the methods of healing the body

   (Recognizing the Main Idea)

183. What does the term *inhabit* mean in this passage?

   (A)   to restrain

   (B)   to release

   (C)   to occupy

   (D)   to defy

   (Determining Word Meaning in Context)

Questions 184 through 186 are based on the following passage.

For more than 20 years, the Angelman Syndrome Foundation (ASF) has made great strides in advancing support for individuals with Angelman syndrome and toward finding a cure. But none to date have proven more successful than accomplishments reached during the past 14 months. During this time, research funded by the ASF discovered a possible treatment for Angelman syndrome, as well as identified the underlying causes of life-threatening symptoms such as seizures. You see, your donation makes all the difference.

184. According to the passage, how long did the successful research team take to find a possible treatment?

(A) 20 years

(B) 5 years

(C) 24 months

(D) 14 months

(Finding Specific Information)

185. What is the main thought of the passage?

(A) Angelman syndrome is an interesting thing.

(B) Donating to the Angelman Syndrome Foundation is important because they might find a cure.

(C) People like to help those with Angelman Syndrome.

(D) Parents and scientists appreciate donations.

(Recognizing the Main Idea)

186. In this passage, what is the meaning of *strides?*

(A) scores

(B) advances

(C) products

(D) witnesses

(Determining Word Meaning in Context)

Questions 187 and 188 are based on the following passage.

When there are larger animals on the premises, the calves ought to be kept by themselves. They should be sustained on their winter feed through the following spring, until the grass furnishes a good bite on a well-compacted sod. The change from hay to grass must be gradual, unless the latter is considerably matured. The extreme relaxation of the bowels from the sudden change frequently produces excessive purging. A slight and temporary relax from the early spring grass is not objectionable.

187. According to the passage, what is winter feed?

(A) hay

(B) grass

(C) calf pellets

(D) leftovers

(Finding Specific Information)

188. According to the passage, why must the change from hay to grass be gradual?

(A) so the calves avoid digestive issues

(B) so the calves don't miss eating hay all of a sudden

(C) so the grass has time to grow

(D) so the calves don't go into shock

(Finding Specific Information)

Questions 189 through 192 are based on the following passage.

The success of Christopher Columbus's initial voyage to the Americas aroused the appetites of many European countries. In hopes of obtaining the riches of the New World, power-hungry leaders chartered numerous expeditions to the unexplored lands. Small settlements and trading posts grew up along the Atlantic and Gulf Coasts as travel between Europe and America became more commonplace. Explorers were able to discover great quantities of precious metals and natural resources, but these finds were not enough to satisfy the growing thirst for more wealth.

189. What does the author mean by the phrase *New World?*

(A) Europe

(B) America

(C) the Gulf Coast

(D) the Atlantic Coast

(Finding Specific Information)

190. What would be a good title for the paragraph?

(A) "The Insatiable Appetite for Power and Wealth"

(B) "The Establishment of American Colonies"

(C) "The European Drive to Explore the New World"

(D) "The Discovery of the New World"

(Recognizing the Main Idea)

191. What is the main idea of the passage?

(A) Christopher Columbus traveled to America frequently.

(B) Christopher Columbus's voyage to America inspired many voyages to take place.

(C) People in Europe were hungry for riches.

(D) There were a lot of trading posts established between Europe and America.

(Recognizing the Main Idea)

192. In the paragraph, the word *appetite* means

(A) a desire for food or drink.

(B) a desire to satisfy a bodily craving.

(C) a feeling of craving something.

(D) a diversion.

(Determining Word Meaning in Context)

Questions 193 and 194 are based on the following passage.

It is commonly agreed upon by health experts that second-hand smoke is a serious public health risk. When yet another research team concluded in their publication that there posed a link between exposure to second-hand smoke and a shortened life span in other regions, a team of State Representatives proposed a new bill banning smoking in most public places, with the thought of promoting a better quality of life and longer length of life span.

193. According to the passage, what do health authorities agree on?

(A) Second-hand smoke is a personal choice.

(B) Second-hand smoke poses a health risk.

(C) People who breathe second-hand smoke have no quality of life.

(D) No one from the State House of Representatives smokes.

(Finding Specific Information)

194. Which of the following is not supported by the passage?

(A) The legislators' argument is about protecting people from second-hand smoke.

(B) Research links second-hand smoke to a shorter life span.

(C) The State Representatives' argument for banning smoking is based on scientific research.

(D) Data shows that other regions that enacted tough anti-smoking reform experienced longer life spans.

(Recognizing the Main Idea)

Questions 195 through 197 are based on the following passage.

Despite the dire predictions of economists that home sales would reach only 4.5 million units in the month of August, a rate of 5.01 million units of existing home sales was reported. The fact that this rate is up from 4.67 million units from the prior month has still not caused a strong reaction by the market at large. However, homebuilders MainCorp, GB Home, and Homeowners Group stock are all reporting big gain. Investors are predicting that the rise in existing home sales will soon bring an acceleration of new home sales.

195. How much more in sales was recorded for August than expected?

(A)   4.50 million

(B)   0.51 million

(C)   5.01 million

(D)   4.67 million

(Finding Specific Information)

196. Which of the following would be the best title for this passage?

(A)   "Investors Favor Homebuilders"

(B)   "A Better Way to Build a Home"

(C)   "MainCorp, GB Home, and Homeowners Group"

(D)   "Led by Homebuilders, Stocks Hit New Highs"

(Recognizing the Main Idea)

197. What is the topic of this passage?

(A)   realtors

(B)   home sales

(C)   home building

(D)   economy

(Recognizing the Main Idea)

Questions 198 through 201 are based on the following passage.

In order to meet the company goals of cutting costs, increasing productivity, and generally improving product quality, a local business is considering implementing a flex-system policy for all employees to work from home or any other location during the day as long as they are in the business office from 12:30 p.m. to 3:00 p.m. on Monday, Wednesday, and Friday. At the present time, employees work at the office from 8:00 a.m. until 5:00 p.m. The management believes that this implementation of the policy will help the company meet its goals of decreasing total costs, increasing productivity, and improving the overall quality of the product.

198. In the passage, which of the following is not a stated goal of management?

(A)   to decrease costs

(B)   to increase profits

(C)   to increase productivity

(D)   to improve product quality

(Finding Specific Information)

199. According to the passage, what are the current hours of the employees?

(A)   12:30 p.m. to 3:00 p.m. Monday through Friday

(B)   12:30 p.m. to 3:00 p.m. Monday, Wednesday, and Friday

(C)   8:00 a.m. to 5:00 p.m.

(D)   8:00 a.m. to 5:00 p.m. Monday, Wednesday, and Friday

(Finding Specific Information)

200. What is the main idea of the paragraph?

(A) The firm wants to reduce everyone's hours.

(B) The firm wants to lay off some staff.

(C) The firm is thinking about retiring.

(D) The firm thinks implementing flex-time will help its business.

(Recognizing the Main Idea)

201. Which of the following, if true, most weakens the argument of the firm's management?

(A) Some new costs will arise as a result of telecommuting.

(B) A similar firm tried a version of flex-time and abandoned it after a month for unknown reasons.

(C) The firm in question performs work that requires frequent and extensive in-person collaboration, including multiple in-office client meetings each week.

(D) The firm in question works on projects that often take weeks to complete.

(Drawing an Implication from a Stated Idea)

202. According to the passage, in what month are the most animals present?

(A) March

(B) June

(C) September

(D) January

(Finding Specific Information)

203. What is an *avian* population in this passage?

(A) animals

(B) reptiles

(C) amphibians

(D) birds

(Determining Word Meaning in Context)

204. Where does the migration take place?

(A) North America

(B) Asia

(C) the Pacific Ocean

(D) Antarctica

(Drawing an Implication from a Stated Idea)

Questions 202 through 204 are based on the following passage.

January is the month in which the avian population attains its maximum. Geese, ducks, teal, pelicans, cormorants, snake-birds, and ospreys abound in the rivers and jhils; the marshes and swamps are the resort of millions of snipe and other waders; the fields and groves swarm with flycatchers, chats, starlings, warblers, finches, birds of prey, and the other migrants, which in winter visit the plains from the Himalayas and the country beyond.

Questions 205 and 206 are based on the following passage.

Those men built better than they knew. The foundation was properly laid, and the structure, while not finished, is an imposing one. A great many people believe that this structure has been completed, that we have reached our possibilities in fruit raising. This is only half true. We are still building on this splendid foundation erected by those few enthusiasts.

205. According to the passage, what is the foundation for?

(A)   a building

(B)   fruit raising

(C)   an unfinished landmark

(D)   a farm

(Finding Specific Information)

206. In this passage, what does *splendid* mean?

(A)   half-built

(B)   excellent

(C)   trying

(D)   difficult

(Determining Word Meaning in Context)

Questions 207 through 209 are based on the following passage.

On the Tuesday — my last day in prison — I saw him at exercise. He was worse than before, and again was sent in. Since then, I know nothing of him, but I found out from one of the prisoners who walked with me at exercise that he had had twenty-four lashes in the cook-house on Saturday afternoon, by order of the visiting justices on the report of the doctor. The howls that had horrified us all were his.

207. According to the passage, where is the main character?

(A)   in a mental ward

(B)   in a rehabilitation program

(C)   in jail

(D)   on vacation

(Finding Specific Information)

208. According to the passage, how many lashes did the other character receive?

(A)   twenty

(B)   twenty-four

(C)   forty-two

(D)   none of the above

(Finding Specific Information)

209. What is the main idea of this passage?

(A)   It was the main character's last day in prison.

(B)   A man in the prison was sent somewhere where he was beaten.

(C)   Everyone went for a walk during exercise.

(D)   The howls horrified the prisoners.

(Recognizing the Main Idea)

Questions 210 through 212 are based on the following passage.

The "Beat and Thrust" is another variety of attack. Supposing the adversary's blade to be firmly joined to yours, when you wished to deliver a straight thrust, there would then be danger of your falling upon his point. This danger is avoided by giving a slight beat on his blade the instant preceding your extension of arm, of course to be followed en suite by the longe.

210. What is a "Beat and Thrust?"

(A)   a type of skilled move

(B)   a dance move

(C)   a job description

(D)   a way to knead dough

(Finding Specific Information)

211. What is the author describing in the paragraph?

(A) how to kill people

(B) how to play polo

(C) how to win video games

(D) how to fence

(Recognizing the Main Idea)

212. In this passage, what is an *adversary*?

(A) a friend

(B) an opponent

(C) a martial artist

(D) a militant

(Determining Word Meaning in Context)

Officials in the healthcare industry are finding it necessary to look for ways to increase their revenues while reducing their expenses. To do this, they have looked to automation. Automation in the economic society that we now live in is essential to making the best use of economic production while keeping down costs. Officials propose that using considerably greater automation of healthcare would help solve the financial problems facing the industry. This idea should be rejected. If the industry were to use a lot more automation, patients would lose trust in the healthcare system as they would not receive the personal care that studies have shown patients desire to have.

213. Which of the following expresses the main point of the argument portrayed in this passage?

(A) Patients desire customized in-person care.

(B) Healthcare should not be heavily automated.

(C) Trends in the general economy do not apply to the healthcare industry.

(D) Healthcare executives are becoming too greedy.

(Recognizing the Main Idea)

That "two can live on less than one" is not true — but it is nearer the truth than the idea that two can find ultimate happiness together more easily than either can find an approximation of happiness alone. No one who has observed or thought on this subject will deny that it is a thousand times better not to be married at all than to be married to the wrong person.

214. What can you conclude from the passage?

(A) Two can live on less than one.

(B) To be single is always better than to be married.

(C) People can find happiness alone.

(D) It is better to be married than single.

(Recognizing the Main Idea)

Questions 215 and 216 are based on the following passage.

Individuals learn and form opinions about government and acquire their political values in a process called *political socialization.* First, political views come from the home where children hear casual discussions between members of the family regarding political issues, concerns, and praise or complaints about politicians. What children hear, whether positive or negative, will have an immense effect on their political views and decisions.

215. According to the paragraph, what can be concluded?

(A) Parents should not discuss government or politics with their children.

(B) Children are influenced by what they hear.

(C) Government policies are often topics of conversation in the home.

(D) Political socialization is important for children to understand government policies.

(Recognizing the Main Idea)

216. What can be inferred from the passage?

(A)   Government policies are first formed at home.

(B)   Children need to be protected from political discussions.

(C)   Parents or guardians may shape their children's opinion of government.

(D)   Parents should involve their children in political discussions.

(Drawing an Implication from a Stated Idea)

Questions 217 and 218 are based on the following passage.

All cyclists know that the many miles of traveling they do on their bikes will eventually wear down the tread on the tires. It is a common belief that the tires will wear down because of the continual friction and heat generated by the contact between the tire and the pavement as cyclists put miles on their bikes. One extreme cyclist suggested a new theory that this wearing down of the bicycle tires was the result of chemicals from the road and rain residue.

217. What is the main idea of the passage?

(A)   The author describes two theories for why bike tires wear.

(B)   Chemicals ruin bike tires.

(C)   You need to replace your bike tires.

(D)   The road can be rough on bike tires.

(Recognizing the Main Idea)

218. Which of the following would best evaluate the trueness of the proposed theory?

(A)   Ride a road bike aggressively through spring rain storms.

(B)   Ascertain whether chemicals from the road's composition also reside within the bike's frame.

(C)   Place chemicals from rain water and pavement on a bike's idle tires.

(D)   Ride a bike for miles until it breaks.

(Drawing an Implication from a Stated Idea)

Questions 219 through 221 are based on the following passage.

Perhaps you never have thought of yourself as a salesman. You may not have realized the importance *to you* of knowing and practicing the principles of skillful selling. Only one percent of the people in the United States *call* themselves salesmen or saleswomen. Yet in order to succeed, each of us must sell his or her particular qualifications. Your knowledge and use of the selling process are essential to assure your success in life.

219. What is the main topic of the passage?

(A)   being a successful salesman

(B)   being a successful marketer

(C)   practicing exercise

(D)   being a successful artist

(Recognizing the Main Idea)

220. In this passage, what does the term *essential* mean?

(A)   constant

(B)   necessary

(C)   contradictory

(D)   advanced

(Determining Word Meaning in Context)

221. According to the passage, how can you be successful in selling a job?

(A) Get plenty of rest on the couch.

(B) You must report to your job every day.

(C) You must be able to call yourself a salesman.

(D) You must be able to sell your qualifications.

(Drawing an Implication from a Stated Idea)

Questions 222 through 224 are based on the following passage.

Would you ever think that dark chocolate might actually be good for your heart? Short-term clinical trials have indeed shown that dark chocolate can reduce blood pressure and improve blood flow. There is even documentation claiming that consuming dark chocolate may help prevent plaque formation in arteries. This kind of information may help you feel less guilty about eating a chocolate bar.

222. What is the main idea of the passage?

(A) Dark chocolate is delicious.

(B) Scientists study candies.

(C) Plaque prevention is important.

(D) Dark chocolate may be beneficial to your health.

(Recognizing the Main Idea)

223. In the passage, what does *formation* mean?

(A) a straight line

(B) development

(C) clogging

(D) reduction

(Determining Word Meaning in Context)

224. What can be inferred from the passage?

(A) People need to eat a lot of dark chocolate.

(B) Long-term studies have not been conducted.

(C) Scientists like to study chocolate.

(D) Chocolate is the only thing that can reduce clotting.

(Drawing an Implication from a Stated Idea)

Questions 225 through 227 are based on the following passage.

Data has been accumulating about the positive health benefits associated with laughter. A good laugh has many short-term effects. Aside from making you feel better, laughter induces physical changes in your body. Laughter can soothe tension, relieve stress, improve your immune system, stimulate organ function, and promote a healthy attitude. Laughter isn't a temporary pick-me-up; it is also good for your body over the long haul.

225. What is the main topic of the passage?

(A) immune system

(B) body functions

(C) laughter

(D) positive reinforcement

(Recognizing the Main Idea)

226. In this passage, what does the term *induces* mean?

(A) produces

(B) erases

(C) calms

(D) monitors

(Determining Word Meaning in Context)

227. What can be concluded about laughter, according to the paragraph?

    (A)   Laughing is contagious.

    (B)   Laughing has a great effect on bodily functions.

    (C)   Laughing doesn't have any long-term effects.

    (D)   You should try to laugh more.

(Drawing an Implication from a Stated Idea)

Questions 228 and 229 are based on the following passage.

Mr. Darling used to boast to Wendy that her mother not only loved him but respected him. He was one of those deep ones who know about stocks and shares. Of course no one really knows, but he quite seemed to know, and he often said stocks were up and shares were down in a way that would have made any woman respect him.

228. What is the main idea of the passage?

    (A)   Mr. Darling was talking to Wendy.

    (B)   Mr. Darling demanded respect.

    (C)   Mr. Darling knew a lot about stocks.

    (D)   Mr. Darling's wife respected him.

(Recognizing the Main Idea)

229. According to the passage, you could infer that

    (A)   Mr. Darling was a likeable person.

    (B)   Mr. Darling was getting a divorce.

    (C)   Wendy did not respect Mr. Darling.

    (D)   Wendy did not like her mother.

(Drawing an Implication from a Stated Idea)

Questions 230 and 231 are based on the following passage.

A world for habitation, then, is a world whereon living organisms can exist that are comparable in intelligence with men. But "men" presuppose the existence of living organisms of inferior grades. Therefore, a world for habitation must first of all be one upon which it is possible for living organisms, as such, to exist.

230. What would be a good title for this passage?

    (A)   "Mysterious Living Organisms"

    (B)   "Why Do Men Always Think They're Better?"

    (C)   "Is There Life on Other Planets?"

    (D)   "Where Is My Ham and Cheese Sandwich?"

(Recognizing the Main Idea)

231. What is the main thought of the paragraph?

    (A)   In order for a world to have habitation, living organisms must be as smart as men.

    (B)   In order for a world to have habitation, it must have living organisms.

    (C)   Living organisms are not as important as humans.

    (D)   Men are fairly intelligent.

(Recognizing the Main Idea)

Questions 232 through 234 are based on the following passage.

You will find it is a good plan, as fast as you think of a thing that you want to take, to note it on your memorandum. In order to avoid delay or haste, cast your eyes over the list occasionally to see that the work of preparation is going on properly. It is a good plan to collect all of your baggage into one place as fast as it is ready, for if it is scattered, you are apt to lose sight of some of it and leave without it.

232. What can you conclude from the passage?

    (A) It is a good idea to plan ahead.

    (B) Leaving spontaneously is fun.

    (C) You should work harder to succeed.

    (D) Taking notes is a great way to learn.

(Recognizing the Main Idea)

233. In the passage, what does the term *cast* mean?

    (A) to throw

    (B) to fish

    (C) to look

    (D) to roll

(Determining Word Meaning in Context)

234. What might the author be explaining in the passage?

    (A) how to start a project

    (B) how to pack for a big trip

    (C) how to make a list

    (D) how to become organized

(Drawing an Implication from a Stated Idea)

Questions 235 and 236 are based on the following passage.

Rice, one of the world's most important food crops, has been grown for probably thousands of years. Early records show that it was cultivated in India as early as 326 B.C. It was introduced into Spain in A.D. 700. But it wasn't until the late 1600s that rice was finally planted in American soil.

235. What is the main topic of the passage?

    (A) American soil

    (B) rice

    (C) crops

    (D) history

(Recognizing the Main Idea)

236. What other word could the author have used for *cultivated*?

    (A) developed

    (B) planted

    (C) worked

    (D) manufactured

(Determining Word Meaning in Context)

Questions 237 through 239 are based on the following passage.

They had eaten and were lounging in content on the soft sand just beyond the curl of the waves when Sssuri lifted his head from his folded arms as if he listened. Like all those of his species, his vestigial ears were hidden deep in his fur and no longer served any real purpose; the mind touch served him in their stead. Dalgard caught his thought, though what had aroused his companion was too rare a thread to trouble his less acute senses.

237. What is the main idea of the passage?

(A) They were lying on the sand.

(B) Their minds were capable of trans-
ferring information.

(C) Their ears don't work.

(D) The two had just finished eating when
one of them "heard" something.

(Recognizing the Main Idea)

238. According to the passage, where is this
scene taking place?

(A) the ocean

(B) the lighthouse

(C) the beach

(D) the woods

(Drawing an Implication from a Stated Idea)

239. From the passage, you can assume that

(A) The characters are two men.

(B) The characters are not human.

(C) The characters are big and strong.

(D) The characters are well-educated.

(Drawing an Implication from a Stated Idea)

*Questions 240 and 241 are based on the following
passage.*

The descriptive portion of the work contains a
succinct, though comprehensive, treatment of
the various scientific and popular features of the
Park. While it is sufficient for all the requirements
of ordinary information, it purposely refrains from
a minute discussion of those details which have
been, or are now being, exhaustively treated by
the scientific departments of the government.

240. What is the main idea of the passage?

(A) The information given is satisfactory,
but it does not get into specific details.

(B) The information given is left up to
the demands of the scientists.

(C) The Park is very popular.

(D) The government regulates the Park.

(Recognizing the Main Idea)

241. In this passage, what does *succinct* mean?

(A) mellow

(B) extensive

(C) brief

(D) inadequate

(Determining Word Meaning in Context)

*Questions 242 and 243 are based on the following
passage.*

Learning to read people is also a simpler process
than learning to read books because there are
fewer letters in the human alphabet. Though man
seems to the untrained eye a mystifying mass of
"funny little marks," he is not difficult to analyze.
This is because there are after all but a few kinds
of human feelings. Some form of hunger, love,
hate, fear, hope or ambition gives rise to every
human emotion and every human thought.

Now our actions follow our thoughts. Every
thought, however transitory, causes muscular
action, which leaves its trace in that part of the
physical organism which is most closely allied to it.

242. The word *analyze,* as used in this passage,
most nearly means

(A) to muddle

(B) to confuse

(C) to evaluate

(D) to approach

(Determining Word Meaning in Context)

243. Which of the following statements is supported by the passage?

(A) It is extremely difficult to analyze what people feel at any given time.

(B) A person shows his emotions only in his expressions.

(C) There are innumerable emotions and many ways in which they show on individuals.

(D) People's thoughts are reflected in their appearance.

(Drawing an Implication from a Stated Idea)

Questions 244 and 245 are based on the following passage.

Jelly Bellies, in the amount of three and a half tons, were delivered to the White House for the inaugural festivities for President Reagan in 1981. One of the most popular flavors to this day, blueberry, was actually developed specifically for the president's inauguration so that they could have red, white, and blue jelly beans at the celebration.

244. In this passage, what does *inauguration* mean?

(A) work

(B) celebration

(C) meeting

(D) interview

(Determining Word Meaning in Context)

245. What does this passage imply?

(A) President Reagan preferred blueberry Jelly Bellies.

(B) Jelly Bellies were the most popular candy in 1981.

(C) Blueberry Jelly Bellies did not exist before 1981.

(D) President Reagan liked Jelly Bellies.

(Drawing an Implication from a Stated Idea)

Questions 246 and 247 are based on the following passage.

Several words are entirely obsolete. *Alybbeg* no longer means a bed, nor *askew* a cup. *Booget* nowadays would not be understood for a basket; neither would *gan* pass current for mouth. *Fullams* was the old Cant term for false or loaded dice and, although used by Shakespeare in this sense, is now unknown and obsolete.

246. In this paragraph, what does *obsolete* mean?

(A) damaged

(B) remote

(C) outdated

(D) forgetful

(Determining Word Meaning in Context)

247. From the paragraph, what can you assume the author is describing?

(A) strange recipes

(B) old words

(C) relative sayings

(D) candid statements

(Drawing an Implication from a Stated Idea)

Puffins, Auks, and Murres are all sea birds and are only found inland when blown there by some severe storm of winter. At this season numbers of them are apt to lose their bearings and may sometimes be found with their feet frozen in some inland ponds.

248. According to the passage,

(A) all sea birds will die if found inland.

(B) some sea birds become disoriented when driven inland.

(C) sea birds' feet will freeze if they go in a pond.

(D) Puffins' feet freeze easily.

(Drawing an Implication from a Stated Idea)

Two separate studies were done to determine the effect, if any, that smoking had on the concentration abilities of men and women. The studies observed 1,024 individuals who had a daily smoking habit for at least 3 years, as well as a control group of 1,024 people who had never smoked. The studies concluded that persistent and regular smoking did indeed cause increased difficulties in the concentration abilities of men and women.

249. Which of the following, if true, most severely weakens the researchers' conclusion?

   (A) After developing a severe addiction to smoking for 15 years, many individuals have a decreased ability to concentrate.

   (B) A separate research study found that smokers and nonsmokers exhibited statistically significant differences in their incarceration rates.

   (C) A separate research study found that individuals with preexisting attention and concentration disorders exhibited significantly higher rates of trying cigarettes and subsequently becoming addicted to smoking.

   (D) The addiction to smoking and the cravings this addiction engenders are often on the minds of habitual smokers.

(Drawing an Implication from a Stated Idea)

Our government has many massive responsibilities. Among these are: protecting citizens, maintaining order, regulating the economy, providing public goods and services, and even socializing the nation's youth. To provide these services, the government needs billions of dollars. In order to raise the money needed, taxes are levied by both the federal and state governments. The federal tax system is run by the Internal Revenue Service (IRS) and the United States Treasury. These government offices are directly responsible for overseeing that individuals and companies pay their taxes according to the mandates of the law.

250. What necessity does this passage justify?

   (A) socializing the nation's youth

   (B) penalizing for evasion of paying taxes

   (C) raising taxes

   (D) bigger government

(Drawing an Implication from a Stated Idea)

Chapter 3

Mathematics Knowledge: Counting on a Variety of Questions

∙∙

The Mathematics Knowledge subtest is part of the Armed Forces Qualification Test (AFQT), so you really need to do well on it if you want to enlist (which you likely do since you bought this particular product). The Mathematics Knowledge subtest may be the broadest test offered in the ASVAB, at least from a variety standpoint. It asks questions about basic math, geometry, and algebra, including but not limited to fractions, square roots, factorials, bases, number sequencing, and inequalities. So if you want to get a high score on this subtest, you need to brush up on every possible question type Mathematics Knowledge has to offer.

The Questions You'll Work On

Although the Mathematics Knowledge subtest includes many categories under its umbrella, the questions generally come in one of four forms:

- **Math basics:** These questions cover ratios, irrational numbers and squares, order of operations, number sequencing, scientific notation, and general addition and subtraction methods.

- **Fractions:** These questions ask you to multiply, divide, add, subtract, and convert fractions.

- **Algebra:** The basic, yet often challenging, questions in this category involve solving inequalities and equations, factoring, solving for x, and working with exponents.

- **Geometry:** The questions in this group have to do with measuring things and defining the properties of and relationships among points, lines, angles, shapes, and the like.

What to Watch Out For

Follow these pointers as you work on the questions in this chapter:

- Follow the order of operations, which you can remeber from the acronym **PEMDAS** (**P**arentheses, **E**xponents, **M**ultiplication, **D**ivision, **A**ddition, and **S**ubtraction), as you work through problems that have more than one operation.

- Keep track of your negative and positive signs, making sure you carry over or convert the signs when needed.

- Follow step-by-step calculations of each operation so you don't overlook a number and get the wrong answer.

- Reduce your fractions to their lowest terms.

Math Basics

251. What number is expressed by $(4 \cdot 10^3) + (1 \cdot 10^2) + (6 \cdot 10^1)$?

(A) 1,460

(B) 416

(C) 421

(D) 4,160

252. What is the greatest common factor of 24 and 60?

(A) 6

(B) 24

(C) 12

(D) 10

253. What is the value of the equation $9 - 2 \cdot 4 = ?$

(A) 28

(B) 3

(C) 17

(D) 1

254. Which of these answers has a value between 0.01 and 0.1?

(A) 0.3

(B) 0.4

(C) 0.003

(D) 0.06

255. Convert the following to a mathematical expression:

three times the quantity five plus two, then that quantity minus seven squared

(A) $3(5 + 2) - 7^2$

(B) $3 \times 5 + 2 - 7^2$

(C) $3 + 5 \times 2 - 7^2$

(D) $3(5 \times 2) - 7^2$

256. Solve:

$(4 - 3)^2 \, (2) - 1$

(A) 3

(B) 1

(C) 7^2

(D) 4

257. In order to be considered an equation, a mathematical expression must have what?

(A) parentheses

(B) a variable

(C) an equal sign

(D) integers

258. Solve:

$-|-6| =$

(A) -6

(B) 5

(C) 6

(D) -5

259. Solve:

$(4 \times 3) \times 3 - 6 \times (9 \div 3)$

(A) 54

(B) 14

(C) 18

(D) 28

260. Solve:

$\left(\left(3^5 \right)^2 \right)^6$

(A) 3^{13}

(B) 3^{42}

(C) 3^{60}

(D) 3^{224}

261. Simplify:

$\sqrt{75}$

(A) $\sqrt{3}$

(B) $5\sqrt{3}$

(C) $3\sqrt{5}$

(D) $\sqrt{5}$

262. Solve:

$0 - (-15) =$

(A) 1

(B) −1

(C) −15

(D) 15

263. Solve:

$3(2 - 5) + 14 =$

(A) 5

(B) 7

(C) −5

(D) −7

264. What is 403,000,000,000,000 in scientific notation?

(A) 4.03×10^{14}

(B) 403×10^{14}

(C) 4.03×10^{-14}

(D) 40.3×10^{14}

265. Simplify:

$\sqrt{12}$

(A) $\sqrt{6}$

(B) $2\sqrt{6}$

(C) $2\sqrt{3}$

(D) $2\sqrt{4}$

266. Simplify:

$\left(2^{-6}\right)^{-8} =$

(A) 2^{-2}

(B) 2^{48}

(C) 2^{-14}

(D) 2^{2}

267. What is the reciprocal of $\frac{1}{8}$?

(A) $\frac{1}{8}$

(B) 8

(C) 16

(D) 0.08

268. What is the square root of 4?

(A) 0

(B) 1

(C) 2

(D) 3

269. What is the average of the following?

101, 15, 62, 84, and 55

(A) 55

(B) 63.4

(C) 75.5

(D) 5

270. 1 hour 30 minutes + 3 hours 40 minutes + 2 hours 45 minutes =

(A) 6 hours 45 minutes

(B) 6 hours 55 minutes

(C) 7 hours 50 minutes

(D) 7 hours 55 minutes

271. Divide:

$(4.2 \times 10^{-6}) \div (2.1 \times 10^{-3}) =$

(A) 2.0×10^{-9}

(B) 2.0×10^{-18}

(C) 2.0×10^{-3}

(D) 2.1×10^{-3}

272. Convert 0.7 to a percent.

(A)   0.7%

(B)   7%

(C)   70%

(D)   700%

273. Evaluate:

$\left|10 - \left(42 \div |1 - 4|\right)\right|$

(A)   1

(B)   2

(C)   3

(D)   4

274. Solve:

$|5 - 11| = ?$

(A)   −6

(B)   6

(C)   16

(D)   −16

275. How many students failed the test if the passing score was 70%?

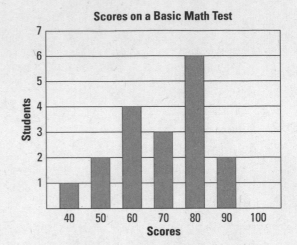

Scores on a Basic Math Test

(A)   10

(B)   9

(C)   8

(D)   7

276. Solve the exponential expression: 4^5

(A)   20

(B)   1,024

(C)   256

(D)   1,240

277. Solve:

$2(5 - 3)^2$

(A)   16

(B)   8

(C)   −8

(D)   −16

278. Continue the pattern:

1, 1, 2, 3, 3, 4, 5 . . .

(A)   6, 6, 7

(B)   10, 15, 20

(C)   6, 7, 8

(D)   5, 6, 7

279. Continue the pattern:

. . . 5, 10, 9, 15, 20, 19, 25

(A)   30, 35, 41

(B)   30, 29, 35

(C)   26, 30, 35

(D)   26, 30, 31

280. Continue the pattern:

a + b − c, b + c − d, c + d − e . . .

(A)   d + e + f

(B)   f + g − h

(C)   d + e − f

(D)   d + e − c

281. Continue the pattern:

98b, 88a, 78d, 68c, 58f . . .

(A)   48e, 38f, 28g

(B)   58f, 48g, 38h

(C)   58g, 48i, 38h

(D)   48e, 38h, 28g

282. Continue the pattern:

$x = 7$, $x = 14$, $y = 6$, $y = 12$, $x = 5$, $x = 10$, $y = $ . . .

(A)   4, $y = 8$, $x = 3$

(B)   4, $x = 3$, $x = 6$

(C)   8, $y = 16$, $x = 7$

(D)   11, $y = 7$, $x = 8$

283. Solve:

(−4) + (−6) + (−10) =

(A)   −20

(B)   20

(C)   10

(D)   −10

284. $5 \times 6 + 11 − 4 = $

(A)   37

(B)   41

(C)   45

(D)   66

285. Solve:

−1(3 − 1) + 9 =

(A)   7

(B)   6

(C)   5

(D)   4

286. Write 105,000 in scientific notation.

(A) 10.5×10^4

(B) 105×10^5

(C) 1.05×10^5

(D) 1.05×10^{-5}

287. Solve:

$2^3 \times 2^4$

(A) 2^7

(B)   128

(C) 2^1

(D)   both A and B

288. Simplify:

$\sqrt{200}$

(A) $\sqrt{10 \times 2}$

(B) $10\sqrt{10 \times 2}$

(C) $10\sqrt{2}$

(D) $2\sqrt{10}$

289. Multiply:

100×55

(A) 555

(B) 5,500

(C) 55,100

(D) 550

290. Multiply:

$1,010 \times 1,015$

(A) 1,250,100

(B) 1,150,500

(C) 1,050,500

(D) 1,025,150

291. What is the symbol for the absolute value of *x?*

(A) $|x|$

(B) x

(C) $\sqrt{x}$

(D) (x)

292. What is the following symbol?

$\leq$

(A) greater than

(B) less than

(C) greater than or equal to

(D) less than or equal to

293. Solve:

$\sqrt{49}$

(A) 7×7

(B) 7

(C) 98

(D) 7^2

294. Solve:

$6^2 + 5^3$

(A) 150

(B) 40

(C) 161

(D) 90

Fractions

295. $5 \div 0 = ?$

(A) 5

(B) 0

(C) $\dfrac{0}{5}$

(D) undefined

296. Solve:

$$\frac{32}{30 - 2(3+4)} =$$

(A) $2\dfrac{1}{2}$

(B) 4

(C) $\dfrac{1}{2}$

(D) 2

297. Solve:

$$\frac{3}{8} + \frac{7}{12} =$$

(A) $\frac{10}{20}$

(B) $\frac{1}{2}$

(C) $\frac{10}{24}$

(D) $\frac{23}{24}$

298. Solve:

$$\left(\frac{a^p}{b^q}\right)^{-n} =$$

(A) $\frac{a^{pn}}{b^{qn}}$

(B) $\frac{b^{qn}}{a^{pn}}$

(C) $-\frac{b^{qn}}{a^{pn}}$

(D) $\frac{bn^q}{an^p}$

299. Convert to a decimal:

$$\frac{3}{5}$$

(A) 0.20

(B) 0.50

(C) 0.60

(D) 0.80

300. Change 0.45 to a fraction.

(A) $\frac{9}{20}$

(B) $\frac{7}{10}$

(C) $\frac{3}{10}$

(D) $\frac{3}{5}$

301. Evaluate $\frac{x^2 - 2x}{y^2 + 2y}$, if $x = 3$ and $y = -1$.

(A) 5

(B) -3

(C) -6

(D) 4

302. Solve:

$$7\frac{1}{7} \div 3\frac{3}{14}$$

(A) $\frac{64}{52}$

(B) $1\frac{5}{8}$

(C) 9

(D) $2\frac{2}{9}$

303. Solve for x:

$$\frac{7}{8} = \frac{x}{40}$$

(A) 5

(B) 35

(C) 7

(D) 36

304. Solve:

$$\frac{3^2 \times 3^4 \times 2}{3^{-1} \times 3^6 \times 2^{-3}} =$$

(A) 20

(B) 24

(C) 48

(D) 52

305. Solve:

$$-\frac{15}{14} \div \left(-\frac{20}{21}\right) =$$

(A) 1

(B) $1\frac{1}{8}$

(C) $1\frac{3}{8}$

(D) $1\frac{1}{2}$

306. Solve:

$$\frac{3^4 \times 2^4}{3^2 \times 2^3} =$$

(A) $\frac{6^8}{6^5}$

(B) 15

(C) $16\frac{1}{3}$

(D) 18

307. What is 40% as a fraction?

(A) $\frac{2}{5}$

(B) $\frac{5}{8}$

(C) $\frac{3}{8}$

(D) $\frac{4}{100}$

308. Solve:

$$(110 \times 6)\frac{1}{6} =$$

(A) 110

(B) 660

(C) 55.7

(D) 360

309. Solve:

$$\frac{-3(-4)}{-2} =$$

(A) −12

(B) 12

(C) −6

(D) 6

310. Reduce the fraction:

$$\frac{63}{84}$$

(A) $\frac{1}{2}$

(B) $\frac{3}{4}$

(C) $\frac{1}{4}$

(D) $\frac{2}{5}$

311. Divide:

$$\frac{4x^3 - 3x^2 + 2x}{x}$$

(A) $5x^3 - 4x + 3x$

(B) $4x^4 - 3x^3 + 2x^2$

(C) $4x^2 - 3x + 2$

(D) $x^2 + 2^3 - 3$

312. Divide:

$$2\frac{1}{4} \div 2\frac{4}{7} =$$

(A) $4\frac{5}{11}$

(B) $\frac{3}{7}$

(C) $\frac{7}{8}$

(D) $\frac{18}{7}$

313. Which of the following is an improper fraction?

(A) $1\frac{5}{28}$

(B) $\frac{9}{7}$

(C) $\frac{1}{2}$

(D) $\frac{100}{100}$

314. Simplify:

$$\frac{4x^3}{16x^{-2}}$$

(A) $4x$

(B) $64x^{-6}$

(C) $\frac{1}{4}x^5$

(D) $\frac{1x}{16}$

315. Solve:

$$\frac{(-5)(2)(3)}{-1} =$$

(A) -15

(B) -1

(C) 30

(D) -30

316. Change the mixed number to an improper fraction:

$4\frac{7}{8}$

(A) $\frac{32}{8}$

(B) $\frac{39}{8}$

(C) $\frac{7}{8}$

(D) $\frac{7}{32}$

317. Change $\frac{5}{8}$ to a decimal.

(A) 1.6

(B) 0.625

(C) 0.375

(D) 0.833

Algebra

318. Solve: $8y = 16$

(A) $y = 16$

(B) $y = 2$

(C) $y = 4$

(D) $y = 8$

319. Add: $3x + 7x$

(A) $10x^2$

(B) $4x^2$

(C) $21x$

(D) $10x$

320. Divide: $8x \div 2y$

(A) $\frac{4x}{y}$

(B) $\frac{8xy}{2y^2}$

(C) $16xy$

(D) $4xy$

321. Solve for x:

$2x - 6 = x + 5$

(A) 3

(B) 11

(C) 7

(D) 5

322. Simplify:

$(1 + x)(3 + 2x)$

(A) $2x^2 + 4$

(B) $2x^2 + 5x + 3$

(C) $2x^2 + x + 3$

(D) $2x^2 + 5x + 4$

323. Simplify:

$4a(x - 2) =$

(A) $4ax - 8a$

(B) $8ax$

(C) $2ax^2$

(D) $2ax(2)$

324. Evaluate: $6x^2 - xy$, if $x = 2$ and $y = -3$.

(A) 24

(B) 30

(C) 18

(D) 138

325. Solve for y:

$5y^2 = 80$

(A) 16

(B) 400

(C) 8

(D) 4

326. Solve by factoring:

$x^4 - 16 = 0$

(A) $x = \pm 2$

(B) $x = \pm 4$

(C) $x = \pm 5$

(D) $x = \pm 8$

327. $(a + b)^2 =$

(A) $(a^2 + b^2)$

(B) ab^2

(C) $2(a + b)$

(D) $a^2 + 2ab + b^2$

328. Solve:

$\sqrt{x^2 + 9} = 5$

(A) 2

(B) 4

(C) 6

(D) 8

329. Solve for x:

$x + 4 = 15$

(A) 19

(B) 60

(C) 11

(D) 3.75

330. Evaluate $3x^2$, if $x = -2$.

(A) 12

(B) -12

(C) 6

(D) -6

331. Factor:

$5y^3 - 5y^2 - 10y$

(A) $2y + 5y^2$

(B) $5y(y - 2)(y + 1)$

(C) $(1y^2 - 5)(1y^2 + 5)$

(D) $5y(y - 2)(y - 1)$

332. Distribute:

$-2x(x-1) =$

(A) $-2x^2 - 1$

(B) $2x^2 + 2x$

(C) $-2x^2 - 2x$

(D) $-2x^2 + 2x$

333. Simplify:

$(w+4)(w-4)$

(A) $w^2 - 4^2$

(B) $w^2 - 8$

(C) $(w^2 - 8)^2$

(D) $w^2 - 16$

334. What is the simplest way to write the reciprocal of x^{-4}?

(A) x^4

(B) $\dfrac{x^4}{1}$

(C) $\dfrac{x^{-4}}{100}$

(D) $\dfrac{1}{x^4}$

335. Multiply:

$(3a^3)(-2a) =$

(A) $6a^{-4}$

(B) $-6a^4$

(C) $-6a^{-4}$

(D) $6a^{-2}$

336. What is the equivalent of $(a+b)^2$?

(A) $(a+b)(a+b)$

(B) $a^2 + b^2$

(C) $a^2 + 2ab + b^2$

(D) A and C

337. Find x if $2(x+4) = 6$.

(A) 1

(B) -1

(C) 2

(D) -2

338. If $p = -5$ and $q = -4$, then $p(p-q) =$

(A) 5

(B) -20

(C) -5

(D) -40

339. If the ratio of s to d is the same as the ratio of d to n, then which of the following must be true?

(A) $sn = d^2$

(B) $s + d = d + n$

(C) $sn = 2d$

(D) $sd - dn$

340. Choose the true statement if $a = \frac{1}{2}$, $b = \frac{2}{3}$, and $c = \frac{5}{8}$.

(A) $a < c < b$

(B) $b < c < a$

(C) $c < b < a$

(D) $c < a < b$

341. What does c equal if $(x-5)^2 = x^2 - 10x + c$?

(A) -10

(B) 10

(C) -25

(D) 25

342. Solve for x:

$$x + \frac{1}{2} = -\frac{2}{3}$$

   (A) $-1\frac{1}{3}$

   (B) $-\frac{7}{6}$

   (C) $-\frac{3}{5}$

   (D) $-\frac{1}{5}$

343. Simplify:

$2(a^3) + 5(a^3)$

   (A) $7a^3$

   (B) $10a^6$

   (C) $3a$

   (D) $7a^6$

344. How many terms are in the expression $x^2 + bx - c^4$?

   (A)   1

   (B)   2

   (C)   3

   (D)   4

345. If $h + s = k$ and $h = s$, then:

   (A) $k = 2s$

   (B) $k = 2s + 7$

   (C) $k = k + s$

   (D) $k = s - h$

346. What does the following represent in exponential form?

$\sqrt[3]{x}$

   (A) $\sqrt{3x}$

   (B) $x^{1/3}$

   (C) x^{300}

   (D) x^3

347. Combine like terms:

$4a + 3ab + 5ab + 6a$

   (A) $10a + 8ab$

   (B) $18ab$

   (C) $8a + 10ab$

   (D) $2ab - 2a$

348. Multiply:

$(8y^2)(x^4y)$

   (A) $8xy$

   (B) $8x^4y^3$

   (C) $4xy$

   (D) $8y^8x$

349. Solve for n:

$$\frac{4}{5}n + 8 = 12$$

   (A)   4

   (B)   6

   (C)   5

   (D)   2

350. Solve for x:

$8(8) = \frac{x}{2}$

   (A)   64

   (B)   128

   (C)   32

   (D)   8

Geometry

351. Find the area of the rhombus if $AC = 18$ cm and $BD = 16$ cm.

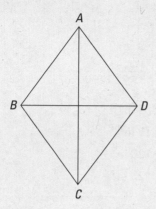

- (A) 72 cm²
- (B) 144 cm²
- (C) 288 cm²
- (D) 168 cm²

352. According to the figure, lines a and b are

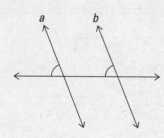

- (A) transversal
- (B) intersecting
- (C) parallel
- (D) right angles

353. According to the figure, if angle B is 38°, angle A is

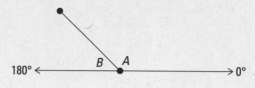

- (A) 142°
- (B) 38°
- (C) 218°
- (D) 55°

354. What is the sum of angle A and angle D?

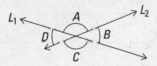

- (A) 90°
- (B) 180°
- (C) 270°
- (D) 360°

355. If the angle C is 140°, what is the sum of angles B and D?

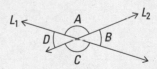

- (A) 40°
- (B) 80°
- (C) 180°
- (D) 280°

356. In which quadrant would the following coordinates lie?

(–4, –2)

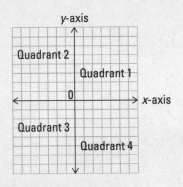

(A)   Quadrant 1

(B)   Quadrant 2

(C)   Quadrant 3

(D)   Quadrant 4

357. What is the value of *YZ*? (Note: This figure is not drawn to scale.)

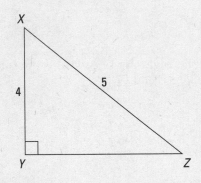

(A)   3

(B)   2

(C)   6

(D)   5

358. What is the volume of the cube?

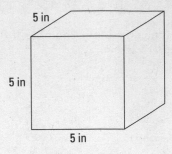

(A)   25 in³

(B)   15 in²

(C)   125 in³

(D)   225 in³

359. What is the area of the trapezoid?

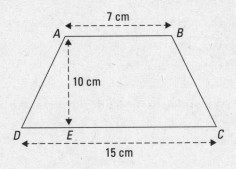

(A)   32 cm²

(B)   157 cm²

(C)   110 cm²

(D)   220 cm²

360. Find the total area of the isosceles triangle if $AD = 10$ and $DC = 3$.

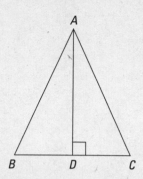

(A) 60

(B) 30

(C) 15

(D) 25

361. Find AD rounded to the nearest tenth.

$DC = BD$

$AB = 20$ cm

$BC = 16$ cm

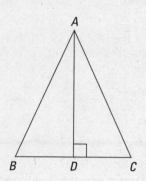

(A) 17.5

(B) 18.3

(C) 19

(D) 19.3

362. Find the area of a circle with a radius of 5 cm.

(A) 87.5 cm²

(B) 78.5 cm²

(C) 17.5 cm²

(D) 8.5 cm²

363. Find the volume of this cylinder.

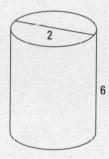

(A) 17.54

(B) 18.84

(C) 75.36

(D) 42.54

364. Find the volume of this cube.

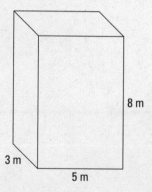

(A) 120 m³

(B) 50 m³

(C) 240 m³

(D) 24 m³

365. What is the perimeter of the figure?

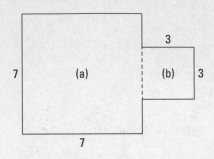

(A) 37

(B) 36

(C) 40

(D) 34

366. Find the area of the figure.

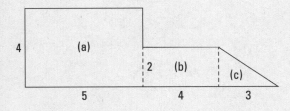

(A) 35

(B) 30

(C) 38

(D) 31

367. Find the volume of the figure.

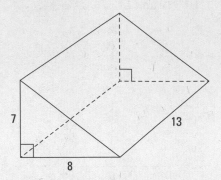

(A) 728

(B) 364

(C) 104

(D) 350

368. Find the circumference of a circle if the diameter is 8 inches.

(A) 50.24

(B) 35.74

(C) 25.12

(D) 22.5

369. What is the radius of a circle whose circumference is 16 inches?

(A) 2.45

(B) 2.55

(C) 3.67

(D) 8

370. What type of triangle has no equal sides and no equal angles?

(A) isosceles

(B) equilateral

(C) scalene

(D) right

371. In any triangle, the sum of the interior angles adds up to how many degrees?

(A) 90

(B) 180

(C) 270

(D) 360

372. Which of the following equations on a graph would show a line passing through point (–1, 4)?

(A) $x + y = 5$

(B) $-x + 3 = y$

(C) $y = x - 5$

(D) $y = x^2 + 5$

373. In which quadrant do the coordinates (7, –8) lie?

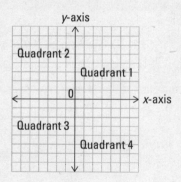

(A) Quadrant 1

(B) Quadrant 2

(C) Quadrant 3

(D) Quadrant 4

374. Find the distance between the two points (2, 3) and (2, –4).

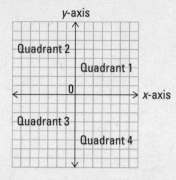

(A) 5

(B) 7

(C) –5

(D) –7

375. One complementary angle is 62 degrees. What is the other angle?

(A) 158 degrees

(B) 28 degrees

(C) 62 degrees

(D) 26 degrees

Chapter 4

Arithmetic Reasoning: Tackling Word Problems

· ·

The Arithmetic Reasoning subtest is an important part of the ASVAB because it's also part of the Armed Forces Qualification Test (AFQT), which determines your eligibility for military service. The purpose of this subtest is to measure your ability to apply mathematical principles to real-world situations. How many eggs does Betty need to bake a cake for 50 people? How long will it take Joe to run around the track if he runs 5 miles per hour? Your job is to read each word problem, determine what the question asks, and calculate the correct answer. The questions you find in the Arithmetic Reasoning subtest are general word problems, which require both arithmetic and reasoning. The arithmetic comes in handy as you figure out how to solve different types of mathematical problems, and good reasoning helps you decide what numbers to plug into each calculation.

The Questions You'll Work On

In testing your ability to perform calculations based on real-life problems, the Arithmetic Reasoning subtest includes the following three types of questions:

- ✔ **Algebra word problems:** These problems generally deal with the unknown — in other words, solving for *x*. First, you have to figure out what the question is asking; then you have to set up an equation to find your answer.

- ✔ **Geometry word problems:** These problems ask you to figure out distances, circumference, area, volume, and other geometry-related values. In many geometry questions, so-and-so needs to build something or go somewhere, and you need to figure out how big or how far.

- ✔ **Fact-finding word problems:** These problems deal with everything that isn't algebra or geometry. This is where basic math, including ratios, proportions, interest, percentages, and probability, come into play.

What to Watch Out For

Keep in mind the following tips as you work on the questions in this chapter:

- ✔ Set up your equations correctly by plugging the right numbers into the right spots. Sometimes the wrong answer choices are answers that you'd get if you made a common mistake.

- ✔ Make sure your answer is realistic based on the question being asked.

- ✔ Pay attention to units of measurement and convert to other units when necessary.

- ✔ Read the question carefully to verify what it's asking you to find. For example, the question may ask how much is left rather than how much was used.

Algebra Word Problems

376. If Jeff can finish his assignment in half an hour, what part can he finish in 20 minutes?

(A) $\frac{1}{4}$

(B) $\frac{2}{3}$

(C) $\frac{3}{4}$

(D) $\frac{1}{6}$

377. If Tim and Sue start off $\frac{1}{4}$ mile apart in the field, and Tim runs at 4.25 miles/hour and Sue runs at 4.75 miles/hour, how long will they run before they meet each other?

(A) 1 minute 30 seconds

(B) 1 minute 40 seconds

(C) 2 minutes 5 seconds

(D) 1 minute 15 seconds

378. If Ed puts $50 in the bank at a 5% yearly interest rate, how long must he wait before his account is worth $60?

(A) 3 years

(B) 15 years

(C) 6 years

(D) 4 years

379. Tickets to the ballgame are $8 for students and $12 for adults. If you sold three times as many student tickets as adult tickets and you made a total of $540, how many adult tickets did you sell?

(A) 45

(B) 19

(C) 15

(D) 24

380. Taylor has $3.30 in his ash tray for small change. If he has three times as many dimes as quarters and no other coins, how many quarters does he have?

(A) 12

(B) 5

(C) 10

(D) 6

381. Bill takes 2 hours to travel 30 miles by boat. How long will it take him to travel 72 miles?

(A) 2.3 hours

(B) 1.7 hours

(C) 5.5 hours

(D) 4.8 hours

382. One-fourth of a number added to itself has the sum of 410. What is the number?

(A) 328

(B) 335

(C) 280

(D) 4,265

383. Larry travels 60 miles per hour going to a friend's house and 50 miles per hour coming back, using the same road. He drove a total of 5 hours. What is the distance from Larry's house to his friend's house, rounded to the nearest mile?

(A) 110

(B) 126

(C) 136

(D) 154

384. The numbers 12, 23, 17, and x have an average equal to 15. What is x?

(A) 11

(B) 7

(C) 8

(D) 15

385. Louisa can paint a square wall with sides of 12 feet in 45 minutes. How many minutes will it take her to paint a square section of this wall with sides of 4 feet?

    (A) 10 minutes

    (B) 20 minutes

    (C) 5 minutes

    (D) 15 minutes

386. Linda and Dale have been on diets. Dale weighs 165 pounds. If three times Linda's weight is twice Dale's weight, how much does Linda weigh?

    (A) 110 pounds

    (B) 115 pounds

    (C) 125 pounds

    (D) 105 pounds

387. A store sells 10 square yards of carpet installed for $275. At this price, what will 25 square yards of carpet cost?

    (A) $675.50

    (B) $550.00

    (C) $687.50

    (D) $700.00

388. To buy a new car priced at $32,000, Martha takes out a five-year loan with an interest rate of 6.5%. By the time she owns the car, how much will she have paid including principal and interest?

    (A) $45,000

    (B) $41,500

    (C) $40,000

    (D) $42,400

389. Austin borrowed some money from Wendell. He agreed to pay him back one and a half times the original sum, plus $50. He paid Wendell a total of $458. What was the original amount he borrowed?

    (A) $272

    (B) $325

    (C) $350

    (D) $290

390. A real estate agent received a 5% commission on the selling price of a house. If his commission was $8,800, what was the selling price of the house?

    (A) $210,000

    (B) $157,000

    (C) $176,000

    (D) $80,600

391. The cost of 4 shirts, 4 pairs of dress pants, and 2 ties is $560. The cost of 9 shirts, 9 pairs of dress pants, and 6 ties is $1,290. What is the total cost of 1 shirt, 1 pair of dress pants, and 1 tie?

    (A) $150

    (B) $230

    (C) $175

    (D) $195

392. If 40 of 120 laborers work overtime, about what percentage of the laborers works overtime?

    (A) 33%

    (B) 35%

    (C) 50%

    (D) 40%

393. Sophia has some books, and Alfonzo has twice as many. Together, they have 18 books. How many books does Sophia have?

(A) 5

(B) 10

(C) 2

(D) 6

394. A troop hiked to a camp. They returned by a path that was 2.5 miles shorter than the original path they had taken. If they hiked 7 miles in all, how many miles did they walk to the camp?

(A) 4.5

(B) 3

(C) 5

(D) 4.75

395. At target practice, Ted missed the target 11 times fewer than his total number of shots. If 3/4 of the number of shots fired was 9 times the number of misses, how many shots were fired?

(A) 6

(B) 12

(C) 14

(D) 10

396. A large office has 36 desks, some single and some double. If the seating capacity of the room is 42, how many single desks are there?

(A) 6

(B) 30

(C) 26

(D) 18

397. If the cost of a particular computer program is $\frac{1}{9}$ the cost of a home computer system without the program and if the computer system plus the program costs $810, how much does the program alone cost?

(A) $95

(B) $65

(C) $81

(D) $36

398. What is the second of four consecutive odd numbers whose sum is 88?

(A) 19

(B) 21

(C) 27

(D) 13

399. Lenny has 3 more quarters than dimes. If he has $3.55 in all, how many quarters does he have?

(A) 8

(B) 7

(C) 11

(D) 10

400. A train left New York at 9 a.m. At 11 a.m., a second train left, going 24 miles an hour faster than the first train. It passed the first train at 3 p.m. How many miles from New York did the fast train pass the slow train?

(A) 245

(B) 236

(C) 288

(D) 291

401. In the 12 weeks of summer vacation, the number of clear days was 8 more than 3 times the number of rainy days. How many rainy days were there?

(A) 18

(B) 21

(C) 19

(D) 15

402. Joe's mother sent him a total of 132 cookies. She sent 18 fewer oatmeal cookies than peanut butter cookies. How many oatmeal cookies did she send to Joe?

(A) 75

(B) 62

(C) 55

(D) 57

403. The ratio of the number of yards in a given distance to the number of meters is 3,937:3,600. How many yards are there in 720 meters?

(A) 787.4 yards

(B) 855.2 yards

(C) 829.4 yards

(D) 756.2 yards

404. The interest on Jerry's fixed sum of money depends on the length of time the money is invested. If it draws $60 in 4 months, how much will it draw in 1.5 years?

(A) $320

(B) $240

(C) $270

(D) $200

405. Robert's boat can go 9 miles per hour (mph) in still water. He can go 44 miles downstream in a river in the same time as it would take him to go 28 miles upstream. What is the speed of the current in the river?

(A) 5 mph

(B) 2 mph

(C) 3 mph

(D) 2.5 mph

406. Two machines are used to attach parts in a factory. One requires 8 hours to attach the needed parts; the other requires 6 hours. How long would it take the two machines working together to attach the parts?

(A) $3\frac{3}{4}$ hours

(B) $4\frac{1}{2}$ hours

(C) $3\frac{5}{6}$ hours

(D) $3\frac{3}{7}$ hours

407. Noah doubled the number of magazine subscriptions he sold each week for four weeks. If he sold 32 subscriptions during the fourth week, how many did he sell the first week?

(A) 4

(B) 8

(C) 5

(D) 32

408. Alice made a new bean soup mixture by adding 15 pounds of lima beans that cost $9.22 per pound and 3 pounds of pinto beans that cost $5.80 per pound. What is the price per pound of Alice's new bean soup mixture?

(A) $8.25

(B) $8.65

(C) $9.40

(D) $9.05

409. A shipment of railroad ties measuring 400,000 board feet contained as many carloads as there were board feet in a tie. If each car held 250 ties, what was the total number of ties?

(A) 100,000

(B) 10,000

(C) 15,000

(D) 25,000

410. Two Alaskan dogs hauled freight 20 miles. If it had taken them 2 hours longer, the distance traveled per hour would have been $\frac{5}{6}$ of a mile less. How long did it take them?

(A) 4 hours

(B) 3.5 hours

(C) 8 hours

(D) 6 hours

411. When Bob received his shipment of 50,000 tomatoes, 20% were too badly bruised to sell. How many could he still sell?

(A) 35,000

(B) 45,000

(C) 30,000

(D) 40,000

412. If Riverside Automotive has 78 employees and twice as many men work for them as women, how many men work for Riverside Automotive?

(A) 35

(B) 52

(C) 26

(D) 24

413. Two dentists have a total of 16 patients to see in one day. Dr. Owen has to see 2 more patients than Dr. Green. How many patients does Dr. Owen see?

(A) 6

(B) 10

(C) 7

(D) 9

414. George gives 10% of his gross earnings to charity. If his net earnings are $425 after paying 12% in taxes, how much will he have after giving to his favorite charity?

(A) $395.50

(B) $376.70

(C) $387.55

(D) $377.49

415. Mr. Barclay sold goods for $21 and lost a percent equal to the number of dollars he paid for the goods. How much did the goods cost him?

(A) $70

(B) $55

(C) $40

(D) $95

416. Find a fraction whose value is $\frac{2}{3}$ and whose numerator is 3 greater than half its denominator.

(A) $\frac{10}{16}$

(B) $\frac{6}{9}$

(C) $\frac{12}{18}$

(D) $\frac{12}{16}$

417. Find two consecutive integers whose sum is equal to 129.

(A) 64, 65

(B) 61, 68

(C) 65, 66

(D) 63, 64

418. Mr. Cameron purchased a shirt for $20. He sold it for $26. By what percentage did he increase the price?

(A) 5

(B) 20

(C) 30

(D) 25

419. During a car trip, Asher drove for 2 hours, made a stop for lunch, and then drove 200 miles in 3 hours. Find how many miles he traveled before lunch if the average speed for the entire journey was 70 miles per hour.

(A) 210 miles

(B) 150 miles

(C) 175 miles

(D) 165 miles

420. The sum of the first and third of three consecutive odd integers is 131 less than three times the second integer. Find the first of the three integers.

(A) 131

(B) 111

(C) 129

(D) 117

421. Mason ate 100 peanut butter cups in five days. Each day he ate six more than he ate the previous day. How many peanut butter cups did Mason eat on the first day?

(A) 16

(B) 12

(C) 8

(D) 20

422. Nathanael and his three friends order the same thing for lunch except Nathanael has an extra slice of pizza for $1.25. If the total bill is $10.45, what is Nathanael's portion of the bill?

(A) $3.55

(B) $3.50

(C) $2.75

(D) $3.75

423. Ella's family recipe for macaroni and cheese makes 4 servings of 310 calories each. Ella decided to make 112% of the amount in the recipe rather than her usual 100%. Approximately how many calories are in Ella's batch of macaroni and cheese?

(A) 1,860

(B) 1,544

(C) 1,389

(D) 1,490

Geometry Word Problems

424. A rectangular conference room has a perimeter of 200 feet. The shortest two sides of the room add up to 50 feet. What is the length of each of the longest two sides?

(A) 60 feet

(B) 85 feet

(C) 75 feet

(D) 90 feet

425. If a 5-foot tall bush casts a 2-foot shadow, how tall is a tree standing next to the bush that casts an 8-foot shadow at the same time?

(A) 25 feet

(B) 15 feet

(C) 20 feet

(D) 10 feet

426. Aiden is purchasing carpet for his den. How much carpet will he need to cover the room if it's 12 feet long by 10 feet wide?

(A) 22 square feet

(B) 120 square feet

(C) 125 square feet

(D) 240 square feet

427. The shooting range is putting up a wall that's 10 feet by 16 feet. If each brick is 3 inches wide by 5 inches long, how many bricks would you need to complete the wall?

(A) 1,600

(B) 1,255

(C) 3,050

(D) 1,536

428. Joe ran around a pentagon-shaped track with sides each measuring 1,760 feet. If he made three complete trips around the track, how far did he run?

(A) 37,500 feet

(B) 15,300 feet

(C) 20,150 feet

(D) 26,400 feet

429. What is the width of a rectangular vegetable garden whose perimeter is 150 feet and length is 50 feet?

(A) 100 feet

(B) 25 feet

(C) 200 feet

(D) 50 feet

430. A line segment is 75 inches long. Divide this line segment into two parts whose lengths have a ratio of 3 to 2. How long is the shortest segment of the line?

(A) 15

(B) 30

(C) 45

(D) 20

431. The area of a square is 121 square feet. Find the length of each side.

(A) 12 feet

(B) 14 feet

(C) 11 feet

(D) 20 feet

432. Find the hypotenuse of a right triangle if side F measures 6 and side S measures 8.

(A) 5

(B) 21

(C) 12

(D) 10

433. A can of pork and beans has a radius of 3 inches and a height of 7 inches. What is the volume of the can?

(A) 198 cubic inches

(B) 156 cubic inches

(C) 21 cubic inches

(D) 42 cubic inches

434. A carpenter is building a ramp to a platform that is 9 feet off the ground. The ground is perfectly level, and he begins 16 feet away from the structure. How long will the face of the ramp be?

(A)   25 feet

(B)   20.33 feet

(C)   21.1 feet

(D)   18.36 feet

435. A rancher is driving along the edge of a round sinkhole on his property. The sinkhole's diameter is 14 kilometers. If he walked around the sinkhole, how far would he walk?

(A)   34 kilometers

(B)   54 kilometers

(C)   44 kilometers

(D)   35 kilometers

436. What is the area of a rectangle whose length is 10 inches and whose width is 6 inches?

(A)   16 square inches

(B)   66 square inches

(C)   60 square inches

(D)   4 square inches

437. A playing court is 24 feet longer than twice its width. The distance around the court is 210 feet. What is the width of the court?

(A)   27 feet

(B)   33 feet

(C)   29 feet

(D)   18 feet

438. What is the volume of a box with edges that are each 5 inches long?

(A)   25 cubic inches

(B)   10 cubic inches

(C)   200 cubic inches

(D)   125 cubic inches

439. A steam pipe was enclosed in a casing. The diameter of the pipe was $\frac{2}{3}$ of the diameter of the casing. The radius of the casing was 2 inches less than the diameter of the pipe. What was the diameter of the casing?

(A)   8 inches

(B)   12 inches

(C)   18 inches

(D)   10 inches

440. A playground is 101 feet longer than it is wide. If its width were decreased by 25 feet, the length would be twice its width. What are the dimensions of the playground?

(A)   252 feet × 151 feet

(B)   250 feet × 151 feet

(C)   231 feet × 332 feet

(D)   301 feet × 200 feet

441. Joe was hired to paint the trim around the base of the courtyard wall. How many feet of trim must Joe paint?

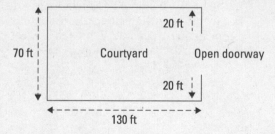

(A)   350 feet

(B)   400 feet

(C)   310 feet

(D)   370 feet

442. What will it cost to carpet a room 10 feet wide and 12 feet long if carpet costs $12.51 per square yard?

(A) $166.80

(B) $213.50

(C) $186.23

(D) $165.12

443. What is the surface area of the box?

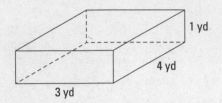

1 yd
4 yd
3 yd

(A)   38 square yards

(B)   42 square yards

(C)   13 square yards

(D)   12 square yards

444. The width of a large American flag is $\frac{3}{5}$ its length. The area of the flag is 1,500 square feet. What are the dimensions of the flag?

(A)   35 feet × 55 feet

(B)   50 feet × 30 feet

(C)   75 feet × 100 feet

(D)   60 feet × 100 feet

445. Michael is going to fence the area shown in the figure. If side A is 12 feet long, side B is 2 feet longer than side A, and side C is 1 foot longer than side B, how many feet of fence will Michael have to purchase?

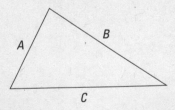

A
B
C

(A)   41 feet

(B)   24 feet

(C)   44 feet

(D)   35 feet

446. Jeffrey wants to surprise his wife with new carpeting in her family room. He can purchase the carpet for $3.50 per square yard, plus $12 per hour for labor. Assuming the job will take 4 hours to complete, how much will Jeffrey spend on this surprise?

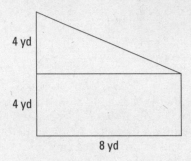

4 yd
4 yd
8 yd

(A) $216.00

(B) $245.50

(C) $155.75

(D) $325.00

447. If a triangle has interior angles of 30 and 50 degrees, what is the measurement of the third angle?

(A)   10 degrees

(B)   110 degrees

(C)   80 degrees

(D)   100 degrees

448. What is the circumference of this circle?

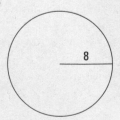

8

(A)   50.27

(B)   25.25

(C)   52.40

(D)   36

449. An electric motor makes 3,000 revolutions per minute. How many degrees does it rotate in one second?

(A) 15,000

(B) 12,000

(C) 6,000

(D) 18,000

450. If the radius of a certain circle is 12, what is the diameter of the same circle?

(A) 6

(B) 24

(C) 18

(D) 36

Fact-Finding Word Problems

451. 40% of what number is 80?

(A) 120

(B) 200

(C) 220

(D) 240

452. If 10% of the 2,400 people who entered a drawing won a prize, how many did not win a prize?

(A) 240

(B) 2,160

(C) 24

(D) 2,240

453. Susan goes out to lunch and receives a bill for $23.00. What is the total amount she pays if she includes a 20% tip?

(A) $23.20

(B) $27.40

(C) $27.60

(D) $21.40

454. If 30 people at a gathering of 70 people are vegetarians, approximately what percent of the people are vegetarians?

(A) 4%

(B) 10%

(C) 35%

(D) 43%

455. The average price of a new car is $30,303. What is that price to the nearest hundred?

(A) $30,000

(B) $31,000

(C) $30,300

(D) $30,310

456. Mrs. Smith invested $50 in the stock market. The first year, her investment shrank by 10%. The next year, it grew by 10%. How much does she have now?

(A) $49.50

(B) $50.00

(C) $50.50

(D) $40.50

457. It takes Steve 56 hours to paint his fence. If his 3 children each work 7 hours per day with him, how many days will it take the family to paint the fence, assuming the children keep up with their dad's pace?

(A) 2

(B) 4

(C) 2.5

(D) 1

458. A tablet is on sale for 20% off its normal price of $400. If the sales tax is 5%, what is the final cost of the tablet?

(A) $300

(B) $336

(C) $350

(D) $420

459. If a phone poll of 20,000 calls resulted in 4,000 responses, what was the percentage of responses to actual calls?

(A) 20%

(B) 10%

(C) 5%

(D) 40%

460. Mike took Jen bowling for the first time. He bowled two games with scores of 157 and 175. Jen had never bowled before and scored 78 and 98. What was Mike's average score?

(A) 88

(B) 127

(C) 156

(D) 166

461. Josiah worked 32 hours last week. He earned $368. If he earned $437 this week, how many hours did he work?

(A) 38

(B) 40

(C) 35

(D) 36

462. Edward's electric bill for the month of July was $90.12. The electric company charges a flat monthly fee of $20.00 for service plus $0.14 per kilowatt-hour of electricity used. Approximately how many kilowatt-hours of electricity did Edward use in July?

(A) 361.11

(B) 424.12

(C) 500.86

(D) 567.17

463. The sum of three consecutive integers is 87. What is the first integer?

(A) 28

(B) 30

(C) 21

(D) 25

464. A number decreased by 439.5 gives the result of 1,293.1. What is the number?

(A) 1,234.5

(B) 799.6

(C) 876.6

(D) 1,732.6

465. A new car depreciates at the rate of $2,500 per year. If the original price of the car was $30,000, what is the value after six years (assuming the bank loan is paid off)?

(A) $15,000

(B) $20,000

(C) $10,000

(D) $5,000

466. Rod won the lottery of $60,000. He invested part at 8% and placed the remainder in tax-free bonds at 7%. His annual income from the investment was $4,700. How much was invested at 8%?

(A) $50,000

(B) $10,000

(C) $5,000

(D) $45,000

467. Jack eats three hot dogs per minute, while Jeff eats two hot dogs per minute. How many total hot dogs do they eat in 12 minutes?

(A) 35

(B) 40

(C) 60

(D) 65

468. Water flows into Mom's sink at 6 ounces per minute and drains out at 2 ounces per minute. The sink holds 180 ounces. How long does it take to fill the sink?

- (A) 40 minutes
- (B) 45 minutes
- (C) 39 minutes
- (D) 50 minutes

469. A fruit bowl has 6 oranges and 4 apples. If one piece of fruit is selected at random and then a second piece of fruit is selected at random, what are the chances that both pieces of fruit will be oranges?

- (A) 1 in 6
- (B) 1 in 3
- (C) 3 in 10
- (D) 1 in 5

470. What is the price of a $200 item after successive discounts of 10% and 15%?

- (A) $75
- (B) $175
- (C) $153
- (D) $150

471. It takes an average of 3 person-hours to produce 1 ton of an item. How many people would be required to produce 36 tons in 6 hours?

- (A) 23
- (B) 12
- (C) 6
- (D) 18

472. What is the cost of 16 pounds of candy at $2.98 per pound?

- (A) $47.68
- (B) $16.98
- (C) $47.90
- (D) $45.97

473. At 9 a.m. one day in January, the thermometer registered 12° above zero. For the next four hours, the temperature rose at the rate of 2° an hour, and then it began to fall 3° an hour. Find the temperature at 5 p.m.

- (A) 18°
- (B) 8°
- (C) 6°
- (D) 10°

474. Mrs. Jones is 28 years older than her daughter. In 11 years, she will be 3 times as old as her daughter. How old is Mrs. Jones now?

- (A) 31
- (B) 42
- (C) 29
- (D) 35

475. Cindy is making four music CDs. Each contains $2\frac{3}{4}$ hours of music. How many hours of music does she need to fill the CDs?

- (A) 11
- (B) 12
- (C) 8
- (D) 5.5

476. The first term of an arithmetic sequence is 200, and the common difference is –10. Find the value of the 20th term.

- (A) 30
- (B) 10
- (C) 410
- (D) 80

477. Matt played 4 video games at a video arcade. If his scores were 120, 125, 135, and 140, what was his mean score?

- (A) 120
- (B) 128
- (C) 130
- (D) 135

478. A furniture company charges a delivery fee of 5% of an order's total price. What is the charge for delivering a mattress priced at $850, a bedroom set priced at $1,155, and a recliner priced at $355 to the same location?

(A) $2,360

(B) $120

(C) $118

(D) $125

479. Julius Caesar was born in the year 100 BC and was 56 years old when he was assassinated. In what year was he assassinated?

(A) 156 BC

(B) 144 BC

(C) 44 BC

(D) 44 AD

480. Robert made $300 on one investment. He lost $500 on a second and made $400 on a third. What were his earnings on the three investments?

(A) $200 loss

(B) $200 gain

(C) $500 gain

(D) $150 loss

481. A box contained four green balls, three red balls, and two purple balls. Jason removed one purple ball from the box and did not put the ball back in the box. He then removed another ball from the box. What is the probability that the second ball Jason removed was purple?

(A) $\frac{1}{24}$

(B) $\frac{1}{9}$

(C) $\frac{1}{8}$

(D) $\frac{2}{7}$

482. Jimmy fills up his truck at $3.45 per gallon. His truck holds 42 gallons of gas. If he already had 9 gallons of gas in his tank, how much does Jimmy spend at the pump?

(A) $104.92

(B) $97.85

(C) $113.85

(D) $144.90

483. Quinton invested $650 at $7\frac{1}{2}\%$ simple interest. How much will he have after 5 years?

(A) $756.00

(B) $695.45

(C) $893.75

(D) $821.15

484. If Samuel travels 55 miles per hour, approximately how long will it take him to travel 250 miles?

(A) 4.5 hours

(B) 5 hours

(C) 4 hours

(D) 5.5 hours

485. Ralph has found that he can sell 250 tickets when he sells them for $25 each. However, if he sells them for $22, he can sell 450. How much more money in sales does he make when he sells the tickets at a discount?

(A) $2,450

(B) $3,600

(C) $450

(D) $3,650

486. Nat's goal was to complete $\frac{4}{5}$ of his math problems before dinner. When dinner was served, he had completed $\frac{5}{7}$ of the problems. How much more of his assignment does he have left to do?

(A) $\frac{1}{5}$

(B) $\frac{1}{7}$

(C) $\frac{4}{14}$

(D) $\frac{2}{10}$

487. Billy left the house without his wallet. When he went to purchase his lunch, he had to dig into his change stash to buy it. How much did he have left if he had 15 quarters, 15 dimes, 22 nickels, and 12 pennies and the lunch cost $5.52?

(A) $0.45

(B) $1.15

(C) $0.95

(D) $1.03

488. If Bentley is going to get a scholarship, he needs to make at least 93% in his math class. If he got a 97 on his first test, an 88 on the second, and a 90 on the third, what must his score be on the final if it counts for 1/3 of the grade?

(A) 94

(B) 95

(C) 98

(D) 96

489. Find two numbers whose sum is 26 and whose product is 165.

(A) 11, 15

(B) 12, 14

(C) 10, 16

(D) 17, 9

490. 20% of 2 is equal to what?

(A) 20

(B) 10

(C) 0.4

(D) 0.04

491. Cade bought $1\frac{3}{4}$ pounds of cheddar cheese, 3.75 pounds of mozzarella and $4\frac{1}{2}$ pounds of American cheese. How many pounds of cheese did Cade buy?

(A) 10

(B) 7.5

(C) 11.25

(D) 6.75

492. Cooper was going to buy a car for $5,800 at a buy here/pay here car lot. The car dealer offered him two options for buying the car. He could pay the full amount in cash, or he could pay $1,000 down and $230 a month for 24 months on the installment plan. How much more would he pay for the car on the installment plan?

(A) $1,200

(B) $720

(C) $860

(D) $640

493. Cole is reading a 445-page book. He has already read 157 pages. If he reads 24 pages a day, how long will it take him to finish the book?

(A) 55 days

(B) 288 days

(C) 24 days

(D) 12 days

494. If it takes 24 seconds to write a tweet and 8 seconds to send it, what is the greatest number of tweets that can be written and sent in 6 minutes?

(A) 15

(B) 12

(C) 11

(D) 8

495. Using his $50 gift card, Justin bought 5 apps for $1.99 each and a new set of headphones for $10. After these purchases, what was the remaining balance on his gift card?

(A) $5.05

(B) $30.05

(C) $25.55

(D) $28.55

496. A car averages 20 miles per gallon of gas in city driving and 30 miles per gallon in highway driving. At these rates, how many gallons of gas will the car use on a 300-mile trip if 45 miles of the trip distance is highway driving and the rest is city driving?

(A) 14.25

(B) 11

(C) 12.50

(D) 15.50

497. Jasmine started a cleaning service. During her first month in business, Jasmine spent $380 on supplies and drove 800 miles at an average cost of $0.30 per mile. In addition, her business phone and other expenses were $198. That month Jasmine completed 60 jobs, earning $50 per job. What was Jasmine's profit during her first month in business?

(A) $818

(B) $2,488

(C) $2,182

(D) $2,042

498. What is the number of red balloons on a float that contains 25 balloons if 56% of the balloons are not red?

(A) 14

(B) 9

(C) 16

(D) 11

499. Working together, 2 groomers can groom 8 dogs in 3 hours. How many hours would it take 3 groomers to groom 12 dogs at this rate?

(A) 3

(B) 4

(C) 2

(D) 2.5

500. A train traveling at 30 miles per hour enters a tunnel that is 1 mile long. The length of the train is 1 mile. How many minutes after the front of the train enters the tunnel does the back of the train exit the tunnel?

(A) 2

(B) 6

(C) 4

(D) 8

Chapter 5

General Science: Knowing about the World around You

The General Science subtest on the ASVAB is used to calculate some military composite scores for job-qualification purposes. Not surprisingly, this subtest measures your knowledge of various topics, including plants and animals, the human body, the solar system, clouds and rain, and chemical structures. Generally speaking, you'll either know the answer to the question right off the bat, or you won't. Memorizing common facts related to each topic under the General Science umbrella can help you score well on this test.

The Questions You'll Work On

The topics covered in the General Science subtest vary greatly, but for the most part, the questions fall into one of these categories:

- ✓ **Science basics:** This question type may ask for definitions or general science principles.
- ✓ **Biology:** These questions deal with major body systems, genetics, and cell structures as well as plants, animals, and their relationship to their environment.
- ✓ **Chemistry:** These ask about reactions, elements, energies, and chemical changes.
- ✓ **Astronomy:** This question type deals with the solar system and the universe beyond.
- ✓ **Geology:** The questions in this category cover the physical changes of the Earth, including its history.
- ✓ **Meteorology:** These questions quiz you on the atmosphere and its phenomena, including weather and climate.

What to Watch Out For

Keep in mind the following pointers as you work through the questions in this chapter:

- ✓ Latin roots may help you find the correct answers to some questions. For instance, if you know that the root *hydro* means water, you may be able to eliminate any unrelated choices right away.
- ✓ Metric prefixes can help you solve a problem, especially if you remember that *deci* is one-tenth, *deca* is ten, and so on.
- ✓ Some answer choices don't necessarily pertain to the question at hand. Read the question carefully and use your common sense to eliminate these distracters right away.

Science Basics

501. What does a hypothesis become if it holds up to repeated testing?

(A) law

(B) fact

(C) theory

(D) principle

502. Which of the following is a unit of length?

(A) meter

(B) liter

(C) gram

(D) watt

503. Which of the following is a unit of volume?

(A) meter

(B) liter

(C) gram

(D) watt

504. Which of the following is a unit of mass?

(A) meter

(B) liter

(C) gram

(D) watt

505. Which of these metric prefixes means one-tenth?

(A) milli-

(B) centi-

(C) deci-

(D) deca-

506. Which of the following metric prefixes means one million?

(A) kilo-

(B) mega-

(C) hecto-

(D) deca-

507. What is one milligram?

(A) one-tenth of a gram

(B) one-thousandth of a gram

(C) one-hundredth of a gram

(D) one-millionth of a gram

508. What do geologists study?

(A) outer space

(B) the physical history of the Earth

(C) weather

(D) dinosaurs

509. What do meteorologists study?

(A) outer space

(B) the physical history of the Earth

(C) weather

(D) dinosaurs

510. What do paleontologists study?

(A) outer space

(B) the physical history of the Earth

(C) weather

(D) dinosaurs

511. What job would you apply for if you wanted to study the life and culture of the past?

(A) genealogist

(B) archeologist

(C) ecologist

(D) ichthyologist

512. What is the term for the force that gravity exerts on a mass?

(A) weight

(B) compound

(C) neutron

(D) kinetic

Biology

513. What is agriculture?

(A) the study of plants

(B) the study of animals

(C) the study of bugs

(D) the study of farming

514. What is botany?

(A) the study of plants

(B) the study of animals

(C) the study of bugs

(D) the study of farming

515. What is ecology?

(A) the study of plants

(B) the study of heredity

(C) the study of bugs

(D) the study of the environment

516. What is entomology?

(A) the study of fish

(B) the study of heredity

(C) the study of bugs

(D) the study of genes

517. What do geneticists study?

(A) fish

(B) heredity

(C) health

(D) biology

518. Lions, tigers, and polar bears can be categorized as what?

(A) carnivores

(B) herbivores

(C) omnivores

(D) insectivores

519. Which of the following terms means defining groups of biological organisms?

(A) class

(B) ecology

(C) taxonomy

(D) biodiversity

520. Which of the following is true about the classification system of biology?

(A) Every animal is categorized according to the proper definition.

(B) Many disagreements occur among scientists about where an organism belongs.

(C) Every organism belongs to the *mammalian* classification.

(D) Every organism belongs to the *felidae* classification.

521. What kingdom of the classification system has more than one million species?

(A) animals

(B) plants

(C) protists

(D) fungi

522. If an organism has cell walls made of cellulose, what would scientists classify it as?

(A) animal

(B) plant

(C) protist

(D) fungus

523. To what kingdom do bacteria belong?

(A) plants

(B) monerans

(C) protists

(D) fungi

524. To which kingdom does an amoeba belong?

(A) plants

(B) monerans

(C) protists

(D) fungi

525. What kingdom doesn't include organisms that photosynthesize?

(A) monerans

(B) plants

(C) protists

(D) fungi

526. The brain is a part of what body system?

(A) circulatory system

(B) musculoskeletal system

(C) respiratory system

(D) central nervous system

527. The heart is part of what body system?

(A) circulatory system

(B) musculoskeletal system

(C) respiratory system

(D) central nervous system

528. The rectum is part of what body system?

(A) circulatory system

(B) digestive system

(C) respiratory system

(D) central nervous system

529. Bones are part of what body system?

(A) circulatory system

(B) musculoskeletal system

(C) respiratory system

(D) central nervous system

530. What do humans exhale while breathing?

(A) oxygen

(B) carbon dioxide

(C) waste

(D) germs

531. Where in the body do you find DNA?

(A) a cell's nucleus

(B) cytoplasm

(C) cell membrane

(D) cell wall

532. What is cytoplasm mostly composed of?

(A) oxygen

(B) carbon dioxide

(C) water

(D) air

533. What part of the cell protects the cell's contents?

(A) cell membrane

(B) DNA

(C) prokaryotes

(D) cytoplasm

534. What do plant cells contain that animal cells do not?

(A) nuclei

(B) cytoplasm

(C) chlorophyll

(D) lysosomes

535. What part of a cell combines amino acids into proteins?

(A) ribosome

(B) chloroplast

(C) mitochondria

(D) nucleoplasm

536. What is the term for the process in which a cell converts nutrients into energy?

(A) metabolism

(B) cellular respiration

(C) photosynthesis

(D) osmosis

537. Which process occurs when carbon dioxide and water are converted into glucose and oxygen?

(A) metabolism

(B) cellular respiration

(C) photosynthesis

(D) osmosis

538. What term describes when water or another solvent moves through the cell membrane?

(A) metabolism

(B) cellular respiration

(C) photosynthesis

(D) osmosis

539. What term describes when one nucleus of a cell divides, forming two?

(A) metabolism

(B) mitosis

(C) recession

(D) division

540. What term describes the division of cells to create egg cells and sperm cells?

(A) meiosis

(B) mitosis

(C) metabolism

(D) mitochondria

541. What do the father's sex chromosomes determine about his offspring during reproduction?

(A) the color of the offspring's hair

(B) the color of the offspring's eyes

(C) whether the offspring is a boy or girl

(D) whether the offspring will have a genetic defect

542. What term is used to describe a gene that is not strong enough to express itself?

(A) dormant

(B) dominant

(C) recessive

(D) progressive

543. Which of the following terms refers to the functional unit of inheritance that controls the transmission of one or more traits in the human body?

(A) DNA

(B) gene

(C) cells

(D) chromosome

544. What is the term for a small space in the cells of an organism that contains fluid?

(A) chromatin

(B) ribosome

(C) mitochondria

(D) vacuole

545. What parts of a cell are rich in fats, proteins, and enzymes?

(A) chromatin

(B) ribosome

(C) mitochondria

(D) vacuole

546. Which term refers to the collection of veins that join together to form a large vessel that collects blood from the heart muscle?

(A) right ventricle

(B) left atrium

(C) coronary sulcus

(D) coronary sinus

547. What tissue separates the atria from the ventricles in a mammalian heart?

(A) endocardium

(B) cardiac skeleton

(C) fibrous pericardium

(D) intravenous tubercle

548. Where is the aorta of the heart located in the body?

(A) from the neck to the heart

(B) from the heart to the abdomen

(C) from the heart to the leg

(D) only in the heart

Chemistry

549. At what point on the Fahrenheit scale does water boil?

(A) 32 degrees

(B) 100 degrees

(C) 212 degrees

(D) 273 degrees

550. At what point on the Celsius scale does water boil?

(A) 32 degrees

(B) 100 degrees

(C) 212 degrees

(D) 273 degrees

551. What is another term for "absolute zero?"

(A) 0 freezing

(B) 0 centigrade

(C) 0 frostbite

(D) 0 kelvin

552. How do you convert from Celsius to Fahrenheit?

(A) $C = -32 - \frac{100}{32}$

(B) $F = \frac{9}{5}C + 32$

(C) $F = \frac{100}{32} + \frac{9}{5}$

(D) $C = \frac{9}{5} + F$

553. How do you convert from Fahrenheit to Celsius?

(A) $C = (F - 32)\frac{5}{9}$

(B) $F = \frac{9}{5}C + 32$

(C) $F = \frac{100}{32} + \frac{9}{5}$

(D) $C = \frac{9}{5} + F$

554. What is the term for a chemical substance that is broken down into its simplest form?

(A) weight

(B) element

(C) mass

(D) gene

555. What is the smallest particle of an element that can exist either in combination or alone?

(A) nucleus

(B) atom

(C) proton

(D) neutron

556. What is the atomic number of an element equal to?

(A) the number of protons

(B) the number of neutrons

(C) the number of atoms

(D) the number of compounds

557. What is the only element with an atomic number of 1?

(A) oxygen

(B) hydrogen

(C) lithium

(D) helium

558. What is the term for negatively charged particles that float around an atom's nucleus?

(A) protons

(B) neutrons

(C) electrons

(D) compounds

559. What is the purpose of the periodic table?

(A) It lists the periods of time.

(B) It shows which chemicals should not be mixed together.

(C) It classifies the elements.

(D) There is no real purpose.

560. What is the atomic number for uranium?

(A) 26

(B) 80

(C) 92

(D) 108

561. What is the atomic number for sodium?

(A) 2

(B) 11

(C) 22

(D) 112

562. What is the atomic number of helium?

(A) 1

(B) 2

(C) 3

(D) 4

563. What is another name for kinetic energy?

(A) real energy

(B) fake energy

(C) the energy of motion

(D) dormant energy

564. What happens to the molecules of an element after the element undergoes a physical change, such as heating or cooling?

(A) They turn into different molecules.

(B) They multiply.

(C) They don't change.

(D) None of the above.

565. What is the lanthanide series?

(A) a group of rare gases on the periodic table

(B) a group of rare earth metals on the periodic table

(C) a group of deadly gases on the periodic table

(D) a group of radioactive elements on the periodic table

566. What is the term for an element or molecule that results from a chemical reaction?

(A) reactant

(B) product

(C) molecule

(D) chemical

567. What happens scientifically when water freezes?

(A) It experiences only a chemical change.

(B) It experiences only a physical change.

(C) The molecules change.

(D) The water evaporates.

568. Which metallic element is similar to uranium?

(A) plutonium

(B) lead

(C) cadmium

(D) sulfur

569. Which element is necessary to the human body for proper nerve and muscle function?

(A) magnesium

(B) carbon

(C) helium

(D) neon

570. What is the densest metal known to man?

(A) iron

(B) osmium

(C) titanium

(D) copper

571. What metal is liquid at ordinary temperatures?

(A) iron

(B) copper

(C) mercury

(D) gold

Astronomy

572. What do astronomers study?

(A) outer space

(B) the physical history of the Earth

(C) weather

(D) dinosaurs

573. Which term refers to the plasma that continuously erupts from the sun's surface into space?

(A) solar stream

(B) solar wind

(C) solar power

(D) solar gas

574. Approximately how much bigger is the sun's diameter compared to the Earth's?

(A) 25 times

(B) 50 times

(C) 100 times

(D) 200 times

575. What are asteroids, planets, moons, and stars grouped as astronomically?

(A) celestial bodies

(B) satellites

(C) variable stars

(D) galaxies

576. How many known moons does Jupiter have?

(A) 11

(B) 32

(C) 67

(D) 74

577. Why are regions of the Earth unequal in daylight and darkness?

(A) because the Earth rotates on a tilted axis

(B) because the sun changes direction halfway through the year

(C) because the Earth's orbit is slower during different seasons

(D) because the Earth's axis moves around during rotation

578. What two main components do the four terrestrial planets in our solar system contain?

(A) iron and sulfur

(B) iron and rock

(C) rock and oxygen

(D) rock and carbon

579. What are the "gas giant" planets also called?

(A) terrestrial planets

(B) ghost planets

(C) jovian planets

(D) asteroid planets

580. What planet can be viewed by the naked eye from the Earth?

(A) Mercury

(B) Uranus

(C) Neptune

(D) Jupiter

581. How do astronomers classify Pluto?

(A) the smallest planet

(B) a dwarf planet

(C) a non-planet

(D) a moon

582. Pluto's diameter is what fraction of Earth's diameter?

(A) 1/10

(B) 1/6

(C) 1/2

(D) 3/4

583. How far away is Venus from the sun?

(A) the first planet

(B) the second planet

(C) the fifth planet

(D) the sixth planet

584. What is the largest moon in the solar system?

(A) Earth's moon

(B) Jupiter's moon, Ganymede

(C) Saturn's moon, Titan

(D) Pluto's moon, Charon

585. What are the "Galilean satellites?"

(A) Saturn's moons

(B) Jupiter's moons

(C) Neptune's moons

(D) Uranus's moons

586. What is a meteor also known as?

(A) a comet

(B) an asteroid

(C) a shooting star

(D) a satellite

587. What is a meteorite?

(A) a smaller meteor

(B) a meteor that strikes the Earth

(C) the particles that form a meteor

(D) none of the above

588. What causes a blue tail to trail behind a comet?

(A) Vapors from its nucleus are blown by solar winds.

(B) Rock in the comet heats up when it gets closer to the sun.

(C) A comet is made of fire.

(D) Comets do not have blue tails.

589. What comet is visible to the naked eye from Earth every 75 or 76 years?

(A) Faye

(B) Gale

(C) Johnson

(D) Halley

590. Where is the asteroid belt located?

(A) between the sun and Mercury

(B) between Earth and Mars

(C) between Mars and Jupiter

(D) between Uranus and Neptune

591. What is the largest asteroid named in the asteroid belt?

(A) Pluto

(B) Vesta

(C) Pallas

(D) Ceres

592. What do scientists sometimes call asteroids?

(A) minor planets

(B) comets

(C) rocks

(D) ice balls

Geology

593. What is the Earth's surface called?

(A) crust

(B) mantle

(C) magma

(D) top

594. What layer makes up the most mass of planet Earth?

(A) core

(B) mantle

(C) magma

(D) chamber

595. What are the cracks in the Earth's crust called?

(A) cracks

(B) chambers

(C) pockets

(D) faults

596. What is the Earth's core made of?

(A) oxygen

(B) iron

(C) frozen rock

(D) molten lava

597. What is the Earth's mantle made of?

(A) lava

(B) fire

(C) rock

(D) ice

598. What part of the Earth forms volcanoes?

(A) tectonic plates

(B) lava pockets

(C) mantle cracks

(D) magma faults

599. What is lava made of?

(A) fire

(B) gas

(C) rock

(D) ice

600. Earthquakes, volcanic activity, mountain-building, and oceanic trench formation occur along what part of the Earth?

(A) near the ocean

(B) over tectonic plates

(C) in areas of high elevation

(D) none of the above

Meteorology

601. What layer of the Earth divides the atmosphere and outer space?

(A) ionosphere

(B) exosphere

(C) thermosphere

(D) stratosphere

602. What is the term used to describe the many layers of air outside of the Earth's crust?

(A) troposphere

(B) stratosphere

(C) thermosphere

(D) atmosphere

603. What layer of the Earth is closest to the exosphere?

(A) ozone

(B) thermosphere

(C) stratosphere

(D) troposphere

604. What is the Earth's main protection against meteorites?

(A) mesosphere

(B) exosphere

(C) thermosphere

(D) stratosphere

605. What is the atmospheric layer called from the Earth's crust to approximately 8 miles up, where most weather changes are made?

(A) troposphere

(B) stratosphere

(C) mesosphere

(D) none of the above

606. What are fast-flowing, narrow air currents located in the Earth's atmosphere called?

(A) density

(B) air mass

(C) jet streams

(D) air chambers

607. What is the term used to describe how closely packed the air molecules are in the atmosphere?

(A) thermo-generation

(B) air density

(C) air mass

(D) cold front

608. What is the term used to describe when two different air masses meet in the atmosphere?

(A) pressure

(B) density

(C) hurricane

(D) front

609. What measures atmospheric pressure?

(A) barometer

(B) anemometer

(C) manometer

(D) none of the above

610. What are the clouds that look thin and wispy called?

(A) cirrus

(B) cumulus

(C) cumulonimbus

(D) stratus

611. What are the white, puffy clouds that you can imagine as personified shapes in the sky called?

(A) cirrus

(B) cumulus

(C) stratus

(D) puffus

612. What does the prefix nimbo- or the suffix -nimbus mean?

(A) precipitation

(B) high altitude

(C) low altitude

(D) cold front

613. What kind of clouds tends to stretch low and look like a gray blanket?

(A) cirrus

(B) cumulus

(C) stratus

(D) altocirrus

614. Mid-level clouds exist between 6,500 and 20,000 feet. What is the prefix used to describe this type of cloud?

(A) cirro-

(B) alto-

(C) nimbo-

(D) middo-

615. What type of cloud doesn't produce precipitation?

(A) cirrus

(B) cumulus

(C) stratus

(D) none of the above

Chapter 6

Auto and Shop Information: Nailing Down Vehicle and Workshop Basics

The ASVAB Auto and Shop Information subtest goes into calculating some military composite scores that are used for job-qualification purposes. Approximately half of the questions are based on automobile and engine information, including everyday knowledge about the way engines work. Most of the time, the auto-related information is fairly basic, as long as you know what the different parts of a car do and how they relate to the nearby parts. The other half of the test includes shop- and carpentry-based questions. These basic questions test your knowledge of tools and their functions. The purpose of this subtest is to measure your knowledge of the various topics related to the auto and shop fields.

The Questions You'll Work On

Here are the two categories of questions you'll encounter on the Auto and Shop Information subtest and work on in this chapter:

- ✔ **Auto:** The auto questions ask about engine parts, vehicle and engine function or malfunction, wear and tear, and the physical aspects of vehicle motion and nature.
- ✔ **Shop:** The shop questions test your knowledge of carpentry, building materials, tool identification, and the functions of those materials and tools.

What to Watch Out For

The following tips can help you as you work on the questions in this chapter:

- ✔ Use common sense when viewing tool images. A ratchet isn't going to look like a washer.
- ✔ Think about vehicle part placement when working through tough problems. A part with exhaust function isn't going to be near the brake pads.
- ✔ Use the names of parts or tools to help you choose the correct answer. For instance, the term *snips* may make you think of cutting something, and that's exactly what they do. Likewise, a *compressor* decreases volume, increasing the pressure of gases in an engine.

Auto

616. How many cylinders does a V8 engine have?

(A) 2

(B) 3

(C) 6

(D) 8

617. A car uses too much oil when which parts are worn?

(A) pistons

(B) piston rings

(C) main bearings

(D) connecting rods

618. Which of the following is a common component of a standard internal combustion engine, such as the one found in an automobile?

(A) piston

(B) hammer

(C) turbine

(D) hydraulic jack

619. Which automotive system uses the following components: water pump, radiator, and thermostat?

(A) the engine cooling system

(B) the interior heating system

(C) the exhaust system

(D) the braking system

620. What is the main function of engine oil?

(A) to measure engine temperature

(B) to lubricate engine parts

(C) to avoid engine combustion

(D) to clean engine fuel

621. What component in an engine opens as the connecting rod pulls the piston down, drawing the gas and air mixture into the cylinder?

(A) exhaust

(B) intake valve

(C) crankshaft

(D) flywheel

622. What does the acronym ZEV stand for?

(A) zero electronic vehicle

(B) zero emission vehicle

(C) zero electronic variable

(D) zero emission variable

623. Better fuel efficiency in a vehicle could best be attributed to what?

(A) a lighter load

(B) better gas prices

(C) more electronic computers

(D) an aftermarket gas pedal

624. In the term *CV joints,* what does *CV* stand for?

(A) continuously variable

(B) cruise velocity

(C) constant velocity

(D) controlled variable

625. Why do spark plugs misfire in a vehicle?

(A) They are dirty.

(B) They are improperly gapped.

(C) They are too old.

(D) All of the above.

626. What is undercoating?

   (A) a type of primer used to make a surface shiny

   (B) a process used to remove dings and dents

   (C) a technique used to create a smooth surface

   (D) a spray used to prevent rust

627. Why might you be hesitant to offer a jump start to another vehicle?

   (A) The battery terminals are not corroded.

   (B) One of the vehicles has a digital ignition system.

   (C) One of the vehicles makes a clicking sound when attempting to start.

   (D) The vehicle is really dirty.

628. What would you check on a vehicle if it were constantly overheating?

   (A) the thermostat

   (B) the radiator fluid

   (C) the cooling system for leaks

   (D) all of the above

629. Internal combustion engines are used in cars, trucks, construction equipment, and many other devices. What are they fueled by?

   (A) gasoline

   (B) diesel fuel

   (C) natural gas

   (D) all of the above

630. What part of an engine is shown here?

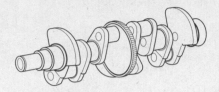

   (A) exhaust manifold

   (B) crankshaft

   (C) spark plug

   (D) intake valve

631. When would you consider changing your engine's push rods?

   (A) when they are excessively corroded

   (B) when your car will not operate

   (C) when they become bent

   (D) all of the above

632. What is most likely to occur if a spark plug's gap is too wide?

   (A) It could damage the motor.

   (B) It could misfire.

   (C) The car could swerve.

   (D) A fire could start in the engine.

633. Where does coolant pass through in order to cool an internal combustion engine?

   (A) radiator

   (B) engine block

   (C) exhaust valve

   (D) intake valve

634. What lowers the freezing point of water-based liquid?

   (A) ice

   (B) vinegar

   (C) antifreeze

   (D) plasma

635. Where does the oil flow in an engine after it leaves the oil pump?

(A) crankshaft

(B) intake valve

(C) push rod

(D) piston

636. What engine part opens to release exploded gases as the connecting rod moves the piston back up?

(A) flywheel

(B) crankshaft

(C) exhaust valve

(D) push rod

637. What assembly is pictured?

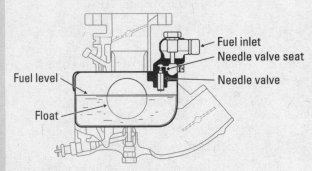

(A) exhaust

(B) compressor

(C) carburetor

(D) radiator

638. Which automotive part is pictured?

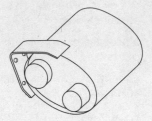

(A) crankshaft

(B) flywheel

(C) oil pump

(D) muffler

639. What is used as an emission control device?

(A) filter

(B) brake

(C) steering

(D) wheel

640. What vital component do disc brakes contain?

(A) ventilation

(B) calipers

(C) drums

(D) converters

641. Which of the following terms refers to the maximum rpm value the engine can reach without exploding?

(A) danger zone

(B) redline

(C) thermostat

(D) fire level

642. In a manual engine, what is located in between the engine and the transmission?

(A) clutch

(B) drive shaft

(C) U joint

(D) differential

643. What does an automatic transmission affect when it applies a different gear ratio to the input shaft?

(A) ignition

(B) combustion

(C) rpm value

(D) air injection

644. What component in a vehicle allows the drive wheels to rotate at different speeds?

(A) differential

(B) axial bearing

(C) torque converter

(D) transmission

645. What component of a vehicle is pictured?

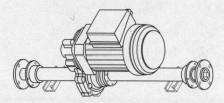

(A) exhaust

(B) differential

(C) crankcase

(D) clutch

646. What is the standard battery voltage for an average vehicle?

(A) 6

(B) 8

(C) 12

(D) 14

647. What electromechanical device converts mechanical energy to electrical energy in a vehicle?

(A) distributer

(B) alternator

(C) coil

(D) condenser

648. Which of the following parts is in an electronic ignition system?

(A) condenser

(B) starter

(C) coil

(D) distributor

649. What component routes high voltage in a vehicle from the ignition coil to the spark plugs in the correct firing order?

(A) distributor

(B) rotor

(C) cylinder

(D) capacitor

650. What is the primary purpose of an intake manifold?

(A) to burn fuel

(B) to distribute the air/fuel mixture

(C) to ignite the spark plugs

(D) to circulate coolant

651. Identify this automotive part.

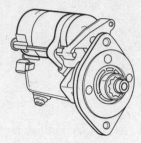

(A) catalytic converter

(B) crankshaft

(C) starter

(D) water pump

652. What converts hydraulic pressure and flow into angular displacement and torque?

(A) pneumatic motor

(B) hydraulic motor

(C) electric motor

(D) gas motor

653. What measures how much force is acting on an object and causing it to rotate?

(A) force

(B) torque

(C) velocity

(D) inertia

654. Which term refers to the computer that controls virtually every system in most modern vehicles?

(A) Electrical System Enhancer

(B) Emission Control Unit

(C) Engine Control Unit

(D) Electronic Sensor Enhancer

655. Why would you never add cold water to a hot engine?

(A) It could cool the engine too quickly.

(B) It could cause rust.

(C) It could crack the engine block.

(D) It could damage the water hoses.

656. What is the standard proportion for the water and coolant mixture in a radiator?

(A) 15/85

(B) 25/75

(C) 50/50

(D) 80/20

657. What hoses under the hood of a vehicle should you be extremely cautious of when replacing?

(A) radiator

(B) air conditioning

(C) water pump

(D) fuel pump

658. What is another name for Freon?

(A) CFC-12

(B) R-134a

(C) H20-1

(D) MM-90

659. What forms a cushion around the crankshaft and connecting rod to keep these parts from causing friction and wearing away?

(A) water

(B) heat

(C) oil

(D) coolant

660. What does the *W* mean in the oil multi-viscosity rating 10W-40?

(A) wheel

(B) water

(C) warranty

(D) winter

661. Identify the vehicle part pictured here.

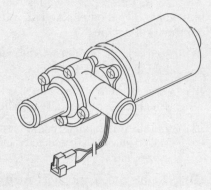

(A) water pump

(B) fuel filter

(C) radiator

(D) air conditioner

662. Identify the vehicle part shown here.

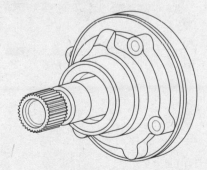

(A) water pump

(B) fuel filter

(C) oil pump

(D) air compressor

663. Which of the following devices is used for lifting all or part of a vehicle off the ground?

(A) motor mount

(B) jack

(C) jumper

(D) manifold

664. Which device measures the specific gravity of a liquid?

(A) ammeter

(B) hydrometer

(C) odometer

(D) dosimeter

665. Which of the following terms refers to a rubber, cork, paper, or metal plate that's inserted between two parts in order to prevent leakage?

(A) fuse

(B) gap

(C) gasket

(D) bearing

666. Which of the following allows the drive wheels to turn faster without forcing the engine to increase its rpm?

(A) clutch

(B) overdrive

(C) radial

(D) powertrain

667. What does *psi* stand for?

(A) pounds per square inch

(B) polymer shifting injector

(C) power shift injector

(D) power stabilizing ignition

668. Identify the vehicle part shown here.

(A) spark plug

(B) shock absorber

(C) coil

(D) steering axis

669. What controls the amount of gasoline that goes into the cylinders?

(A) push rod

(B) throttle

(C) transmission

(D) camshaft

670. What is the purpose of a fuel gauge?

(A) to indicate if the fuel is dirty

(B) to indicate the amount of fuel

(C) to indicate if there is a fuel leak

(D) to indicate if the fuel needs to be flushed

671. What are the steering wheel and steering shaft connected to?

(A) tie rod

(B) wheels

(C) transmission

(D) ball joints

672. If you jack up a vehicle and try to rock the tire and there's a lot of play, what should you replace or repair?

(A) tires

(B) bearings

(C) brakes

(D) rotors

673. What is the difference, besides fuel, between a diesel engine and an internal combustion engine?

(A) Spark plugs are not used in a diesel engine to ignite the fuel.

(B) Oil is used in a diesel engine to power the engine instead of fuel.

(C) In a diesel engine, oil is mixed with fuel to cause the vehicle to carry more load.

(D) Double the spark plugs are used in a diesel to give it more power.

Shop

674. Which tool is the most suitable for general metalwork?

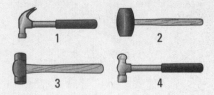

(A) 1

(B) 2

(C) 3

(D) 4

675. What is the part shown here called?

- (A) split lock washer
- (B) internal shake-proof washer
- (C) external shake-proof washer
- (D) flat washer

676. What is the purpose of this tool?

- (A) to drill holes in metal
- (B) to drill holes in wood
- (C) to place rivets
- (D) none of the above

677. Which of the following is not a carpenter's hand tool?

- (A) a level
- (B) a winch
- (C) a chisel
- (D) a compass

678. Which tool listed is the best for cutting metal?

- (A) a back saw
- (B) a hacksaw
- (C) a circular saw
- (D) a handsaw

679. Which hand tool is shown here?

- (A) an offset wrench
- (B) a box wrench
- (C) a crescent wrench
- (D) a socket wrench

680. Which of the following tools is used to smooth or level a piece of wood?

- (A) a hammer
- (B) a plane
- (C) a screwdriver
- (D) a wrench

681. Which tool would you use to measure the tightness of a nut or bolt?

- (A) screwdriver
- (B) pliers
- (C) ratchet
- (D) torque wrench

682. What is the next step after filling in a hole with plastic filler and letting it dry?

- (A) Clean the area with a glass-cleaning solution.
- (B) Sand the area with medium-grain sandpaper.
- (C) Coat the area with a layer of primer.
- (D) None of the above.

683. What is the primary use for a ratchet handle?

(A) to tighten a bolt in a tight space

(B) to crank a vehicle in the air

(C) to move the block on an engine

(D) to attach soffit to fascia

684. What is the purpose of a crosscut saw?

(A) to cut with the grain of wood

(B) to cut against the grain of wood

(C) to cut irregular shapes from metal

(D) to cut smooth angles from plastic

685. What type of saw would you choose if you wanted to cut a big oval out of wood?

(A) crosscut saw

(B) ripsaw

(C) coping saw

(D) hacksaw

686. What is the purpose of a ripsaw?

(A) to cut with the grain of wood

(B) to cut against the grain of wood

(C) to cut irregular shapes from metal

(D) to cut smooth angles from plastic

687. What is this tool called?

(A) scissors

(B) snips

(C) pliers

(D) vises

688. Why would you use slip-joint pliers?

(A) to adjust the range of the jaw to fit different bolt shapes

(B) to secure two pieces of wood while the glue dries

(C) to stabilize a floor when the load is too heavy

(D) to trim the space around pipe fittings

689. What category of tools does this image show?

(A) cutting tools

(B) clamping tools

(C) finishing tools

(D) measuring tools

690. Identify the tool shown here.

(A) needle-nosed pliers

(B) offset screwdriver

(C) torque wrench

(D) handscrew vise

691. If you wanted to make a small impression or dent on a work piece for marking or decorating purposes, what tool would you use?

(A) chisel

(B) punch

(C) drill

(D) nails

692. What type of holes do auger bits create?

(A) oval-shaped

(B) small

(C) large

(D) squared

693. What type of joint is pictured?

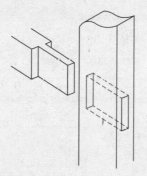

(A) overlap joint

(B) butt joint

(C) dovetail joint

(D) mortise and tenon joint

694. What type of joint is pictured?

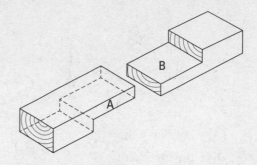

(A) overlap joint

(B) dovetail joint

(C) lap joint

(D) mortise and tenon joint

695. What type of joint is pictured?

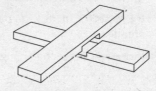

(A) overlap joint

(B) butt joint

(C) lap joint

(D) dovetail joint

696. What type of joint is pictured?

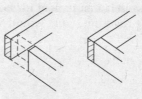

(A) dovetail joint

(B) butt joint

(C) lap joint

(D) mortise and tenon joint

697. What type of joint is pictured?

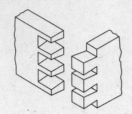

(A) overlap joint

(B) dovetail joint

(C) mortise and tenon joint

(D) lap joint

698. Why is a cross-shaft lug wrench better than a single-shaft wrench?

(A) It gives more leverage.

(B) It holds lug nuts better.

(C) It fits better in storage because it's smaller.

(D) It doesn't scratch the lug nuts.

699. What should you use with a nut to assemble something properly?

(A) nails

(B) screws

(C) hammer

(D) washer

700. If a weld is insufficient for fastening metal parts together, what would the next option be?

(A) nails

(B) rivets

(C) glue

(D) clamps

701. What shape is the head of a lag screw?

(A) circle

(B) oval

(C) hexagonal

(D) octagonal

702. Which of the following is not a bolt head style?

(A) binding

(B) winding

(C) button

(D) flange

703. What type of screw is used to fasten metal parts?

(A) lag screws

(B) wood screws

(C) machine screws

(D) standard screws

704. What is this fastener called?

(A) brad nail

(B) finishing nail

(C) common nail

(D) double-headed nail

705. What do you do when you score a pipe?

   (A)   Measure the circumference.

   (B)   Measure the thickness.

   (C)   Make a groove cut into the surface.

   (D)   Rate the quality from 1 to 10.

706. What is another name for long-nosed pliers?

   (A)   needle-nosed pliers

   (B)   curved-nosed pliers

   (C)   slip-joint pliers

   (D)   cutting pliers

707. Cutting pliers are mostly used to cut what material?

   (A)   wood

   (B)   wire

   (C)   sheet metal

   (D)   plastic

708. What is a common characteristic of vise-grip pliers?

   (A)   long handle

   (B)   serrated jaws

   (C)   curved jaws

   (D)   skinny nose

709. An Allen wrench fits what shape of screw head?

   (A)   circular

   (B)   square

   (C)   hexagonal

   (D)   octagonal

710. What is the name of the tool pictured?

   (A)   socket wrench

   (B)   open-end wrench

   (C)   box-end wrench

   (D)   pipe wrench

711. What is the name of the tool pictured?

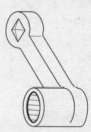

   (A)   socket wrench

   (B)   open-end wrench

   (C)   box-end wrench

   (D)   pipe wrench

712. What is the name of the tool pictured?

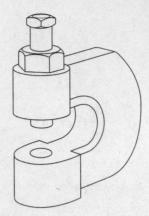

(A) strut clamp

(B) c clamp

(C) ring clamp

(D) compression clamp

713. What is the handle of a socket wrench called?

(A) locking handle

(B) vise handle

(C) ratchet handle

(D) socket handle

714. What is this hammer mostly used for?

(A) metalwork

(B) carpentry

(C) breaking rock

(D) driving nails

715. What is the name of the part pictured?

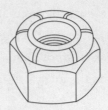

(A) cap nut

(B) spring nut

(C) stop nut

(D) bolt nut

716. What was historically used to make wood glue?

(A) animal hide

(B) salt water

(C) baking soda

(D) casein

717. What is another term for resin?

(A) lacquer

(B) varnish

(C) adhesive

(D) all of the above

718. Which term refers to the measure of thickness of a liquid?

(A) hydrometer

(B) viscosity

(C) fluidity

(D) frequency

719. What would the truss head wood screw shown here be best used for?

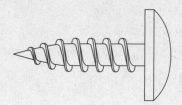

(A) drywall

(B) hinges

(C) playground

(D) aluminum siding

720. What is the name of the tool shown here?

(A) bench vise

(B) pipe vise

(C) pipe cutter

(D) ripsaw

721. What type of nail has a head that's meant to become flush with the fastening material?

(A) common

(B) brads

(C) double-headed

(D) lock

722. What is the term for nails that are larger than 20 penny?

(A) spikes

(B) length

(C) large

(D) common

723. What does the penny system measure?

(A) nail weight

(B) nail size

(C) nail circumference

(D) nail diameter

724. What is the name of the tool shown here?

(A) vise

(B) finisher

(C) level

(D) square

725. What is the name of the tool shown here?

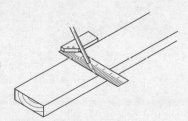

(A) level

(B) clamp

(C) square

(D) vise

726. Why are calipers used?

(A) for larger measurements

(B) for circular measurements

(C) for small measurements

(D) for irregular measurements

727. What do depth gauges measure?

(A) depth of a piece of wood

(B) depth of holes

(C) depth of doorways

(D) depth of pipes

728. What is used to break off sharp concrete edges while concrete is firm but still moist?

(A) shovel

(B) float

(C) edger

(D) groover

729. What tool do you use to drive nails to connect timber together?

(A) claw hammer

(B) nail punch

(C) crow bar

(D) tower pincer

730. The teeth on saws are measured per what?

(A) per 25 mm

(B) per 50 mm

(C) per 75 mm

(D) per 100 mm

Chapter 7

Mechanical Comprehension: Focusing on Physics, Mechanics, and Work

● ●

The Mechanical Comprehension subtest is used on the ASVAB to calculate some military composite scores that are used for job-qualification purposes. The intent of this subtest is to measure your understanding of mechanical operations, including simple machines and mechanisms. To do well on this subtest, you need to know about force, pressure, work, mechanical advantage, and other physics-related basics. An image of a lever, a set of gears, a pulley, or some other item related to physics often accompanies the questions in this subtest. You also need to know how to use different mathematical formulas to determine some answers.

The Questions You'll Work On

Overall, the Mechanical Comprehension subtest tests your knowledge of mechanical physics and applications. Its questions fall into three main categories:

- ✔ **Force:** These basic physics questions ask you about forces from friction, gravity, magnetism, and tension. They also relate force to concepts such as pressure, acceleration, and velocity.
- ✔ **Work:** This type of question deals with work or energy. You may have to determine how the work done relates to force, distance, or power.
- ✔ **Machines**: The questions in this category are all about machines. In many cases, they ask you exactly how machines help make work easier.

What to Watch Out For

The following pointers can help you as you work through the questions in this chapter:

- ✔ Remember the simple formulas, such as power = work ÷ time.
- ✔ Use mathematical principles to solve physics-based problems that you don't quite understand.
- ✔ Pay attention to words like *increase* or *decrease* in the question or answer. The proposed change may lead you to the correct answer.

Force

731. While throwing a football, Dan exerts a forward force of 50 newtons on the ball and pushes it forward a distance of 1.2 meters. How much work does he do on the football?

(A) 45 joules

(B) 60 joules

(C) 50 joules

(D) 50.5 joules

732. How do input force and output force relate to each other?

(A) They are always different.

(B) Output force requires input force to exist.

(C) They are unrelated.

(D) The input is always less than the output.

733. What is the mechanical advantage if 50 newtons are put in and 250 newtons are produced?

(A) 1,000

(B) 500

(C) 5

(D) 50

734. Bill is pushing a box up a ramp with a force of 30 newtons. The box has a weight of 60 newtons. What is the mechanical advantage of the ramp?

(A) 30

(B) 20

(C) 2

(D) 15

735. A force of 30 newtons is applied to a screwdriver to pry the lid off of a gallon can of paint. The screwdriver applies 90 newtons of force to the lid. What is the mechanical advantage of the screwdriver?

(A) 30

(B) 5

(C) 20

(D) 3

736. When Leo is driving his car, he exerts 50 newtons of force on the steering wheel to turn the corner into his driveway. The shaft exerts 300 newtons of force to turn the wheels. What is the mechanical advantage of the system?

(A) 6

(B) 1,500

(C) 150

(D) 60

737. Mechanical advantage is equal to what?

(A) output force divided by input force

(B) input force divided by output force

(C) input force times output force

(D) output force plus input force

738. According to Newton's first law of motion, objects at rest tend to stay at rest unless what?

(A) They are positioned at a high altitude.

(B) A fulcrum is used to lift them.

(C) They are acted upon by an unbalanced force.

(D) None of the above.

739. Aaron needs to move a 400-pound motor with a crowbar that's 5 feet, 9 inches. If he places the fulcrum 9 inches from the motor, how much force must he use to move the motor?

(A)   45 pounds

(B)   60 pounds

(C)   75 pounds

(D)   50 pounds

740. Why does a heavy object require a larger amount of force to get it moving than a light object?

(A)   Heavy objects are usually very large.

(B)   You need a lever to lift a heavy object.

(C)   Heavy objects have a greater amount of inertia.

(D)   Heavy objects have no momentum.

741. A spring has a force constant of 3 pounds per inch. How much force is required to move the spring 12 inches?

(A)   4 pounds

(B)   2.4 pounds

(C)   36 pounds

(D)   102 pounds

742. The attractive force between objects is

(A)   gravity

(B)   friction

(C)   compression

(D)   tension

743. If a force of 210 pounds is exerted over an area of 15 square inches, what is the psi?

(A)   15

(B)   20

(C)   14

(D)   60

744. The shock absorber on a car is a very large spring. If Abra's car hits a pothole with 600 pounds of force and the shock absorber compresses 3 inches, what is its spring constant in pounds per inch?

(A)   200

(B)   600

(C)   20

(D)   1,800

745. Which of the following terms refers to the push or pull on an object that can cause it to accelerate?

(A)   gravity

(B)   force

(C)   speed

(D)   friction

746. Jose is lifting a 405-pound block using a lever. If the block is 3 feet from the fulcrum and Jose is 9 feet from the fulcrum, how much force must he apply to lift the block?

(A)   125 pounds

(B)   75 pounds

(C)   225 pounds

(D)   135 pounds

747. How much force is required to lift the weights?

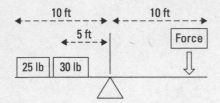

(A) 55 pounds

(B) 75 pounds

(C) 40 pounds

(D) 60 pounds

748. Mrs. Nelson is filling her grocery cart with food. If she uses a force of 26 newtons to move her cart 15.2 meters, how much work does she do?

(A) 390 joules

(B) 395.2 joules

(C) 260 joules

(D) 346 joules

749. A force of 70 newtons is applied to a nutcracker to crack open a pecan. If the mechanical advantage of the nutcracker is 3.5, what force does the nutcracker apply to the pecan?

(A) 70 newtons

(B) 310 newtons

(C) 245 newtons

(D) 325 newtons

750. The red team and the blue team are in a game of tug of war. The red team is pulling with a force of 85 newtons (N), and the blue team is pulling with a force of 90 N. What is the net force?

(A) 175 N

(B) 35 N

(C) 15 N

(D) 5 N

751. If you did 70 joules of work pushing a table 3.5 meters across the room, how much force did you apply?

(A) 2 newtons

(B) 200 newtons

(C) 75 newtons

(D) 20 newtons

752. When an arrow is shot at an upward angle toward the sky, which of the following causes it to come back to the surface of the Earth?

(A) momentum

(B) gravity

(C) centrifugal force

(D) friction

753. 55,000 joules of work are done to move a box 25 meters. How much force is applied?

(A) 2,200 newtons

(B) 2,500 newtons

(C) 5,000 newtons

(D) 2,250 newtons

754. Maddox does 25,000 joules of work pushing a box of his toys 20 meters to his room. How much force was applied?

(A) 1,275 newtons

(B) 50,000 newtons

(C) 1,250 newtons

(D) 5,000 newtons

755. James applies force at one end of a hydraulic jack. The area at the other end of the jack is five times the area where James is applying the force. How much larger is the exerted force than what James is applying?

(A) twice as large

(B) half as large

(C) one-fifth as large

(D) five times as large

756. Deloris wheels her wheelchair up a ramp by using a force of 80 newtons. If the ramp has a mechanical advantage of 7, what is the output force?

(A)   475 newtons

(B)   560 newtons

(C)   45 newtons

(D)   355 newtons

Work

757. Jimmy weighs 90 pounds, and Jolene weighs 60 pounds. They are both seated on a balanced seesaw. If Jimmy is seated 10 feet away from Jolene, how far is Jolene from the fulcrum of the seesaw?

(A)   4 feet

(B)   5 feet

(C)   6 feet

(D)   10 feet

758. James uses effort to lift 80 kilograms. If he uses a simple six-pulley hauling system, then what is the maximum load he can lift with the same effort if he pulls downward on the rope?

(A)   320 kilograms

(B)   480 kilograms

(C)   80 kilograms

(D)   360 kilograms

759. A block and tackle is used to lift a truck engine with a weight of nearly 7,406 newtons. The input force required to lift this weight using the block and tackle is 308.6 newtons. What is the mechanical advantage of the block and tackle?

(A)   23.99

(B)   15

(C)   25

(D)   24.75

760. Heat is a form of what?

(A)   motion

(B)   energy

(C)   calories

(D)   pressurization

761. When you try to mix oil and water together, the oil forms a layer at the top and the water sinks to the bottom because

(A)   oil is denser than water.

(B)   oil is less dense than water.

(C)   oil is more acidic than water.

(D)   oil is less acidic than water.

762. If ball A and ball B are both the same size and weight, what is most likely to happen on these ramps?

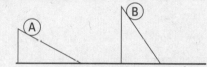

(A)   Ball A will reach the bottom first.

(B)   Ball B will reach the bottom first.

(C)   Both balls will hit the bottom simultaneously.

(D)   Not enough information given.

763. Which of the following does not make use of mechanical advantage?

(A)   using a wheelbarrow to haul dirt

(B)   using a screwdriver to open a can of paint

(C)   pushing a couch across the room

(D)   using a claw hammer to remove a nail

764. How is the mass of an object measured?

(A) liters

(B) joules

(C) kilograms

(D) none of the above

765. In the figure that follows, a 600-pound weight is placed on a 10-pound board that has been evenly balanced between two scales. How much does the left scale measure if the weight is 2/3 closer to the left than to the right?

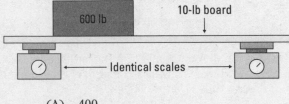

(A) 400

(B) 300

(C) 405

(D) 410

766. Gear A has 12 teeth and Gear B has 6 teeth. If Gear A makes 10 complete revolutions, how many complete revolutions does Gear B make?

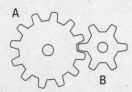

(A) 20

(B) 10

(C) 40

(D) 5

767. When James shifted to a lower gear on his mountain bike, it made his pedaling easier but

(A) also increased his speed of travel.

(B) also decreased his speed of travel.

(C) had no effect on the speed of travel.

(D) made him work harder.

768. Mr. Roth's children — Jake, Paul, and Jill — weigh 80, 60, and 50 pounds, respectively. They all sit on the same side of a seesaw together. Jake sits 3 feet from the fulcrum, Paul sits 5 feet from the fulcrum, and Jill sits 6 feet from the fulcrum. How far from the fulcrum must Mr. Roth sit on the other side to balance the seesaw if he weighs 200 pounds?

(A) 4.2 feet

(B) 5.5 feet

(C) 5 feet

(D) 4 feet

769. The library designed the wheelchair ramp to have a mechanical advantage of 6. The average person using the ramp weighs 180 newtons. How much input force is needed for the ramp?

(A) 30 newtons

(B) 186 newtons

(C) 640 newtons

(D) 60 newtons

770. A construction crew lifts 560 pounds of material several times during a day from a flatbed truck to a 32-foot rooftop. A block and tackle system with 50 pounds of effort force is designed to lift the materials. What is the required actual mechanical advantage?

(A) 11

(B) 11.5

(C) 11.2

(D) 10.4

771. How much force must Kenneth exert to lift the weight?

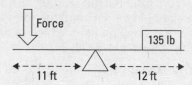

(A) 124.24 pounds

(B) 135.3 pounds

(C) 150 pounds

(D) 147.27 pounds

772. If a ramp measures 9 feet in length and 3 feet in height, how much effort do you need to move an object weighing 210 pounds up the ramp?

(A) 27 pounds

(B) 70 pounds

(C) 45 pounds

(D) 16 pounds

773. Sandy and Sara both want the same doll. Sandy is pulling the doll to the left with a force of 5 newtons, and Sara is pulling the doll to the right with a force of 7 newtons. What is the net force on the doll?

(A) 12 newtons left and right

(B) 12 newtons right

(C) 2 newtons right

(D) 35 newtons left and right

774. Three beams are the same size and 10 feet long. One is made of wood, one of steel, and the third of concrete. If identical loads are applied to these three beams, which of the following will occur?

(A) The wood beam will deflect less than the steel beam.

(B) The steel beam will deflect less than the wood beam.

(C) The wood beam will deflect less than the concrete beam.

(D) The concrete beam will deflect more than the other two.

775. Two ramps can be used to raise a heavy barrel up to a platform. Not taking friction into account, which ramp requires less force to raise the barrel?

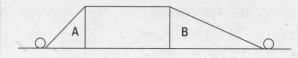

(A) A

(B) B

(C) Both require the same amount of work.

(D) Not enough information given.

776. Devon and Elliott are unloading 125 boxes of books, each weighing 30 pounds, to a pallet 3.5 feet below the truck bed. Elliott has the use of a hand truck and a ramp. Devon is lifting the boxes with no ramp and no hand truck. What is Elliot doing?

(A) more work than Devon

(B) less work than Devon

(C) the same amount of work as Devon

(D) 100 joules of work

777. What would happen to a balloon full of air if you moved it from above a water surface to 5 feet below the water surface?

(A) The volume of the balloon would decrease.

(B) The balloon would explode.

(C) The volume of the balloon would stay the same.

(D) The volume of the balloon would increase.

778. Albert and two friends apply a combined force of 489.5 newtons to move a piano. The amount of work done is 1,762.2 joules. What distance did the piano move?

(A) 3.8 meters

(B) 2.8 meters

(C) 3.6 meters

(D) 4.2 meters

779. Dale uses 1,010 newtons of force to push a box 35 meters across the warehouse floor. How much work does he do on the box?

(A) 35,345 joules

(B) 1,115 joules

(C) 35,250 joules

(D) 35,350 joules

780. A lever being used to lift a heavy box has an input arm length of 5 meters and an output arm length of 1 meter. What is the mechanical advantage of this lever?

(A) 1

(B) 0.5

(C) 5

(D) 10

781. Why does a hydraulic jack work?

(A) Liquids are incompressible.

(B) Liquids maintain the same pressure in a closed system.

(C) Both A and B.

(D) None of the above.

782. Roxie is trying to lift a very heavy rock out of her garden by using a large stick as a lever. If her input arm is 3 meters long and the output arm is 0.75 meters long, what is the mechanical advantage of the lever?

(A) 3

(B) 5

(C) 1.5

(D) 4

783. Mr. Ames made 3 cubes of different sizes out of plastic. The first cube has a weight of 0.75 pounds, the second cube has a weight of 1 pound, and the third cube has a weight of 2 pounds. Which of the following statements is true?

(A) Cube 1 will float and Cubes 2 and 3 will sink.

(B) Cube 3 will float, and Cubes 1 and 2 will sink.

(C) Cubes 1 and 2 will float, and Cube 3 will sink.

(D) All three cubes will either float or sink.

784. On a cold day, Paul uses 40.5 watts of power pulling a sled up a hill in 10.5 seconds. What is the work done by Paul?

(A) 425 joules

(B) 45 joules

(C) 42.50 joules

(D) 425.25 joules

785. A seesaw works best when both people weigh the same. This demonstrates which principle of mechanical motion?

(A) equilibrium

(B) acceleration

(C) centrifugal force

(D) relative velocity

786. A spring is most likely to be used on which of the following?

(A) a pogo stick

(B) an electric cord

(C) a table

(D) a cabinet door

787. What type of gauge is illustrated here?

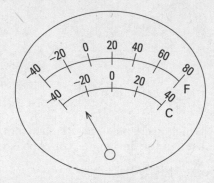

(A) an altitude gauge

(B) a pressure gauge

(C) a flow meter gauge

(D) a temperature gauge

788. Kathy is taking her baby for a stroll. She is using 30 newtons of force to push the stroller 200 meters. How much work is Kathy doing?

(A) 3,000 joules

(B) 750 joules

(C) 6,000 joules

(D) 500 joules

789. What property is responsible for shock absorption?

(A) acceleration

(B) velocity

(C) elasticity

(D) time

790. Mrs. Smith is sweeping the room. She is holding the broom with an input arm length of 0.5 meters. The broom is providing a mechanical advantage of 0.5. What is the length of the broom's output arm?

(A) 1.5 meters

(B) 1 meter

(C) 0.5 meter

(D) 2 meters

791. The amount of force applied to an object multiplied by the distance gives you what value?

(A) acceleration

(B) work

(C) velocity

(D) time

792. Little Johnny holds his toy rake so that its output arm is 0.85 meters. If the mechanical advantage is 0.3, what is the input arm length?

(A) 0.55 meters

(B) 1.23 meters

(C) 0.76 meters

(D) 0.255 meters

793. Little Bobby applied a force of 2,500 newtons on his grandparents' Great Dane, who sat on his lap. How much work did Little Bobby do trying to push the dog if he was unable to move him?

(A) 100 joules

(B) 0 joules

(C) 250 joules

(D) 150 joules

794. Blake is transporting wood to the mill in a trailer. The amount of force needed to pull the wood a distance of 75 meters is 3,000 newtons. How much work will be done on the wood?

(A) 3,075 joules

(B) 225,000 joules

(C) 1,500 joules

(D) 120,000 joules

795. On a given day, at sea level, assuming static conditions, what is the speed of sound?

(A) 1,100 feet per second

(B) 1,200 feet per second

(C) 1,300 feet per second

(D) 1,425 feet per second

796. Two balls of the same density, one large and one small, roll toward each other at the same speed. When they collide, what will happen to the larger ball?

(A) It will be propelled backward.

(B) It will jump over the smaller ball.

(C) It will continue forward.

(D) It will stop.

797. Mom needed her two children to help her move furniture across the room. They had a combined force of 425 newtons. The amount of work they did was 1,062.5 joules. How far did they move the furniture?

(A) 5 meters

(B) 3 meters

(C) 25 meters

(D) 2.5 meters

798. Which of these pairs of magnets will stick together in the positions they are in?

```
A  N     S   N     S

B  S     N   N     S
```

(A) A

(B) B

(C) A and B

(D) neither

799. Which term is the opposite of an increase in speed?

(A) velocity

(B) friction

(C) rotation

(D) deceleration

800. Which principle of mechanical motion is used in the design of a roller coaster?

(A) friction

(B) acceleration

(C) momentum

(D) all of the above

Machines

801. A pump is typically used to accomplish which of the following tasks?

(A) to move liquids uphill

(B) to move liquids downhill

(C) to separate liquids

(D) to clarify liquids

802. If the weight shown in the figure weighs 20 pounds, how many pounds of force would it take to lift the weight?

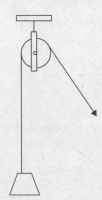

(A) 10

(B) 20

(C) 40

(D) 5

803. What happens to the total amount of work done when you use a machine compared to when you don't use a machine?

(A)   It decreases.

(B)   It stays the same.

(C)   It goes to zero.

(D)   It increases.

804. In the pictured pulley system, which statement is true?

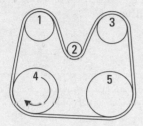

(A)   Pulley 2 would spin faster than Pulley 4.

(B)   Pulley 4 would spin faster than Pulley 3.

(C)   Pulley 1 would spin faster than Pulley 3.

(D)   Pulley 4 would spin faster than Pulley 5.

805. Which of the tanks will overfill?

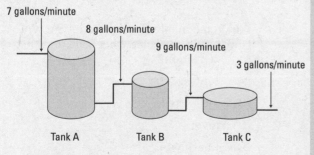

(A)   Tank A

(B)   Tanks A and B

(C)   Tank C

(D)   Tanks B and C

806. As you pull 4 meters of the rope, you lift the weight 2 meters. What is the mechanical advantage of the system?

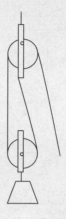

(A)   4

(B)   2

(C)   1

(D)   6

807. A lever has a mechanical advantage of 4. Its input arm is 60 centimeters long. How long is its output arm?

(A)   10 centimeters

(B)   15 centimeters

(C)   20 centimeters

(D)   4 centimeters

808. The mechanic devised a pulley system with a mechanical advantage of 4 to lift an engine that weighs 600 newtons. What input force must he apply to lift the engine?

(A)   100 newtons

(B)   1,200 newtons

(C)   200 newtons

(D)   150 newtons

809. If weight Y weighs 40 pounds, how many pounds of force does the **pulley** require to lift the weight?

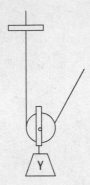

(A)   40 pounds

(B)   80 pounds

(C)   20 pounds

(D)   25 pounds

810. If Gear B turns counterclockwise 10 rotations, how will Gear A turn?

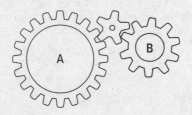

(A)   counterclockwise 5 rotations

(B)   counterclockwise 10 rotations

(C)   clockwise 5 rotations

(D)   clockwise 10 rotations

811. What would be the mechanical advantage of a lever that allows Susan to lift a box weighing 24 newtons with a force of 4 newtons?

(A)   24

(B)   6

(C)   12

(D)   96

812. How much tension do you need on the rope to hold the 200-pound weight in equilibrium?

(A)   100 pounds

(B)   50 pounds

(C)   25 pounds

(D)   33.33 pounds

813. Which mechanical components are typically used between a wheel and an axle to reduce friction?

(A)   hinges

(B)   springs

(C)   levers

(D)   bearings

814. An elevator is most similar to which of the following mechanical devices?

(A)   a spring

(B)   a crane

(C)   a lever

(D)   a hydraulic jet

815. If Gear B turns in a clockwise direction, which of the following is true?

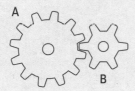

(A)   Gear A turns in a counterclockwise direction at the same speed.

(B)   Gear A turns in a counterclockwise direction at a slower speed.

(C)   Gear A turns in a clockwise direction at the same speed.

(D)   Gear A turns in a clockwise direction at a faster speed.

816. David is using effort to lift a 90-kilogram crate. If he instead were to use a simple five-pulley hauling system, what would be the maximum load that he could lift with the same effort is he were to pull downward on the rope?

(A)   90 kilograms

(B)   450 kilograms

(C)   350 kilograms

(D)   240 kilograms

817. What is the purpose of the crossbelt that connects Pulley X and Pulley Y?

(A)   It makes Pulley Y turn faster.

(B)   It makes Pulley X turn faster.

(C)   It reduces the force on Pulley Y.

(D)   It changes the direction in which Pulley Y turns.

818. Daisy's single-speed bicycle has a front gear with 48 teeth and a rear gear with 12 teeth. If Daisy pedaled at 80 revolutions per minute (rpm), how fast would her rear wheel rotate?

(A)   280 rpm

(B)   320 rpm

(C)   70 rpm

(D)   128 rpm

819. What is the force, in pounds (lb), required to lift the weight?

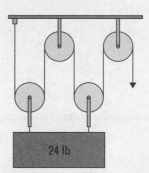

24 lb

(A)   24 pounds

(B)   12 pounds

(C)   18 pounds

(D)   6 pounds

820. What mechanical motion principle do the brakes in a car use?

(A) centrifugal force

(B) momentum

(C) friction

(D) oscillation

821. Which handle will require less force to lift?

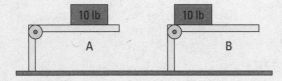

(A) A

(B) B

(C) Both will require the same.

(D) Not enough information is given.

822. A sprocket on a bicycle is most similar to which of the following simple devices?

(A) gear

(B) spring

(C) lever

(D) all of the above

823. Two pipes are used to drain water from a 150-gallon barrel. The opening of Pipe A is 2 inches in diameter, and the opening of Pipe B is 4 inches in diameter. How much faster does liquid leave the barrel through Pipe B compared to Pipe A?

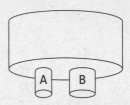

(A) Liquid flows out of Pipe B twice as fast.

(B) Liquid flows out of Pipe B eight times as fast.

(C) Liquid leaves both pipes at the same rate.

(D) Liquid flows out of Pipe B four times as fast.

824. Gear A has 20 teeth, Gear B has 60 teeth, and Gear C has 10 teeth. If Gear A moves at 60 revolutions per minute (rpm), how fast does Gear C revolve?

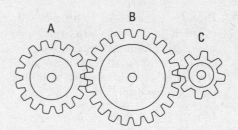

(A) 80 rpm

(B) 75 rpm

(C) 100 rpm

(D) 120 rpm

825. When using a fixed pulley, the amount of effort needed to lift a load is equal to the weight of the load. What is the advantage of a fixed pulley?

(A) It supports the load.

(B) It spreads out the work.

(C) It changes the direction of the effort.

(D) It allows you to lift a heavy load with less force.

826. What is the mechanical advantage of the pulley system shown in the diagram?

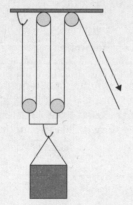

(A) 5

(B) 3

(C) 6

(D) 4

827. The arm of a crane is 18 feet long, and the cable used to lift the arm is attached 12 feet from the crane's cab. For the crane to lift an object weighing 800 pounds, how much force must be applied by the cable?

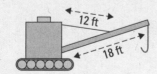

(A) 800 pounds

(B) 1,600 pounds

(C) 1,200 pounds

(D) 1,250 pounds

828. Pulley A has three times the circumference of Pulley B. If Pulley B rotates at 60 revolutions per minute (rpm), how fast must Pulley A rotate?

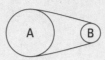

(A) 40 rpm

(B) 120 rpm

(C) 10 rpm

(D) 20 rpm

829. A series of springs with force constants of 2, 6, and 12 pounds per inch support a platform. When a 12-pound block is lowered onto it, how many inches does the platform compress?

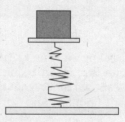

(A) 9 inches

(B) 6 inches

(C) 12 inches

(D) 4 inches

830. Which material would be the best possible for constructing an anchor for a boat?

(A) wood

(B) glass

(C) metal

(D) plastic

831. Two blocks of equal weight are suspended by a pulley. The blocks are 12 vertical feet apart. How far must Block A be pulled down to be at equal height with Block B?

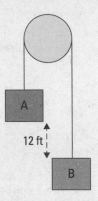

(A) 10 feet

(B) 6 feet

(C) 8 feet

(D) 4 feet

832. Susan can pull a rope with a maximum of 150 pounds of force. Using the pulley system shown here, what is the maximum number of pounds she can lift?

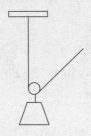

(A) 300

(B) 250

(C) 350

(D) 150

833. What type of outside energy source could be used to operate a pump?

(A) a battery

(B) an electric motor

(C) an internal combustion engine

(D) all of the above

834. A crane lifts a container weighing 1,024 newtons 50 meters. How much work did the crane do?

(A) 51,200 joules

(B) 30,000 joules

(C) 1,075 joules

(D) 45,100 joules

835. A rope is pulling a 320-pound box up an incline that's 16 feet long. If 80 pounds of force are used to move the box up the incline, how tall is the incline?

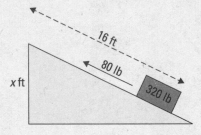

(A) 6 feet

(B) 10 feet

(C) 4 feet

(D) 8 feet

836. Gears A, B, and C are connected by a chain. The diameters of the gears are 2 inches, 4 inches, and 8 inches, respectively. If Gear A is turning at 20 revolutions per minute (rpm), what is the turning rate of Gear C?

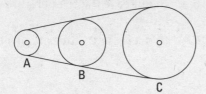

(A)   80 rpm

(B)   5 rpm

(C)   4 rpm

(D)   32 rpm

837. Using a simple pulley system, Sam pulls down with an effort of 80 kilograms to lift a 480-kilogram load. How many pulleys are in the system?

(A)   6

(B)   5

(C)   12

(D)   8

838. A lever with an input arm of 8 meters has a mechanical advantage of 4. What is the output arm's length?

(A)   2 meters

(B)   4 meters

(C)   3 meters

(D)   6 meters

839. Gear A and Gear B are touching. If Gear A has 20 teeth and Gear B has 10 teeth, how many turns does Gear B make when Gear A makes 10 revolutions?

(A)   20

(B)   2

(C)   4

(D)   5

840. Susie is enjoying swinging at the park. When her swing reaches its highest point, it momentarily pauses before swinging back down. What kind of energy does the swing have at this point?

(A)   potential

(B)   kinetic

(C)   static

(D)   chemical

841. When Gene raises a flag up the flagpole, he's using what simple machine?

(A)   lever

(B)   pulley

(C)   gear

(D)   inclined plane

842. What type of pressure is in a liquid that isn't moving?

(A)   static

(B)   metamorphic

(C)   hydraulic

(D)   hydrostatic

843. Which can of juice will pour more easily?

(A)   A

(B)   B

(C)   Both will pour the same.

(D)   Not enough information is given.

844. How can gears be used to change the speed of a machine?

(A) Use two large gears.

(B) Use two gears of different sizes.

(C) Use two gears of the same size.

(D) Use more gears.

845. A valve is used to perform which of the following functions?

(A) to control the flow of a liquid

(B) to aid in the evaporation of a liquid

(C) to increase the temperature of a liquid

(D) to decrease the density of a liquid

Chapter 8

Electronics Information: Amplifying Your Understanding of Electronic Principles

• •

The Electronics Information subtest on the ASVAB is used to calculate some military composite scores that are used for job-qualification purposes. The intent of this subtest is to measure your understanding of basic electronic principles and their relationship and functions in the real world. The questions ask about the electronics field, electrical effects, and materials as well as measurements such as voltage, wattage, and amperage. Diagrams of circuits and electronics symbols may accompany the questions.

The Questions You'll Work On

The questions in this subtest fall into four categories:

✔ **Electronics basics:** These questions test your knowledge of laws and formulas, voltage, power, frequency, impedance, and other concepts.

✔ **Circuits:** These questions often include circuit diagrams and ask you to identify symbols and types of circuits.

✔ **Current:** These questions have to do with generating current, including the different types of current and ways to manipulate it.

✔ **Circuit codes:** These questions ask you to identify electrical symbols, color-coded wires, and other real-world electrical markers.

What to Watch Out For

Keep in mind the following points as you work through the questions in this chapter:

✔ By convention, current goes from a positive terminal to a negative terminal. Electrons flow in the opposite direction.

✔ A closed circuit must exist for electricity to flow.

✔ Current equals voltage divided by resistance. (This is known as *Ohm's law.*)

✔ The following electrical units of measure can help you solve electrical questions:

- *Amps* measure current.
- *Ohms* measure resistance.
- *Watts* measure power.
- *Volts* measure voltage.

Electronics Basics

846. What is the term for the amount of work done per unit charge when electrons move between two points?

(A) time

(B) regulation

(C) volts

(D) ohms

847. What does an ohm measure?

(A) resistance

(B) force

(C) heat

(D) time

848. What is used to amplify a signal?

(A) transformer

(B) transistor

(C) alternating current

(D) remote control

849. What is the unit of measurement for frequency?

(A) hertz

(B) ohms

(C) amperes

(D) watts

850. What are amplifier circuits used to magnify?

(A) current

(B) voltage

(C) power

(D) all of the above

851. Which of the following is an example of a transducer turning electrical energy to sound?

(A) doorbell

(B) tuner

(C) clock

(D) light bulb

852. 5 + 10 + 15 =

Solve the equation and choose the best unit of measurement based on the symbol shown in the figure.

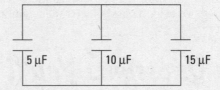

(A) 30 capacitors

(B) 30 volts

(C) 30 microfarads

(D) 30 electrodes

853. What has two components commonly known as an element and a wiper?

(A) variable resistor

(B) integrated circuit

(C) magnetic encoders

(D) basic electrode

854. What does every wired device receive after functional tests?

(A) packaging

(B) voltage rating

(C) color code

(D) seal of approval

855. What is another word for a wire?

(A) conductor

(B) transformer

(C) diode

(D) resistor

856. What can be used to increase or decrease electrical voltage?

(A) accelerator

(B) electrical pole

(C) ignitron

(D) transformer

857. Which of the following is a silvery, highly reactive metallic element that is used as a heat transfer medium?

(A) mercury

(B) iron

(C) lithium

(D) all of the above

858. How is power measured?

(A) diodes

(B) degrees

(C) volts

(D) watts

859. How is electrical energy usually measured?

(A) watt-hours

(B) kilowatt-hours

(C) volt-hours

(D) current-watts

860. What is another word for *electromotive force?*

(A) frequency

(B) heat

(C) voltage

(D) ohms

861. What is the difference between capacitive reactance and inductive reactance?

(A) One opposes changes in voltage, and the other opposes changes in current.

(B) One can only be used with a battery.

(C) One is alternating current, and the other is direct current.

(D) One is only used with magnets.

862. What is another name for *electrolytic decomposition?*

(A) chemical effect

(B) heat effect

(C) magnetic effect

(D) physiological effect

863. What causes wires to become heated when conducting electricity?

(A) chemical effect

(B) heat effect

(C) magnetic effect

(D) physiological effect

864. What occurs when a wire is wrapped around an iron core and a current is sent through the wire?

(A) chemical effect

(B) heat effect

(C) magnetic effect

(D) physiological effect

865. What effect occurs when electricity contracts human muscle tissue?

(A) chemical effect

(B) heat effect

(C) magnetic effect

(D) physiological effect

866. What semiconductor contains at least three terminals called an emitter, a base, and a collector?

(A) a parallel circuit

(B) a transistor

(C) a transducer

(D) a transformer

867. Which of the following means "current equals voltage divided by resistance"?

(A) Kirchhoff's law

(B) power

(C) Ohm's law

(D) resistance in parallel

868. What transducer converts electrical energy to kinetic energy?

(A) heater

(B) buzzer

(C) microphone

(D) motor

869. What does a megahertz (MHz) represent?

(A) 100 hertz

(B) 1,000 hertz

(C) 100,000 hertz

(D) 1,000,000 hertz

870. If two working batteries were connected to a light bulb, as illustrated in this figure, would the light bulb light up?

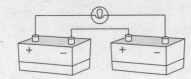

(A) Yes.

(B) No.

(C) Not enough information given.

(D) It would short out.

871. What is the name of an object that conducts electricity poorly at low temperatures?

(A) magnifier

(B) terminal

(C) coulomb

(D) semiconductor

872. What is an electric cell?

(A) battery power

(B) a storage compartment for electricity in a battery

(C) the voltage a battery creates

(D) a measurement of battery power

873. In what electrical object would a filament be found?

(A) oven

(B) clothes iron

(C) computer

(D) lamp

874. Resistance is the ratio of potential difference across a component to the current passing through it. How is it measured?

(A) amps

(B) ohms

(C) volts

(D) degrees

875. If you use a 40-watt light bulb for three hours, how many watt-hours have you used?

(A) 40

(B) 60

(C) 120

(D) 200

876. What is the term for magnetic strength on a two-dimensional surface?

(A) coils

(B) magnetic flux

(C) magnetic effect

(D) electromagnetic induction

877. What is the term for magnetic effects that are perpendicular to the conductor and parallel to each other?

(A) north pole

(B) semiconductor

(C) lines of force

(D) electroplating

878. How can you increase magnetic field strength in a coil?

(A) increase the number of coils

(B) increase the amount of current

(C) condense the coils

(D) all of the above

879. What is the term for excess electricity that is trapped on the surface of an object?

(A) static

(B) magnetic

(C) positive

(D) negative

880. What device compares two voltages or currents and then switches its output to indicate which is larger?

(A) voltmeter

(B) ammeter

(C) comparator

(D) transistor

881. Transistors are usually made of what material?

(A) iron

(B) silk

(C) germanium

(D) wood

882. Magnetic cores usually consist of what substances?

(A) air or iron

(B) copper or iron

(C) air or copper

(D) air or wood

883. What is a potentiometer?

(A) a transistor

(B) a transformer

(C) a variable resistor

(D) a magnetic field

884. What changes resistance according to varying temperatures?

(A) diodes

(B) thermistors

(C) magnetic fluxes

(D) transformers

885. What is a flex sensor?

(A) a resistor

(B) a transistor

(C) a diode

(D) a switch

Circuits

886. What is a circuit?

(A)   a fancy race

(B)   the path of a current

(C)   electric connectors

(D)   the force of a volt

887. What occurs when wires **cross,** causing the electricity to bypass **the intended** circuit?

(A)   explosion

(B)   short circuit

(C)   voltage overload

(D)   watt resistance

888. Which of these devices interrupts electrical current?

(A)   plug

(B)   transformer

(C)   circuit breaker

(D)   diode

889. The following illustration is an example of what?

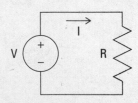

(A)   transformer

(B)   diode

(C)   transistor

(D)   circuit

890. What term describes any device that consumes the energy flowing through a circuit and converts that energy into work?

(A)   meter

(B)   load

(C)   power

(D)   frequency

891. What type of circuit has only one possible path for electrical current to flow?

(A)   parallel

(B)   series

(C)   series-parallel

(D)   complex

892. What causes a circuit breaker to trip?

(A)   You unplug a load from the circuit.

(B)   You turn on all the lights in the house.

(C)   The current running through the circuit generates too much heat.

(D)   The magnetic field is overloaded.

893. Select the correct answer based on the two diagrams of separate bulbs circuits.

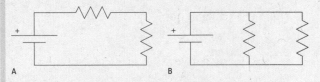

(A)   Circuit A has more bulbs than Circuit B.

(B)   Circuit A has brighter bulbs than Circuit B.

(C)   Circuit B has brighter bulbs than Circuit A.

(D)   Circuit B has a larger battery than Circuit A.

894. What conclusion can you draw based on the following diagram of a flashbulb circuit?

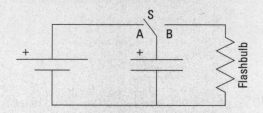

(A) There is no power to the circuit.

(B) The flashbulb is turned off.

(C) Only one battery is working.

(D) The flashbulb is in parallel.

895. What is the electrical version of a valve called?

(A) diode

(B) transformer

(C) capacitor

(D) switch

896. What symbol is not shown in the following circuit diagram?

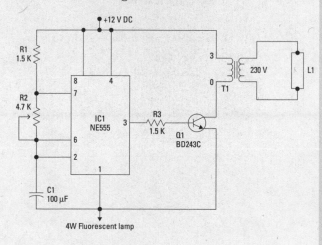

(A) transformer

(B) fuse

(C) resistor

(D) transistor

897. How many amplifiers are shown in the following simple circuit?

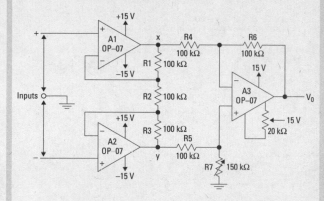

(A) 1

(B) 2

(C) 3

(D) 7

898. The following circuit diagram represents what common household device?

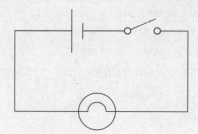

(A) lamp

(B) doorbell

(C) ceiling fan

(D) microwave

899. Which of the following common electric symbols is used only once in the diagram?

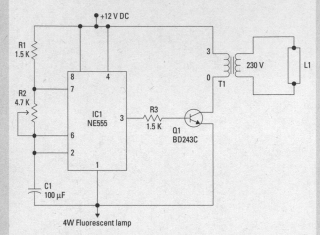

(A) circuit

(B) transformer

(C) resistor

(D) wire

900. What is the term for the part of a circuit that always measures 0 volts?

(A) positive terminal

(B) negative terminal

(C) ground

(D) battery

901. What is commonly used in a circuit in which the flow of electricity needs to be regulated for the device to run properly?

(A) resistance

(B) transformer

(C) diodes

(D) batteries

902. How does a rheostat lower the resistance in an electrical circuit?

(A) It absorbs the electrical current.

(B) It turns off the circuit.

(C) It trips the breaker.

(D) It burns the fuse.

903. According to the diagram, what does the circle with an A symbolize?

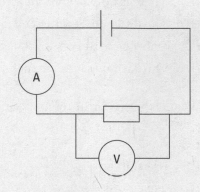

(A) amplifier

(B) antenna

(C) ammeter

(D) alternating current

904. How many ohms are measured in this simple circuit?

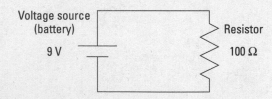

(A) 9

(B) 900

(C) 100

(D) 50

905. In this diagram of a simple circuit, what does the circle with a V symbolize?

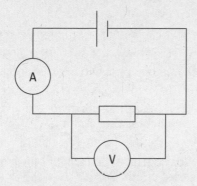

(A)   voltage

(B)   voltmeter

(C)   variable resistor

(D)   variable

906. According to the diagram, what four components make up the circuit?

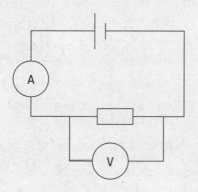

(A)   voltmeter, ammeter, fuse, and potentiometer

(B)   voltmeter, ammeter, ground, and cell

(C)   voltmeter, ammeter, resistor, and cell

(D)   voltmeter, ammeter, battery, and capacitor

907. What does the following schematic represent?

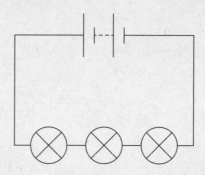

(A)   railroad tracks

(B)   engine wiring

(C)   radio wiring

(D)   lighting system

908. What can be concluded from the following diagram?

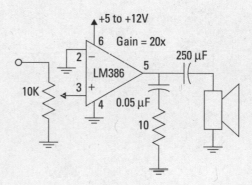

(A)   It produces heat.

(B)   It produces sound.

(C)   It produces light.

(D)   None of the above.

909. What device is the following schematic most likely showing?

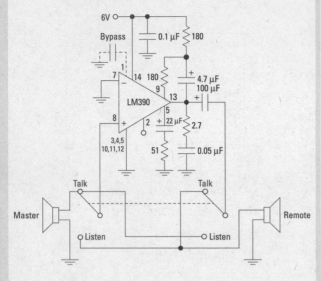

(A) an engine

(B) an intercom

(C) a microwave

(D) an oven

910. How many volts are left after the current makes one loop around the circuit?

(A) 9 volts

(B) 12 volts

(C) 20 volts

(D) 0 volts

911. Which term refers to the process of finding the voltage across and the current through every component in an electrical circuit?

(A) analog circuit

(B) electrical circuit

(C) circuit analysis

(D) circuit integration

912. What is true about parallel circuits?

(A) The voltage decreases along the circuit.

(B) The voltage is applied evenly to each branch.

(C) The voltage increases along the circuit.

(D) The voltage is divided unevenly across the circuit.

913. What occurs when a light blows out in a series circuit?

(A) The series completely breaks.

(B) The remaining components still work.

(C) The power to the blown light is lost.

(D) The battery stores the lost energy from the blown light.

914. What occurs when a light blows out in a parallel circuit?

(A) The series completely breaks.

(B) The remaining components still work.

(C) The power to the blown light is lost.

(D) The battery stores the lost energy from the blown light.

Current

915. Which term refers to the process of electrons moving from one place to another?

(A) gravity

(B) force

(C) exertion

(D) electric current

916. Amperes is a unit of measurement for what?

(A) power

(B) current

(C) resistance

(D) music

917. Frank wanted to set the mood, so he dimmed the lights in his living room. What type of variable resistor did he use?

(A) potentiometer

(B) rheostat

(C) inductor

(D) buzzer

918. What causes electrons in a direct current to flow in a single direction on a wire?

(A) electrical energy

(B) magnetic field

(C) parallel circuit

(D) radiation

919. What process changes incoming alternating current (AC) to direct current (DC)?

(A) magnetic effect

(B) rectification

(C) transformation

(D) impedance

920. Which of the following is a safety device that melts if a flowing current exceeds a specific value?

(A) cell

(B) battery

(C) fuse

(D) transducer

921. What is the term for the number of times a current completes two alternations of direction per second?

(A) capacitance

(B) frequency

(C) power

(D) lap

922. What type of insulator would discourage electric current?

(A) copper

(B) water

(C) wood

(D) iron

923. What is the term for the rate of flow of electrons in a conductor?

(A) coulomb

(B) battery cell

(C) electrical current

(D) amperes

924. What represents the strength of a current?

(A) coulomb

(B) ampere

(C) voltage

(D) wires

925. What measures the flow of current through a circuit?

(A) amperes

(B) coulombs

(C) milliamperes

(D) ammeters

926. What is the term for a material whose internal electric charges do not flow freely and which, therefore, does not conduct an electric current?

(A) semiconductor

(B) insulator

(C) conventional current

(D) short circuit

927. What is the purpose of a rectifier?

(A) amplifies frequency

(B) converts a negative to a positive

(C) converts AC to DC

(D) measures power

928. What is the ratio of electromotive force to current?

(A) impedance

(B) power

(C) magnetism

(D) voltage

929. Most electricity comes in the form of what?

(A) direct current

(B) alternating current

(C) wires

(D) batteries

930. What draws current as it absorbs energy?

(A) inductor

(B) capacitor

(C) transformer

(D) transistor

931. What does the acronym VAC stand for in electronics?

(A) Voltage Alternating Current

(B) Voltage And Current

(C) Variable Aided Current

(D) Voltage Amplified Capacitor

932. In what direction does current go in electron flow notation?

(A) from negative to positive

(B) from positive to negative

(C) any direction

(D) horizontally

933. What is the main function of a diode?

(A) makes alternating current

(B) allows the current to flow in one direction

(C) emits light

(D) provides a power source

934. Divided current in parallel resistors is equal to what?

(A) voltage

(B) wattage

(C) total current

(D) total watt-hours

Circuit Codes

935. What does the following symbol represent?

(A) conductor

(B) volt

(C) ground

(D) transformer

936. What does the following symbol represent?

(A) resistor

(B) inductor

(C) current source

(D) electricity

937. What does the following symbol represent?

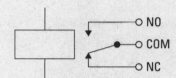

    (A)   alternating current

    (B)   direct current

    (C)   diode

    (D)   resistance

938. What does the following symbol represent?

    (A)   bell

    (B)   relay

    (C)   heater

    (D)   fuse

939. What does the following symbol represent?

    (A)   indicator lamp

    (B)   microphone

    (C)   joined wires

    (D)   inductor

940. What do the color codes on resistors indicate?

    (A)   value

    (B)   tolerance

    (C)   quality

    (D)   all of the above

941. What does the following symbol represent?

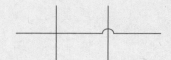

    (A)   joined wires

    (B)   unjoined wires

    (C)   AC power supply

    (D)   DC power supply

942. What is the value for black and white in the resistor band color code?

    (A)   black is 1, white is 2

    (B)   black is 0, white is 1

    (C)   black is 0, white is 9

    (D)   black is 1, white is 9

943. What does the following symbol represent?

    (A)   transistor

    (B)   amplifier

    (C)   potentiometer

    (D)   heater

944. What does the following symbol represent?

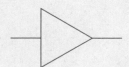

    (A)   transistor

    (B)   current

    (C)   amplifier

    (D)   antenna

945. What does the following symbol represent?

(A) variable capacitor

(B) diode

(C) buzzer

(D) resistor

946. What color wire is not used for any other purpose than grounding to the Earth?

(A) red

(B) white

(C) black

(D) green

947. What color wire from the following choices is not considered a "hot" wire?

(A) red

(B) black

(C) gray

(D) blue

948. What color wire is not commonly used as a switch leg wire?

(A) white

(B) blue

(C) yellow

(D) orange

949. What does it mean to an electrician if black electrical tape is layered at the end of a neutral wire?

(A) It is broken.

(B) It is hot.

(C) It may conduct electricity.

(D) It needs to be replaced.

950. What do the following symbols represent?

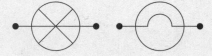

(A) batteries

(B) lamps

(C) wires

(D) speakers

951. What does the arrow over the resistor symbol represent?

(A) indicator

(B) direct current

(C) variable

(D) live

952. What does the following symbol represent?

(A) push switch

(B) push-to-break switch

(C) on/off switch

(D) relay

953. What does the following symbol represent?

(A)   battery

(B)   cell

(C)   buzzer

(D)   heater

954. What does the following symbol represent?

(A)   wire

(B)   cell

(C)   diode

(D)   antenna

955. What do the following symbols represent?

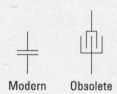

(A)   transformers

(B)   capacitors

(C)   transistors

(D)   lamps

956. What does the U.S. National Electrical Code mandate for color-coded wires?

(A)   hot wires only

(B)   neutral and ground wires only

(C)   hot wires and neutral wires only

(D)   ground wires only

957. What does the following symbol represent?

(A)   fuse

(B)   ground

(C)   outlet

(D)   resistor

958. What does the following symbol represent?

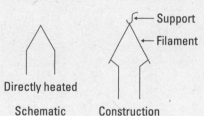

(A)   rheostat

(B)   cathode

(C)   diode

(D)   capacitor

959. What do the following symbols represent?

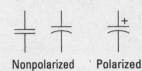

Nonpolarized   Polarized

(A) resistors

(B) capacitors

(C) voltage

(D) batteries

960. What does the following **symbol represent**?

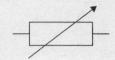

(A) potentiometer

(B) buzzer

(C) rheostat

(D) fuse

Chapter 9

Assembling Objects: Figuring Out How Things Fit Together

· ·

*O*nly the Navy uses the Assembling Objects subtest to calculate military composite scores for a handful of ratings (or jobs). The other branches of the military don't currently use this test, but they may change their minds at any time. The purpose of this subtest is to measure your spatial skills by having you look at pieces of an object and then visualize how they fit together. The questions ask you to identify the correctly assembled drawing after being shown the disassembled diagram. Spatial skills are important for reading and understanding maps, graphs, drawings, and electronic data. So if you're interested in joining the Navy, or just perking up your spatial relations skills, be sure to study for this test.

The Questions You'll Work On

You see two types of drawings (questions) in this subtest:

- **Connectors:** In this type of question, you have to correctly connect two shapes from point A to point B by following the clues given in the disassembled drawing.

- **Shapes:** This type of question gives you cut up pieces of an object and asks you to decide how the pieces fit together. It's a lot like a jigsaw puzzle.

What to Watch Out For

The following tips can help you choose the correct answers as you work through the questions in this chapter:

- Watch out for mirrored objects. Choices with mirrored objects often trick people because they look like the right answer, except that they're flipped around.

- Make sure the shapes in the disassembled drawing are the same size as the ones in your answer.

- If a shape in the disassembled drawing has a line that goes through any part of the shape, make sure the answer reflects that same intersection.

Connectors

961.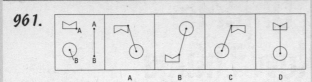

962.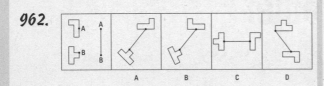

963.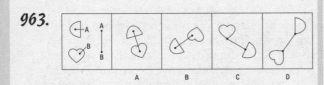

964.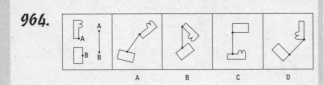

965.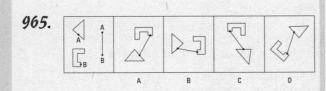

966.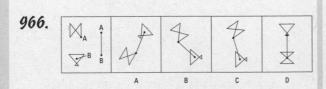

967.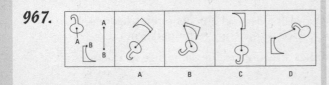

968.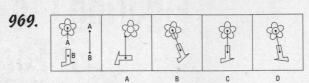

969.

970.

971.

972.

973.

974.

975.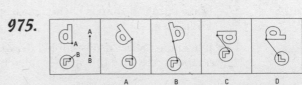

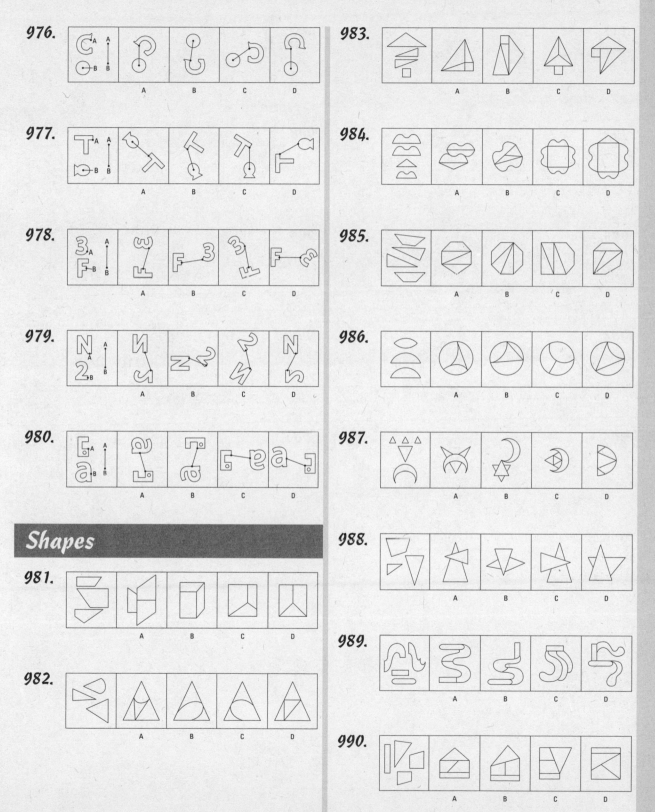

976.

977.

978.

979.

980.

Shapes

981.

982.

983.

984.

985.

986.

987.

988.

989.

990.

991.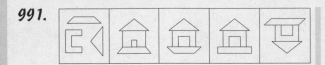

992.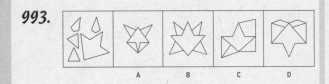

993.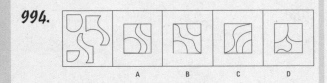

994.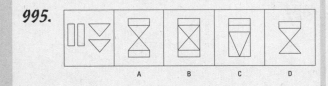

995.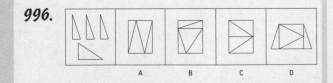

996.

997.

998.

999.

1,000.

1,001.

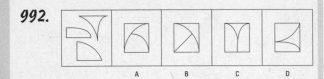

Part II
The Answers

In this part . . .

You've tackled the questions; now you can check your answers. I give you the correct answer and an explanation for every question listed in the first part of this book. If after reviewing your answers, you decide you want more practice before taking the ASVAB, check out the following titles, written by me, myself, and I:

✔ *ASVAB For Dummies*

✔ *ASVAB AFQT For Dummies*

If you discover that you haven't done so well in a certain category, don't worry. The *For Dummies* series offers plenty of excellent resources that can provide more instruction and review. Here are a few that I recommend (all published by Wiley):

✔ *Vocabulary For Dummies* by Laurie E. Rozakis

✔ *Basic Math & Pre-Algebra For Dummies* by Mark Zegarelli

✔ *Algebra I For Dummies* by Mary Jane Sterling

✔ *Geometry For Dummies* by Mark Ryan

✔ *Math Word Problems For Dummies* by Mary Jane Sterling

✔ *Biology For Dummies* by Rene Fester Kratz and Donna Rae Siegfried

✔ *Chemistry For Dummies* by John T. Moore

✔ *Physics I For Dummies* by Steven Holzner

✔ *Electronics For Dummies* by Cathleen Shamieh and Gordon McComb

Visit www.dummies.com for more information.

Chapter 10

Answers

Answers
1–100

1. **A. conscious**

Cognizant is an adjective meaning aware.

2. **C. condense**

Abbreviate is a verb meaning to shorten or condense by omitting letters or words.

3. **A. clearness**

Clarity is a noun meaning clearness in speech, appearance, or thought.

4. **B. complete**

Culminate is a verb meaning to come to the end or completion.

5. **B. passionate**

Ardent is an adjective that means characterized by warmth of feeling, typically expressed in eager, zealous support or activity.

6. **A. hesitate**

Falter is a verb meaning to hesitate or lose courage to act.

7. **B. prevent**

Hamper is a verb meaning to hinder or prevent movement.

8. **C. harmful**

Malicious is an adjective meaning deliberately or intentionally harmful.

9. **D. intrude**

Obtrude is a verb meaning to intrude or become unpleasant or unwelcome.

10. **B. touchable**

Palpable is an adjective meaning able to be touched, felt, or seen.

11. C. drink

Quaff is a verb meaning to enjoy a drink.

12. B. spicy

Savory is an adjective that means having a spicy flavoring.

13. D. change

Vagary is a noun meaning unpredictable change.

14. B. halt

Wean is a verb meaning to halt the dependence of something.

15. C. desire

Yen is a noun meaning a longing or desire.

16. B. various

Diverse is an adjective meaning different or various.

17. B. assign

Entrust is a verb meaning to select and give a responsibility.

18. D. ignore

Disregard is a noun meaning to carelessly ignore.

19. D. cooperative

Amenable is an adjective meaning willing and cooperative.

20. D. independent

Autonomous is an adjective meaning self-governing and independent.

21. B. speak

Orate is a verb meaning to speak.

22. D. exceptional

Superlative is an adjective meaning exceptional or superior.

23. B. besides

Except is a preposition meaning other than or besides.

24. C. disapprove

Criticize is a verb meaning to disapprove or judge poorly.

25. D. allow

Empower is a verb meaning to authorize, enable, or allow.

26. C. flip

Invert is a verb meaning to reverse or turn upside down.

27. C. confess

Divulge is a verb meaning to make known or confess.

28. B. abundant

Prolific is an adjective meaning fruitful, abundant, and productive.

29. B. generous

Munificent is an adjective that means relating to an overwhelming show of generosity.

30. B. joy

Mirth is a noun meaning great joy and cheer.

31. D. perception

Ken is a noun meaning perception or impression.

32. C. force

Momentum is a noun meaning force or thrusting power.

33. D. expedite

Facilitate is a verb meaning to assist in the progress of, to aid, or to expedite.

34. B. finish

Attainment is a noun meaning finish, achievement, or completion.

35. **B. sacrifice**

Forfeit is a noun meaning something given as a sacrifice.

36. **A. false**

Belie is a verb meaning to be false or to misrepresent accuracy.

37. **B. confidence**

Aplomb is a noun meaning the possession of self-confidence and assurance.

38. **C. laziness**

Indolence is a noun meaning slothfulness and laziness.

39. **B. expression**

Phrase is a noun meaning a group of words or an expression.

40. **B. disaster**

Calamity is a noun meaning disaster.

41. **C. inclusive**

Comprehensive is an adjective meaning of large scope or inclusive.

42. **B. compensate**

Remunerate is a verb meaning to compensate or reward.

43. **A. emotion**

Pathos is a noun meaning deep sadness or emotion.

44. **B. swing**

Oscillate is a verb meaning to move back and forth or swing.

45. **B. peace**

Repose is a noun meaning restfulness or peace.

46. **B. halt**

Cease is a verb meaning to stop or conclude.

47. **D. fool**

Dupe is a noun meaning a person who is fooled.

48. **A. shorten**

Truncate is a verb meaning to shorten or abbreviate.

49. **B. hunter**

Predator is a noun meaning hunter or killer.

50. **A. earliest**

Original is an adjective meaning earliest or first.

51. **C. end**

Abolish is a verb meaning to end or destroy.

52. **D. awful**

Abominable is an adjective meaning awful and detestable.

53. **D. suppress**

Quell is a verb meaning to defeat or suppress.

54. **D. sarcastic**

Ironic is an adjective meaning bitterly or cleverly sarcastic.

55. **C. aware**

Sober is an adjective that means having not partaken in alcohol and remaining clear-headed.

56. **B. warn**

Forebode is a verb meaning to predict or warn.

57. **D. relax**

Bask is a verb meaning to relax and enjoy warmth.

58. **C. terseness**

Brevity is a noun meaning briefness in duration, and *terseness* means shortness or few.

59. **B. postpone**

Defer is a verb meaning to put off or postpone.

60. **B. support**

Endorse is a verb meaning to give or declare public approval.

61. **D. glimpse**

Glimmer is a noun that can mean a flicker of light or a faint glimpse.

62. **A. forbidden**

Illicit is an adjective meaning forbidden or illegal.

63. **D. joyful**

Jovial is an adjective meaning joyful, friendly, and of good cheer.

64. **D. moving**

Kinetic is an adjective meaning relating to or characterized by motion.

65. **A. offensive**

Lascivious is an adjective meaning feeling or showing inappropriate, offensive (oftentimes sexual) desire.

66. **B. insignificant**

Nominal is an adjective meaning insignificant or lower than the actual or **expected** value.

67. **A. complicate**

Perplex is a verb meaning to cause difficulty or complications.

68. **C. wise person**

Sage can be a noun or adjective meaning a wise person with gained **wisdom.**

69. **B. hidden**

Ulterior is an adjective meaning hidden beyond admission.

70. **A. corrupt**

Venal is an adjective meaning able to be paid off or corrupt.

71. A. one-year-old

A *yearling* is a creature that is one year of age.

72. A. blind

Ignorant is an adjective meaning unaware and unknowing.

73. C. send

Remit is a verb meaning to send or transfer.

74. B. insensitive

Obdurate is an adjective meaning stubborn and insensitive.

75. A. accept

Accede is a verb meaning to grant approval or allow.

76. B. faithfulness

Fidelity is a noun meaning faithfulness and loyalty in a relationship.

77. C. between

Among is a preposition meaning in the middle of or between.

78. A. repetitive

Redundant is an adjective meaning excessive and repetitious.

79. B. weave

Intertwine is a verb meaning to twist, weave, or mesh around.

80. A. analyze

Peruse is a verb meaning to check out, examine, or analyze.

81. C. refrain

Abstain is a verb meaning to hold back from doing or refrain.

82. B. confused

Stumped is a verb meaning to confuse or bewilder.

83. A. invigorate

Vivify is a verb meaning to refresh and enlighten.

84. B. splendid

Sumptuous is an adjective meaning splendid and lavish to indicate expense.

85. A. question

Query can be a noun or verb; as a noun, it means a question or inquiry.

86. A. alluring

Provocative is an adjective meaning alluring, intriguing, and intending to arouse.

87. C. opinionated

Officious is an adjective meaning overly eager to offer opinions and advice.

88. A. inattentive

Listless is an adjective meaning low in spirits and uninterested.

89. A. immediate

Instant is an adjective meaning urgent and immediate.

90. A. condemn

Censure is a verb meaning to condemn or to disapprove.

91. C. danger

Peril is a noun meaning danger or risk.

92. C. fabricate

Forge is a verb meaning to counterfeit or fabricate.

93. A. digestible

Edible is an adjective meaning able to be eaten.

94. B. compete

Contend is a verb meaning to claim a battle or compete.

95. C. confirm

Corroborate is a verb meaning to back up or confirm a story.

96. C. prevent

Avert is a verb meaning to turn something away or prevent it from happening.

97. C. irritation

Asperity is a noun meaning an irritable and harsh manner.

98. A. applause

Adulation is a noun that means the giving of enthusiastic praise and flattery.

99. D. grief

Sorrow is a noun meaning extreme sadness or grief.

100. C. protection

Coverage is a noun meaning a protection provided against risks.

101. C. superior

Premium is an adjective meaning of exceptional quality or superior.

102. B. high price

Premium is a noun meaning at a higher price or cost.

103. A. snobby

Pretentious is an adjective that means relating to an exaggerated snobbishness or conceited attitude.

104. D. harmful

Malign is an adjective meaning hurtful or injurious.

105. C. excitement

Thrill is a noun meaning sudden excitement or adventure.

106. C. immobility

Inertia is a noun meaning disinclination to move or lifelessness.

107. **B. chaos**

Turmoil is a noun meaning chaos or distress.

108. **C. replace**

Supplant is a verb meaning to replace.

109. **D. importance**

Emphasis is a noun meaning importance or prominence.

110. **C. little**

Scanty is an adjective meaning inadequate or little.

111. **B. insurrection**

Sedition is a noun meaning rebellion and insurrection.

112. **A. erroneous**

Specious is an adjective meaning misleading and deceptive.

113. **C. piece**

Shard is a noun meaning end, fragment, or piece.

114. **B. complete**

Unmitigated is an adjective meaning absolute, unqualified, and complete.

115. **B. immoral**

Noisome is an adjective meaning immoral, bad, or offensive.

116. **C. attraction**

Allure is a noun meaning attraction and appeal.

117. **B. threaten**

Intimidate is a verb meaning to threaten or frighten.

118. **A. law**

Canon is a noun meaning ecclesiastical law or rule.

119. **A. rush**

Delay is a verb meaning to postpone, and the word most opposite in meaning is *rush*.

120. **C. ignore**

Reflect is a verb that means to think deeply about, demonstrate, or give back. *Ignore* would be most opposite in meaning from the choices given.

121. **D. exalt**

Blame can be both a noun and a verb; as a verb, it means to condemn, place responsibility, or accuse. So *exalt* is most opposite in meaning.

122. **A. compliment**

Insult is a noun meaning hateful communication or a verb meaning to abuse with words, so *compliment* is the word most opposite.

123. **B. polite**

Forthright is an adjective meaning straightforward and honest, so of the choices given, *polite* is the closest to the opposite.

124. **B. mild**

Profound is an adjective meaning thoughtful, intellectual, and intense, so *mild* is the most opposite in meaning.

125. **B. reluctant**

Keen is an adjective meaning interested and enthusiastic, so *reluctant* is the choice most opposite in meaning.

126. **A. since 1995**

Choice (B), 1967, is the year model of Al's car. Choice (C), 2005, isn't mentioned anywhere in the passage, and five years ago, Choice (D), is when Al took over the club. Because Joe has been in the club since it was founded and the club was founded in 1995, the answer is Choice (A).

127. **C. Joe likes Al's car but doesn't like Al.**

The passage says that Al is the new president, but he didn't found the club. Therefore, Choice (A) is wrong. The passage doesn't mention anything about whether or not Al and Joe were once friends, Choice (B), or if Joe is dating Al's ex, Choice (D). That leaves only Choice (C) as the winner.

128. **B. the casting that contains the cylinders of an internal combustion engine**

The word *block* appears only once in the passage. Because the author uses the phrase *big block* in reference to a car, you can rule out all the options except Choice (B).

129. **B. Primitive man did not struggle with human relationships.**

The paragraph states that human interaction was not the "chief" problem in their society, but it doesn't state that it was never a problem. So the paragraph doesn't support Choice (B).

130. **B. Prehistoric man's greatest challenges had to do with their environment.**

Both Choices (A) and (C) are accurate statements, but they're serving as supporting statements rather than the main thought. Choice (D) is incorrect, as the passage clearly states that the environment included more than weather. Therefore, Choice (B) is correct.

131. **D. "My Account of the War"**

Choice (A) doesn't make much sense, since the group put up an English flag in the first breach. Choice (B) doesn't work because the passage talks about fighting and dead bodies. Choice (C) is not the best answer because it doesn't directly relate to the passage. Choice (D) is correct because the main character is speaking of his experiences of a particular war.

132. **B. from day to dusk**

The passage states in the beginning that the assault began in the day. Later in the passage, the author explains that the town was theirs by dusk, so you can conclude the time frame was from daytime into dusk.

133. **A. pile**

Heap is a noun meaning a group of things placed, thrown, or lying one on another — in other words, a pile — so Choice (A) is the correct answer.

134. **B. in a war.**

The main character is describing a scene relative to that of a war, even mentioning an English flag, a general, and dead bodies. The paragraph never states he is doing something for the community, is planning to stay at the town, or is in a dream, so you can conclude that the main character is in some sort of war.

135. **A. Some wavelengths of light that produce eye damage in certain animals are more likely to hit the Earth due to ozone decay.**

This statement summarizes the main argument. Further, it is a near rephrase of the last two sentences in the paragraph.

136. **D. More information is needed.**

The author states that wavelengths of light that reach the Earth's surface due to the decay of the ozone layer are believed to cause damage in some animals. The author doesn't say which animals, but he implies that some are affected and others are not. You need more information to answer this question.

137. **A. depletion**

Many people would automatically relate the word *decay* to decomposition; however, another use for the word is to represent a decline from a prosperous condition, making it a synonym of depletion. *Depletion* is a noun meaning a lessening in power, quantity, value, and/or content.

138. **B. Help for the Roanoke Colony was delayed for three years.**

The paragraph makes no mention of Raleigh's death, and no knowledge is given of where the colonists disappeared to. Queen Elizabeth I, not the II, was the "Virgin Queen." Choice (B) is correct as the colonists settled in Roanoke in 1587 and help came in 1590, which was three years later.

139. **D. 5 years**

The paragraph states that the settlers started out in Virginia in 1585. Then near the end of the paragraph, help came to search for the second round of settlers in 1590, leaving you with a difference of 5 years.

140. **C. that the Croatoans had something to do with the disappearance of the settlers**

Because the settlers were not Croatoan, this evidence left near where the settlers set up their colony implies that the Croatoans must have known what happened to the colony.

141. **B. giving in to fear**

The passage states that fear leads a swimmer to stop making rational decisions, the first step in drowning.

142. **C. to splash about helplessly.**

To *flounder* in the water is to splash around helplessly.

143. **D. remaining calm**

The paragraph doesn't discourage the reader from going in the water, nor does it mention having someone nearby. It says knowing how to swim can save your life, but the main focus of the passage is on the importance of remaining calm when trouble strikes.

144. **D. He wanted a code that could be read at night.**

Napoleon wanted to devise a code that could be read at night, so one of his soldiers invented a system of raised dots that later became Braille.

145. **C. one to six**

The passage states that each letter of the alphabet is represented in Braille by raised dots and that each letter uses from one to six dots.

146. **D. He simplified someone else's complicated idea.**

Napoleon rejected the idea for a code that could be read at night because it was too complicated. Louis Braille took that idea and simplified it for the use by blind people.

147. **D. something that can be felt with the fingers.**

The word *tactile* refers to something that can be felt with one's hands.

148. **A. legal authorization**

The statement stresses that you must have a judge's approval, or legal authorization, before you can conduct a search. Choices (B) and (D) are incorrect because having direct evidence or a reasonable belief isn't enough to validate a search. The passage doesn't mention Choice (C).

149. **C. the Fourth Amendment**

The passage is informing readers about the Fourth Amendment.

150. **C. direct evidence of a crime**

The question asks what the judge needs before issuing a search warrant, which is direct factual evidence of a crime, or probable cause. The judge's decision must be based on factual evidence.

151. **D. They're used to reduce the number of individuals running for the office.**

The purpose of the conventions is to clear the field of candidates, or rather to reduce the number of individuals running for the office. Primary elections and caucuses, not conventions, are held in each state, so Choice (A) is wrong. The Constitution doesn't cover this process, so Choice (B) is also wrong. The paragraph doesn't state that candidates are introduced in the conventions, so you can cross out Choice (C).

152. **B. The Republican Party holds a primary election in Florida.**

The passage states that presidential primary elections are held in each state. The passage doesn't say anything regarding the elections being illegal, Choice (A), or needing to be changed, Choice (D). The process of elections isn't outlined in the Constitution, Choice (C), but that doesn't mean that nothing regarding the election is. Therefore, Choice (B) is the only correct answer.

153. C. 20

The passage clearly states that computer scientists have been looking into many ways to run successful businesses for 20 years.

154. A. A program cannot be both creative and profitable.

This answer identifies an essential assumption in the original argument. If writing creative and profitable programs weren't mutually exclusive, then computer scientists could write profitable programs without losing their creative aspect.

155. C. Radiation will not increase risk of cancer.

Choices (A), (B), and (D) are each stated as fact in the paragraph, whereas Choice (C) is a direct contradiction. Therefore, Choice (C) is correct.

156. B. defects

The phrase "preexisting genetic faults" means preexisting defects in the body. In this context, *faults* is a noun meaning physical or intellectual impairments or defects.

157. A. Most cancers are not hereditary.

The passage states that 5 to 10 percent of cancers are hereditary, so most aren't.

158. C. basketball court

Although the author would probably consider a basketball court a play space, it isn't listed in the passage.

159. A. Play spaces improve society.

The main idea of the passage is about how play spaces contribute to the community.

160. B. Communities with play areas within walking distance are better communities.

The passage implies that children and families within a community have better health and well-being when they have play spaces close by.

161. B. helping people

According to the last sentence, the biggest satisfaction of being a nurse comes from knowing you make a difference in people's lives, so Choice (B), helping people, is correct.

162. C. convenient uniforms

The passage describes many benefits of being a nurse, but it doesn't talk about the uniforms nurses may wear.

163. **D. Nursing has many benefits.**

The passage says that nursing has not only good monetary and work benefits but also rewarding self-satisfaction benefits.

164. **B. plenty**

Abundant is an adjective meaning marked by great plenty. The passage describes abundant job opportunities, meaning there are a lot of jobs from which a nurse can choose.

165. **B. 150 feet**

The passage states the men walk 150 feet per minute.

166. **D. steps**

Paces, in this context, is a noun meaning steps in walking.

167. **A. transporting the mixture in a wheelbarrow**

The last sentence states that it costs more to carry the mixture by hand than it does to carry it by wheelbarrow.

168. **B. to spend time in the country**

The last sentence states, "she never needed it as now," talking about being in the country.

169. **C. She was enjoying being in the country.**

The passage is describing the character's history and feelings about the country and explaining how she was enjoying the country and needed to be there.

170. **C. passed time**

Spent is the past tense of the verb *spend* and in this context means to use time or occupy.

171. **C. American bison**

The paragraph states that the explorer's exact whereabouts were unknown, but he did spot the first American bison within 15 miles of the U.S. capital.

172. **B. berries of a plant**

The author describes a plant with berries and explains how the berries were used in the past.

173. **D. They boiled the berries.**

The second sentence in the passage clearly states that the Indians used to boil the berries for food.

174. **A. The plant berries appear in the summer and are useful to humans and animals.**

The main point of the paragraph is that when the berries of the plant ripen, they become useful to humans and animals.

175. **B. obvious**

The word *conspicuous* in the paragraph is an adjective meaning obvious or noticeable.

176. **B. how to handle a horse**

A *colt* is a young horse. The author is explaining how to handle a horse in different circumstances.

177. **A.** *How to Train a Horse*

How to Train a Horse is the best title because the excerpt is clearly explaining tips on how to handle and teach a colt in different situations.

178. **A. frightening**

Formidable, in the context, is an adjective that means causing fear, dread, or apprehension.

179. **B. physical and psychological studies**

The passage states that anyone who is training or educating a child should be familiar with modern studies about the psychological and physical effects on child growth.

180. **D. The interests of a child can aid in his or her development if the adult is educated on certain developmental studies.**

According to the passage, fun games can aid in the successful development of a child if the adult or person charged in training or teaching fun games is educated on the results of scientific studies. A parent or caregiver should know how age-appropriate games can aid in child development.

181. **D. It is unknown.**

According to the passage, it is unclear how the spirit directly affects the matter of the body.

182. **A. the partnership between mind and body**

The author refers to a study in the last sentence. You can conclude from the information given that the study is about the partnership of mind and body.

183. **C. occupy**

Inhabit, in this passage, is a verb meaning to live in or occupy, so Choice (C) is the best answer.

184. **D. 14 months**

The passage states that during the recent time of 14 months, researchers found a possible treatment for Angelman syndrome.

185. **B. Donating to the Angelman Syndrome Foundation is important because they might find a cure.**

The passage describes how the Foundation has made recent strides toward finding a cure thanks to donations.

186. **B. advances**

In the passage, a *stride* is a noun meaning advancement in a stage of progress.

187. **A. hay**

The third sentence describes winter feed as hay, where it says, "The change from hay to grass must be gradual."

188. **A. so the calves avoid digestive issues**

The passage states that excessive purging can occur if a gradual change in feed is not made.

189. **B. America**

Europe's travelers made voyages to America, which was also called the *New World.*

190. **C. "The European Drive to Explore the New World"**

The paragraph covers why Europeans were eager to explore the New World. Many European governments sent explorers to the Americas in the hopes of finding resources that would lead to wealth. Therefore, Choice (C) is correct.

191. **B. Christopher Columbus's voyage to America inspired many voyages to take place.**

The main idea of the passage is that Christopher Columbus's first voyage to America inspired other travelers to go on trips there in order to gain wealth.

192.   C. a feeling of craving something.

The paragraph talks about the power-hungry leaders who took many more expeditions with the hope (craving) of obtaining more riches.

193.   B. Second-hand smoke poses a health risk.

The passage states that most health experts agree that second-hand smoke poses a health risk.

194.   D. Data shows that other regions that enacted tough anti-smoking reform experienced longer life spans.

The passage doesn't imply that existing data shows that quality and length of life improved in other regions due to anti-smoking laws.

195.   B. 0.51 million

The passage clearly states that 4.51 million was expected. The actual rate was 5.01 million, which is just over a half million more than expected.

196.   A. "Investors Favor Homebuilders"

Choice (C), "MainCorp, GB Home, and Homeowners Group," would be contextually true, but it actually serves as a supporting fact rather than the main idea. Choice (A), "Investors Favor Homebuilders," is the correct answer. Everything in the passage supports this main idea.

197.   B. home sales

The topic of this paragraph is home sales.

198.   B. to increase profits

The first and last sentences of the passage state that the goals are to decrease total costs, increase productivity, and improve product quality. The passage doesn't mention increasing profits.

199.   C. 8:00 a.m. to 5:00 p.m.

The passage doesn't state what days the current hours are worked, so they're unknown. The passage does state, however, that the current hours are from 8:00 a.m. to 5:00 p.m.

200.   D. The firm thinks implementing flex-time will help its business.

The passage explains that the company is considering a new plan to help meet its business goals.

201. **C. The firm in question performs work that requires frequent and extensive in-person collaboration, including multiple in-office client meetings each week.**

Because the firm performs work that requires frequent and in-person collaboration, you can reasonably infer that cutting the time spent together at work will have a considerable effect on productivity and quality as workers will have severely restricted access to a crucial component of their work (coworkers).

202. **D. January**

The author states in the first sentence that the population is at its *maximum*, which means most, in January.

203. **D. birds**

Avian is an adjective that means of or pertaining to birds, so an avian population consists of a bunch of birds.

204. **B. Asia**

The passage mentions that some birds migrate to the Himalayas, which are in Asia.

205. **B. fruit raising**

While the passage continues to describe a foundation and structure, the third sentence reveals that the author is talking about fruit raising, which is the process of planting and growing fruit-bearing trees and vines.

206. **B. excellent**

Splendid is an adjective that means possessing or displaying splendor or excellence.

207. **C. in jail**

The main character is describing scenes during his last day in prison, as you can see from the first sentence of the passage.

208. **B. twenty-four**

According to the passage, a prisoner told the narrator that the other man had received twenty-four lashes in the cook-house on Saturday.

209. **B. A man in the prison was sent somewhere where he was beaten.**

The main idea of the passage is to describe an unknown man who was sent somewhere in the prison and whipped.

210. **A. a type of skilled move**

The main idea of the paragraph is to explain a "Beat and Thrust." Even though the author calls it a "variety of attack," the supporting information implies that it's actually a skilled move one may learn.

211. **D. how to fence**

The author is describing moves related to fencing.

212. **B. an opponent**

An *adversary* is one's opponent in a contest, conflict, or dispute.

213. **B. Healthcare should not be heavily automated.**

When a question asks about the main point, it's asking for the conclusion. The middle of the paragraph says that healthcare officials want more automation but that the idea should be rejected. The conclusion provides supporting reasons, so it's obvious the author believes healthcare shouldn't be automated.

214. **C. People can find happiness alone.**

The passage actually states that Choice (A) is not true. Choices (B) and (D) both form too broad conclusions. Choice (C) is correct.

215. **B. Children are influenced by what they hear.**

Choice (B) is a simple restatement of the passage's statement "What children hear, whether positive or negative, will have an immense effect on their political views and decisions."

216. **C. Parents or guardians may shape their children's opinion of government.**

The passage makes no claim as to where government policies are made or how a parent should raise a child, so Choices (A) and (D) are wrong. It also doesn't say parents should protect children from political discussions. Choice (C) is correct, as the passage states "What children hear, whether positive or negative, will have an immense effect on their political views and decisions."

217. **A. The author describes two theories for why bike tires wear.**

The main idea is about bike tires and proposed ideas for why the tread wears down and becomes damaged.

218. **C. Place chemicals from rain water and pavement on a bike's idle tires.**

This method isolates the two competing explanations for the tires' erosion. If the tires erode under this scenario, you know that the exposure to chemicals contributes to erosion.

219. **A. being a successful salesman**

While the paragraph does touch on subjects related to some of the answer choices, the main topic is how you can be a successful salesman, so Choice (A) is correct.

220. **B. necessary**

In this passage, *essential* is an adjective meaning absolutely necessary.

221. **D. You must be able to sell your qualifications.**

Although you may have the ability to report to your job, get plenty of rest, and call yourself a salesman, you must have the ability to sell your qualifications in order to be successful.

222. **D. Dark chocolate may be beneficial to your health.**

The paragraph is about dark chocolate. It explains how studies have shown that it may be beneficial to your health.

223. **B. development**

Formation is a noun meaning the act of giving shape or development.

224. **B. Long-term studies have not been conducted.**

Because the passage states that short-term clinical trials were conducted, it implies that long-term studies have not yet been conducted.

225. **C. laughter**

The main topic of the passage is laughter. It explains that laughter has many short-term effects and implies that laughter may also have long-term effects on the body.

226. **A. produces**

Induce, in this context, is a verb meaning to cause the formation of or to produce.

227. **B. Laughing has a great effect on bodily functions.**

While Choices (A) and (D) may be true, the paragraph more clearly supports Choice (B) by describing the ways laughter helps improve body function. The last sentence implies that long-term effects for laughter are also good, making Choice (C) false.

228. **D. Mr. Darling's wife respected him.**

Although Mr. Darling was speaking with Wendy and the passage claims he knew a lot about stocks, the main point of the passage is that his wife respected him. The passage never claims Mr. Darling demanded anything, so Choice (B) is wrong.

229. **A. Mr. Darling was a likeable person.**

The passage implies that Mr. Darling was a likeable person because he was knowledgeable and respected.

230. **C. "Is There Life on Other Planets?"**

Obviously, Choice (D) is too amazing to work, Choice (B) doesn't really touch on the subject of the passage, and Choice (A) doesn't directly describe the passage. Therefore, "Is There Life on Other Planets?" — Choice (C) — would be the best choice for the title.

231. **B. In order for a world to have habitation, it must have living organisms.**

The main thought of the paragraph is that a world for habitation must include the existence of living organisms.

232. **A. It is a good idea to plan ahead.**

The entire paragraph is explaining what you should do to plan for a future event, so Choice (A) is the best answer.

233. **C. to look**

The word *cast* in this passage is a verb meaning to cause or send forth, as in a direct glance.

234. **B. how to pack for a big trip**

The author describes making a list of items to take and getting baggage ready, all evidence of someone packing for a trip.

235. **B. rice**

The passage is all about rice and its history.

236. **B. planted**

The last sentence tells you that rice was planted in American soil. By comparison, the second sentence says that it was cultivated in India. Therefore, you can conclude that *planted* is the correct answer.

237. **D. The two had just finished eating when one of them "heard" something.**

Choices (A), (B), and (C) are supporting information. The entire passage is describing the two characters, lounging after a meal, when one heard something using "mind touch."

238. **C. the beach**

The passage clearly states that they were lounging in the sand next to the waves.

239. **B. The characters are not human.**

You can assume the characters in the passage are not human because it describes their "species" as having fur and tucked-in ears.

240. **A. The information given is satisfactory, but it does not get into specific details.**

While the passage implies that the government and scientists have something to do with the information given, the main idea is that there's a good amount of information, just not in detail.

241. **C. brief**

Succinct is an adjective meaning briefly and clearly expressed.

242. **C. to evaluate**

Analyze is used as a verb in the passage and means to examine or evaluate.

243. **D. People's thoughts are reflected in their appearance.**

The passage doesn't state Choice (A). Choice (B) is incorrect as a muscular action may be in an area of the body other than the face. The passage says that there are only a few kinds of feelings; therefore, Choice (C) is incorrect. This leaves you with Choice (D), which is correct.

244. **B. celebration**

The word *inauguration* is a noun meaning a ceremonial induction into office; however, the second sentence states that the inauguration was President Reagan's celebration.

245.

C. Blueberry Jelly Bellies did not exist before 1981.

You could infer from the passage that President Reagan liked Jelly Bellies, but the better answer is Choice (C) because the passage states that the blueberry flavor was developed specifically for President Reagan's inauguration in 1981.

246.

C. outdated

Obsolete is an adjective that means out of date and no longer produced or used.

247.

B. old words

The author is clearly describing lesser known words that are no longer in use.

248.

B. some sea birds become disoriented when driven inland.

When found inland against their will, some seabirds, including those listed in the passage, may lose their bearings and be found with their feet frozen in inland ponds.

249.

C. A separate research study found that individuals with preexisting attention and concentration disorders exhibited significantly higher rates of trying cigarettes and subsequently becoming addicted to smoking.

This additional study pinpoints that individuals with preexisting (or already established) concentration difficulties subsequently became addicted to smoking. In other words, the smoking couldn't have caused the attention and concentration difficulties because these difficulties existed before the individuals became addicted.

250.

B. penalizing for evasion of paying taxes

The paragraph isn't discussing socialization, tax hikes, or bigger government but rather the need of taxes to finance important government undertakings. Therefore, Choice (B) is correct.

251.

D. 4,160

Exponents tell you how many times to multiply the number by itself.

10^3 is $10 \times 10 \times 10$ or $1,000$.

10^2 is 10×10 or 100.

10^1 is simply 10.

It's simple to figure the answer now:

$$(4 \cdot 10^3) + (1 \cdot 10^2) + (6 \cdot 10^1)$$
$$= 4,000 + 100 + 60$$
$$= 4,160$$

252. C. 12

The *greatest common factor* is the highest number that divides evenly into two or more numbers. To find the greatest common factor, you must first find the factors of both numbers.

Factors of 24 are 1, 2, 3, 4, 6, 8, 12, 24.

Factors of 60 are 1, 2, 3, 4, 5, 12, 15, 20, 30, 60.

The largest factor they have in common is 12.

253. D. 1

The order of operations is very important when simplifying expressions and equations. You first simplify multiplication and/or division in the order that the operations appear from left to right. Then you perform addition and/or subtraction in the order those operations appear from left to right.

This question uses multiplication and subtraction. Therefore,

$$9 - (2 \cdot 4)$$

$$= 9 - 8$$

$$= 1$$

254. D. 0.06

At first, this question looks really simple to answer, but you have to be careful.

You're being asked to find a number between 0.01 and 0.1.

0.3 and 0.4 are larger than either 0.01 and 0.1.

0.003 is smaller than 0.01 and 0.1.

Therefore, the only answer that could be correct is Choice (D), 0.06.

255. A. $3(5 + 2) - 7^2$

The quantity five plus two is written $(5 + 2)$. Three multiplied by (times) that quantity is written $3(5 + 2)$. The rest of the expression (minus seven squared) is written $- 7^2$.

Remember: An *expression* is a finite combination of symbols that is well-formed according to rules that depend on the context. A *quantity* is a number.

256. B. 1

$$(4 - 3)^2 (2) - 1$$

$$= (1)^2 (2) - 1$$

$$= 1(2) - 1$$

$$= 2 - 1$$

$$= 1$$

257.   **C. an equal sign**

An *equation* is a mathematical sentence with an equal sign in it. A *variable* is a letter used to represent a number. An *integer* is a positive or negative whole number or zero. An equation can have parentheses, a variable, and integers, but it must have an equal sign.

258.   **A. –6**

Absolute value is an operation that evaluates whatever is between the vertical bars and then outputs a positive number.

$-|-6| = -6$ because $|-6| = 6$

259.   **C. 18**

Solve by using the order of operations:

$$(4 \times 3)\, 3 - 6(9 \div 3)$$
$$= (12)3 - 6(3)$$
$$= 36 - 18$$
$$= 18$$

260.   **C. 3^{60}**

Multiply the exponents:

$$\left(\left(3^5\right)^2\right)^6$$
$$= \left(3^{5 \times 2}\right)^6$$
$$= \left(3^{10}\right)^6$$
$$= 3^{60}$$

261.   **B. $5\sqrt{3}$**

Look for a factor of 75 that's a square number; in this case, the number $25 = 5^2$. Replace 75 with its factors 25 and 3 and then take the square root of each factor:

$$\sqrt{75}$$
$$= \sqrt{25(3)}$$
$$= \sqrt{25}\,\sqrt{3}$$
$$= 5\sqrt{3}$$

262.   **D. 15**

To subtract a negative, change both negative signs to positive:

$$0 + (+15) = 15 + 0 = 15$$

263.   **A. 5**

Solve this one by using the order of operations:

$$3(2-5) + 14$$
$$= 3(-3) + 14$$
$$= (-9) + 14$$
$$= 5$$

264.   **A. 4.03×10^{14}**

You place the decimal point after the first number; 10^{14} means you move the decimal point 14 places to the right.

265.   **C. $2\sqrt{3}$**

Look for a factor of 12 that's a square number; in this case, $4 = 2^2$. Write 12 as the product of its factors 4 and 3 and then take the square root of each factor:

$$\sqrt{4 \times 3}$$
$$= \sqrt{4}\sqrt{3}$$
$$= 2\sqrt{3}$$

266.   **B. 2^{48}**

To solve this one, just multiply the exponents:

$$\left(2^{-6}\right)^{-8}$$
$$= 2^{(-6)(-8)}$$
$$= 2^{48}$$

267.   **B. 8**

A *reciprocal* of a fraction is the fraction inverted. The reciprocal of $\frac{1}{8}$ is $\frac{8}{1}$ or 8.

268.   **C. 2**

You should definitely have this one memorized.

$$\sqrt{4} = 2$$

269.   **B. 63.4**

To find the average, add the numbers and divide by 5 (the total number of items in the set):

$$101 + 15 + 62 + 84 + 55 = 317$$
$$317 \div 5 = 63.4$$

270. **D. 7 hours 55 minutes**

Convert the minutes to fractions of an hour (60 minutes) and add:

$$1\frac{30}{60} + 3\frac{40}{60} + 2\frac{45}{60}$$
$$= 6\frac{115}{60}$$
$$= 7\frac{55}{60}$$

271. **C. 2.0×10^{-3}**

First divide the nonexponential terms:

$$4.2 \div 2.1 = 2.0$$

Next, subtract the second exponent from the first:

$$-6 - (-3) = -3$$

The result is 2.0×10^{-3}.

272. **C. 70%**

To convert a decimal to a percent, move the decimal point two places to the right and add a percent sign:

$$0.7 = 70\%$$

273. **D. 4**

Don't let the absolute value signs scare you; just work from the inside out:

$$\left|10 - \left(42 \div |1 - 4|\right)\right|$$
$$= \left|10 - \left(42 \div |-3|\right)\right|$$
$$= \left|10 - \left(42 \div 3\right)\right|$$
$$= \left|10 - (14)\right|$$
$$= |-4|$$
$$= 4$$

274. **B. 6**

$5 - 11 = -6$, but absolute values can't be negative, so the answer is 6.

275. **D. 7**

Using the bar graph, count the number of scores under 70. There's one test at 40%, two tests at 50%, and four tests at 60%.

276. **B. 1,024**

4^5 is the equivalent of $(4)(4)(4)(4)(4)$.

Multiply to get the answer:

$4(4) = 16$

$16(4) = 64$

$64(4) = 256$

$256(4) = 1,024$

277. **B. 8**

Solve by using the order of operations. It's easy to do if you remember the acronym PEMDAS (Parentheses, Exponents, Multiplication, Division, Addition, Subtraction).

$2(5 - 3)^2 = 2(2)^2 = 2(4) = 8$

278. **D. 5, 6, 7**

The pattern is 1, 1, 2, 3, 3, 4, 5, 5, 6, 7, 7, 8 . . .

279. **B. 30, 29, 35**

The pattern is the next two multiples of 5, minus 1:

5, 10, 9, 15, 20, 19, 25, 30, 29, 35, 40 . . .

280. **C. d + e – f**

The pattern is $a + b - c$, $b + c - d$, $c + d - e$, $d + e - f$, $e + f - g$ . . .

281. **D. 48e, 38h, 28g**

The pattern is descending increments of 10 followed by the second letter, then the first letter, then the fourth letter, then the third letter, and so on.

282. **A. 4, y = 8, x = 3**

The first part of the pattern is $x =$, $x =$, $y =$, $y =$, and the second part of the pattern is 7 then doubled, 6 then doubled, 5 then doubled, and so on.

283. **A. –20**

You keep the negative sign when adding negative numbers.

284. **A. 37**

Follow the order of operations:

$(5 \times 6) + 11 - 4$

$= (30 + 11) - 4$

$= 41 - 4$

$= 37$

285. **A. 7**

Follow the order of operations, starting with the subtraction in parentheses:

$-1(3 - 1) + 9$

$- -1(2) + 9$

$= -2 + 9$

$= 7$

286. **C. 1.05×10^5**

Put the decimal point after the 1 and count the number of digits afterward to get the exponent:

1.05×10^5

287. **D. both A and B**

When multiplying exponents with the same base, add the exponents: $2^{3+4} = 2^7$. You can also solve this problem by multiplying $2 \times 2 \times 2 \times 2 \times 2 \times 2 \times 2 = 128$.

288. **C. $10\sqrt{2}$**

Look for a factor of 200 that's a square number; in this case, $100 = 10^2$. Write 200 as the product of its factors 100 and 2 and then take the square root of each factor:

$\sqrt{200} = \sqrt{100 \times 2} = \sqrt{100}\sqrt{2}$

The square root of 100 is 10, and the square root of two isn't a whole number, so the answer it $10\sqrt{2}$.

289. **B. 5,500**

When you multiply by 100, you can drop the one and add the zeros:

$100 \times 55 = 5,500$

290. D. 1,025,150

$$1,010 \times 1,015 = 1,025,150$$

Remember, you can't use a calculator on the ASVAB, so you have to work this one out by hand:

$$
\begin{array}{r}
1,010 \\
\times\ 1,015 \\
\hline
5,050 \\
10,100 \\
000,000 \\
1,010,000 \\
\hline
1,025,150
\end{array}
$$

291. A. $|x|$

Choice (B) is a variable, Choice (C) is a radical sign to find the square root, and Choice (D) shows parentheses with a variable. Choice (A) is the correct symbol for absolute value.

292. D. less than or equal to

The symbol for Choice (A) is >, for Choice (B) is <, and for Choice (C) is ≥. Choice (D) is the correct answer.

293. B. 7

Choice (B) is your only answer here:

$$\sqrt{49} = 7$$

294. C. 161

Multiply 6^2 and 5^3 and then add them together:

$$6 \times 6 = 36$$
$$5 \times 5 \times 5 = 125$$
$$125 + 36 = 161$$

295.   **D. undefined**

You can never divide by zero.

$$\frac{5}{0} = \text{undefined}$$

296.   **D. 2**

You have to complete the work in the denominator before dividing the 32 by that result:

$$\frac{32}{30-2(3+4)}$$

$$=\frac{32}{30-2(7)}$$

$$=\frac{32}{30-14}$$

$$=\frac{32}{16}$$

$$=2$$

297.   **D. $\frac{23}{24}$**

The least common denominator is 24. Change both fractions so that the denominator is 24; then add the fractions.

$$\frac{3}{8}+\frac{7}{12}$$

$$=\frac{3}{8}\times\frac{3}{3}+\frac{7}{12}\times\frac{2}{2}$$

$$=\frac{9}{24}+\frac{14}{24}$$

$$=\frac{23}{24}$$

298.   **B. $\dfrac{b^{qn}}{a^{pn}}$**

Negative exponents flip or invert fractions and then become a positive power to the factors.

$$\left(\frac{a^p}{b^q}\right)^{-n}=\left(\frac{b^q}{a^p}\right)^{n}=\frac{b^{qn}}{a^{pn}}$$

299.   **C. 0.60**

To find the answer, divide 3 by 5:

$$5\overline{)3.0}^{\,0.6}$$

300.   A. $\frac{9}{20}$

$$0.45 = \frac{45}{100}$$

The common factor of 45 and 100 is 5:

$$\frac{45 \div 5}{100 \div 5}$$

$$= \frac{9}{20}$$

301.   B. –3

Plug in the values and solve:

$$\frac{x^2 - 2x}{y^2 + 2y}$$

$$= \frac{3^2 - 2(3)}{(-1)^2 + 2(-1)}$$

$$= \frac{9 - 6}{1 - 2}$$

$$= \frac{3}{-1}$$

$$= -3$$

302.   D. $2\frac{2}{9}$

First, change the mixed numbers to fractions:

$$7\frac{1}{7} \div 3\frac{3}{14}$$

$$= \frac{7 \cdot 7 + 1}{7} \div \frac{3 \cdot 14 + 3}{14}$$

$$= \frac{50}{7} \div \frac{45}{14}$$

Flip or invert the second fraction and change the symbol to multiplication:

$$= \frac{50}{7} \cdot \frac{14}{45}$$

Cross-reduce by using the greatest common factor:

$$= \frac{50 \div 5}{7 \div 7} \cdot \frac{14 \div 7}{45 \div 5}$$

$$= \frac{10 \times 2}{1 \times 9}$$

$$= \frac{20}{9}$$

Convert back to a mixed number:

$$= 2\frac{2}{9}$$

303.   B. 35

To get from 8 to 40, you multiply by 5, so do the same with 7:

$$\frac{7}{8} = \frac{x}{40}$$

$$\frac{7 \cdot 5}{8 \cdot 5} = \frac{x}{40}$$

$$x = 35$$

304.   C. 48

The exponent of a number tells you how many times to multiply the number by itself. A negative exponent means to divide by the number. Therefore, the law of exponents states

$$x^m x^n = x^{m+n}$$

Using this law, you can solve the problem like so:

$$\frac{3^2 \times 3^4 \times 2}{3^{-1} \times 3^6 \times 2^{-3}}$$

$$= \left(3^{2+4-(-1)-6}\right) \times 2^{1-(-3)}$$

$$= 3^1 \times 2^4$$

$$= 3 \times 2 \times 2 \times 2 \times 2$$

$$= 48$$

305.   B. $1\frac{1}{8}$

Do the following to solve this equation:

$$-\frac{15}{14} \div \left(-\frac{20}{21}\right)$$

$$= -\frac{15}{14} \cdot \left(-\frac{21}{20}\right)$$

$$= \frac{15}{14} \cdot \frac{21}{20}$$

$$= \frac{15 \div 5}{14 \div 7} \cdot \frac{21 \div 7}{20 \div 5}$$

$$= \frac{3 \cdot 3}{2 \cdot 4} = \frac{9}{8} = 1\frac{1}{8}$$

306.   D. 18

$$\frac{3^4 \cdot 2^4}{3^2 \cdot 2^3}$$

$$= 3^{4-2} \cdot 2^{4-3}$$

$$= 3^2 \cdot 2$$

$$= 3 \cdot 3 \cdot 2 = 18$$

Answers
301–400

307. A. $\frac{2}{5}$

To turn a fraction into a percent, you first put the percent over 100:

$$40\% = \frac{40}{100}$$

Then reduce the fraction:

$$\frac{40 \div 10}{100 \div 10} = \frac{4}{10}$$

$$\frac{4 \div 2}{10 \div 2} = \frac{2}{5}$$

308. A. 110

Because $\frac{1}{6}$ is the reciprocal of 6, you simply cancel out the 6's:

$$110\left(6 \cdot \frac{1}{6}\right)$$
$$= 110(1)$$
$$= 110$$

309. C. –6

Multiply the top part of the fraction before dividing:

$$\frac{-3(-4)}{-2}$$
$$= \frac{12}{-2}$$
$$= -6$$

310. B. $\frac{3}{4}$

Find the greatest common factor; here, it's 21. Divide the numerator and denominator by that number:

$$\frac{63}{84} = \frac{63 \div 21}{84 \div 21} = \frac{3}{4}$$

311. C. $4x^2 - 3x + 2$

First, factor out x:

$$\frac{4x^3 - 3x^2 + 2x}{x}$$

$$= \frac{x(4x^2 - 3x + 2)}{x}$$

Then you can simply cancel out the two x's not in parentheses to get $4x^2 - 3x + 2$.

312. C. $\frac{7}{8}$

First, convert the mixed numbers to fractions:

$$2\frac{1}{4} \div 2\frac{4}{7} = \frac{9}{4} \div \frac{18}{7}$$

To divide, invert the second fraction and then multiply:

$$\frac{9}{4} \cdot \frac{7}{18} = \frac{63}{72}$$

Reduce to $\frac{7}{8}$.

313. B. $\frac{9}{7}$

An *improper fraction* is a fraction in which the numerator is larger than the denominator.

314. C. $\frac{1}{4}x^5$

First reduce the coefficients:

$$\frac{4}{16} = \frac{1}{4}$$

Next, subtract the exponents (bottom from top):

$$3 - (-2) = 5$$

The result is $\frac{1}{4}x^5$.

315. C. 30

Multiply the top numbers to get –30. Because you divide by –1, the answer becomes positive.

316. B. $\frac{39}{8}$

Multiply and add to find the numerator:

$$(4 \times 8) + 7 = 32 + 7 = 39$$

Keep the same denominator.

317.   **B. 0.625**

To change $\frac{5}{8}$ to a decimal, divide 5 by 8:

$$
\begin{array}{r}
0.625 \\
8\overline{)5.000} \\
-48 \\
\hline
20 \\
-16 \\
\hline
40 \\
-40 \\
\hline
0
\end{array}
$$

318.   **B. $y = 2$**

To solve, divide both sides by 8:

$$\frac{8y}{8} = \frac{16}{8}$$
$$y = 2$$

319.   **D. $10x$**

To solve, add the numerals $3 + 7$, keeping the variable x: $3x + 7x = 10x$.

320.   **A. $\frac{4x}{y}$**

Divide the coefficients:

$$8 \div 2 = \frac{8}{2} = 4 \text{ or } \frac{4}{1}.$$

Divide the variables:

$$x \div y = \frac{x}{y}$$

Multiply the answers:

$$\left(\frac{4}{1}\right)\left(\frac{x}{y}\right)$$

Simplify:

$$\frac{4x}{y}$$

321.   **B. 11**

Isolate x on one side of the equation:

$$2x - 6 = x + 5$$
$$2x - 6 - x = x + 5 - x$$
$$x - 6 = 5$$
$$x - 6 + 6 = 5 + 6$$
$$x = 11$$

322. B. $2x^2 + 5x + 3$

Remember the acronym FOIL (First, Outer, Inner, Last).

First, you multiply:

F: $1(3) = 3$

O: $1(2x) = 2x$

I: $x(3) = 3x$

L: $x(2x) = 2x^2$

Then you add:

$3 + 2x + 3x + 2x^2$

Finally, combine the like terms and put the terms in order starting with the x^2 term:

$2x^2 + 5x + 3$

323. A. $4ax - 8a$

Simplify using the distributive property:

$4a(x - 2)$

$= (4a)x - (4a)(2)$

$= 4ux - 8u$

324. B. 30

Plug in the values given and solve:

$6x^2 - xy = 6(2^2) - 2(-3) = 6(4) - 2(-3) = 24 + 6 = 30$

325. D. 4

Divide both sides by 5 to isolate y^2 on one side of the equation; then take the square root of both sides:

$5y^2 = 80$

$\dfrac{5y^2}{5} = \dfrac{80}{5}$

$y^2 = 16$

$y = \pm\sqrt{16}$

$y = \pm 4$

Because $y = -4$ isn't an option, the answer is $y = 4$.

326. A. $x = \pm 2$

$$x^4 - 16 = 0$$
$$(x^2 - 4)(x^2 + 4) = 0$$
$$(x - 2)(x + 2)(x^2 + 4) = 0$$

Set each of the factors equal to 0 and solve for x:

$$x - 2 = 0, x = 2$$
$$x + 2 = 0, x = -2$$
$$x^2 + 4 = 0, x^2 = -4, x = \pm\sqrt{-4}$$

The answer from the last factor isn't a real number, so you can throw it out. The answer is $x = \pm 2$.

327. D. $a^2 + 2ab + b^2$

Use FOIL and solve:

$$(a + b)^2$$
$$= (a + b)(a + b)$$
$$= a^2 + ab + ab + b^2$$
$$= a^2 + 2ab + b^2$$

328. B. 4

Square both sides and solve:

$$\sqrt{x^2 + 9} = 5$$
$$x^2 + 9 = 25$$
$$x^2 + 9 - 9 = 25 - 9$$
$$x^2 = 16$$
$$x = \pm\sqrt{16}$$
$$x = \pm 4$$

Because $x = -4$ isn't an option, the answer is $x = 4$.

329. C. 11

This one's easy; just subtract 4 from both sides:

$$x + 4 = 15$$
$$x + 4 - 4 = 15 - 4$$
$$x = 11$$

330.

A. 12

Just substitute -2 for x:

$3x^2$

$= 3(-2)^2$

$= 3(4)$

$= 12$

331.

B. $5y(y-2)(y+1)$

Factor out $5y$ because it's the greatest common factor:

$5y^3 - 5y^2 - 10y$

$= 5y(y^2 - y - 2)$

$= 5y(y-2)(y+1)$

332.

D. $-2x^2 + 2x$

Multiply both parts of the expression in parentheses by $-2x$:

$-2x(x-1)$

$= -2x(x) + (-2x)(-1)$

$= -2x^2 + 2x$

333.

D. $w^2 - 16$

Using FOIL, simplify:

$(w+4)(w-4)$

$= w^2 - 4w + 4w - 16$

$= w^2 - 16$

334.

A. x^4

Remember, a base to a negative exponent is the reciprocal of the base to a positive exponent, so $x^{-4} = \dfrac{1}{x^4}$. The reciprocal of $\dfrac{1}{x^4}$ is $\dfrac{x^4}{1}$, which you can simplify to x^4.

335. **B.** $-6a^4$

To multiply these terms, multiply the coefficients and add the powers of the same variables:

$$3(-2) = -6$$

$$(a^{3+1}) = a^4$$

Then combine the two:

$$-6a^4$$

336. **D. A and C**

Don't be fooled by Choice (B).

But don't choose Choice (A) too quickly either. $(a + b)^2$ is equal to $(a + b)(a + b)$, but if you perform FOIL, you also get $a^2 + 2ab + b^2$.

337. **B.** -1

First, divide both sides by 2:

$$2(x+4) = 6$$

$$\frac{2(x+4)}{2} = \frac{6}{2}$$

$$x + 4 = 3$$

Next, isolate x and solve:

$$x + 4 - 4 = 3 - 4$$

$$x = -1$$

338. **A. 5**

Simply plug in the given values and solve, remembering the rules about negative numbers:

$$p(p - q)$$

$$-5(-5 - (-4))$$

$$= -5(-1)$$

$$= 5$$

339. **A.** $sn = d^2$

Change the ratios into fractions and set them equal to each other; then solve by cross-multiplying the values:

$$\frac{s}{d} = \frac{d}{n}$$

$$sn = dd$$

$$sn = d^2$$

340.   **A.** $a < c < b$

First, convert the fractions to decimals; then arrange them from smallest to largest:

$$a = \frac{1}{2} = 0.5$$

$$b = \frac{2}{3} = 0.666$$

$$c = \frac{5}{8} = 0.625$$

$$a < c < b$$

341.   **D. 25**

You can find the constant c by multiplying $(x - 5)$ by itself:

$$(x - 5)^2 = (x - 5)(x - 5) = x^2 - 10x + 25, \text{ because } (-5)(-5) = 25$$

342.   **B.** $-\frac{7}{6}$

First isolate x:

$$x + \frac{1}{2} = -\frac{2}{3}$$

$$x + \frac{1}{2} - \frac{1}{2} = -\frac{2}{3} - \frac{1}{2}$$

$$x = -\frac{2}{3} - \frac{1}{2}$$

Then find the common denominator and solve:

$$x = -\frac{4}{6} - \frac{3}{6}$$

$$x = -\frac{7}{6}$$

343.   **A.** $7a^3$

If expressions have the same bases and exponents, simply add the coefficients:

$$2(a^3) + 5(a^3)$$

$$= (2 + 5)(a^3) = 7a^3$$

344.   **C. 3**

The three terms in the expression are x^2, bx, and $-c^4$.

345.   **A.** $k = 2s$

If $s + h = k$, and $s = h$, then $s + s = k$.

346. **B.** $x^{1/3}$

The symbol represents an exponent that is one-third of x, the value inside the radical: $\sqrt[3]{x} = \sqrt[3]{x^1} = x^{1/3}$.

347. **A.** $10a + 8ab$

Group the two term categories (a and ab):

$$3ab + 5ab = 8ab$$
$$4a + 6a = 10a$$

348. **B.** $8x^4y^3$

Simply add the exponents of like variables together.

349. **C.** 5

Do the following to solve this equation for n:

$$\frac{4}{5}n + 8 = 12$$
$$\frac{4}{5}n + 8 - 8 = 12 - 8$$
$$\frac{4}{5}n = 4$$
$$5\left(\frac{4}{5}n\right) = 4(5)$$
$$4n = 20$$
$$n = 5$$

350. **B.** 128

First multiply the left side of the equation; then isolate x to find the answer:

$$8(8) = \frac{x}{2}$$
$$64 = \frac{x}{2}$$
$$128 = x$$

351. **B.** 144 cm^2

The area of a rhombus is $\frac{d_1 d_2}{2}$, where d represents the diagonals of the rhombus.

Plug in the values and solve:

$$\frac{(18)(16)}{2} = \frac{288}{2} = 144 \text{ cm}^2$$

352. **C.** parallel

Two lines in a plane that don't intersect or touch at a point are called *parallel lines*. The figure shows the curved symbol at two intersections representing equal angles. Because these corresponding angles are equal, you know the lines are parallel.

353. **A. 142°**

Together, angles A and B equal 180°. Therefore, you subtract 38° from 180°, and angle A equals 142°.

354. **B. 180°**

When two lines intersect, the two adjacent angles are *supplementary,* which means they add up to 180°.

355. **B. 80°**

Angles C and D are supplementary, which means they add up to 180°. So find angle D by subtracting the measure of angle C, 140°, from 180°:

$$\text{m}\angle D = 180° - 140° = 40°$$

Angles B and D are across from each other, so they're equal. Therefore, their sum is $40° + 40° = 80°$.

356. **C. Quadrant 3**

Negative x goes left on the x-axis, and negative y goes down on the y-axis, so the answer is Quadrant 3.

357. **A. 3**

Use the Pythagorean theorem:

$$a^2 + b^2 = c^2$$
$$4^2 + b^2 = 5^2$$
$$16 + b^2 = 25$$
$$16 + b^2 - 16 = 25 - 16$$
$$b^2 = 9$$
$$b = \sqrt{9}$$
$$b = 3$$

358. **C. 125 in³**

The volume of a cube equals length times width times height, or the length of a side cubed (to the third power):

$$V = 5^3$$
$$V = 5 \cdot 5 \cdot 5$$
$$V = 25 \cdot 5$$
$$V = 125 \text{ in}^3$$

359.   **C. 110 cm²**

The area of a trapezoid is

$$A = h\left(\frac{b_1 + b_2}{2}\right)$$

Plug in the values and solve:

$$A = 10\left(\frac{7+15}{2}\right)$$

$$A = 10\left(\frac{22}{2}\right)$$

$$A = 10(11)$$

$$A = 110 \text{ cm}^2$$

360.   **B. 30**

The area of a triangle is $A = \frac{1}{2}bh$, and $DC = BD$. Therefore, the length of the base is $2 \times 3 = 6$.

$$A = \frac{1}{2}(6 \cdot 10)$$

$$A = \frac{60}{2}$$

$$A = 30$$

361.   **B. 18.3**

Because BD is equal to DC, you can determine BD simply by dividing BC in half:

$$BD = \frac{BC}{2} = 8.$$

Use the Pythagorean theorem:

$$a^2 + b^2 = c^2$$

$$a^2 + 8^2 = 20^2$$

$$a^2 + 64 = 400$$

$$a^2 = 336$$

$$a = \sqrt{336}$$

The answer choices are between 17.5 and 19.3, so $\sqrt{336}$ must be between those numbers. For reference, find the squares of 18 and 19: $18^2 = 324$, and $19^2 = 361$. Because 336 is a little more than 324, you know that $\sqrt{336}$ must be a little more than 18. Therefore, the answer is Choice (B), 18.3.

362.   **B. 78.5 cm²**

The formula for the area of a circle is $A = \pi r^2$.

Plug in the values and solve:

$$A = (3.14)(5)^2$$
$$A = (3.14)(25)$$
$$A = 78.5 \text{ cm}^2$$

363.   **B. 18.84**

The formula for finding the volume of a cylinder is $V = \pi r^2 h$.

Plug in the values and solve:

$$V = \pi(1)^2(6)$$
$$V = (3.14)(6)$$
$$V - 18.84$$

364.   **A. 120 m³**

Use the formula for volume to solve this one:

$$V = lwh$$
$$V = 3(5)(8)$$
$$V = 120 \text{ m}^3$$

365.   **D. 34**

To find the perimeter, add the lengths of the sides:

Perimeter of (a) = $7 \times 4 - 3 = 25$

Perimeter of (b) = $3 \times 3 = 9$

Total = $25 + 9 = 34$

366.   **D. 31**

To find the area of a rectangle, you multiply length times width:

Area of (a) = $5 \times 4 = 20$

Area of (b) = $2 \times 4 = 8$

To find the area of a triangle, you multiply 1/2 times the base times the height:

Area of $(c) = \frac{1}{2}(3 \times 2) = 3$

Now add the areas:

Total = $20 + 8 + 3 = 31$

367. B. 364

The volume of a prism is $V = Ah$, where A represents the area of the triangle end.

First, find the area of the triangle:

$$A = \frac{1}{2}b \times h$$

$$A = \frac{1}{2}(7 \times 8) = 28$$

Then multiply by the height of the prism:

$$V = 28 \times 13 = 364$$

368. C. 25.12

Use the formula for circumference to solve this problem (d is the diameter):

$$C = \pi d$$

$$C = (3.14)(8)$$

$$C = 25.12$$

369. B. 2.55

Use the formula for circumference to solve this problem (r = radius and C = circumference):

$$C = 2\pi r$$

$$16 = 2(3.14)r$$

$$16 = 6.28r$$

$$r = 2.547 \text{ rounded to } 2.55$$

370. C. scalene

An *isosceles triangle* has two equal sides and angles, an *equilateral triangle* has three equal sides and angles, a *right triangle* has one measurement of 90 degrees, and an *obtuse triangle* (not mentioned in the choices) has one measurement of more than 90 degrees.

371. B. 180

All angles of a triangle always add up to 180 degrees.

372. B. $-x + 3 = y$

In this problem, replace x and y with the values of the coordinates; then choose the equation that's true:

$$x + y = 5$$
$$-1 + 4 \neq 5$$
$$-x + 3 = y$$
$$-(-1) + 3 = 4$$
$$y = x - 5$$
$$4 \neq -1 - 5$$
$$y = x^2 + 5$$
$$4 \neq (-1)^2 + 5$$

373. D. Quadrant 4

The coordinates $(7, -8)$ are read "7 right, 8 down," so the point lies in Quadrant 4.

374. B. 7

You could spend extra time graphing the points and manually counting the distance, but a mathematician would urge you to create the following equation to determine the distance between the y-coordinates:

$$|-4 - 3| = |-7| = 7$$

Because the x-coordinates are the same, they aren't a factor in the distance.

375. B. 28 degrees

Complementary angles are angles that add up to 90 degrees:

$$90 - 62 = 28 \text{ degrees}$$

376. B. $\frac{2}{3}$

To solve this problem, you set up a proportion:

$$\frac{1 \text{ job}}{30 \text{ minutes}} = \frac{x(\text{part of the job})}{20 \text{ minutes}}$$

Then just cross-multiply to solve for x:

$$30x = 20$$
$$x = \frac{20}{30} = \frac{2}{3}$$

377. **B. 1 minute 40 seconds**

Use the distance formula to solve this problem: $d = rt$, where d is distance, r is rate, and t is time.

Tim's distance = $4.25t$

Sue's distance = $4.75t$

Because Tim and Sue run a combined distance of $\frac{1}{4}$ mile, you can write this problem like so:

$$4.25t + 4.75t = \frac{1}{4}$$

Combine like terms and then solve for t:

$$9t = \frac{1}{4}$$

$$\left(\frac{1}{9}\right)9t = \frac{1}{4}\left(\frac{1}{9}\right)$$

$$t = \frac{1}{36}$$

Then convert hours into minutes:

$$\frac{1}{36} \text{ hour} \cdot \frac{60 \text{ minutes}}{1 \text{ hour}} = \frac{60}{36} \text{ minutes}$$

$$= 1\frac{2}{3} \text{ minutes}$$

Finally, convert $\frac{2}{3}$ minute to seconds:

$$\frac{2}{3} \text{ minute} \cdot \frac{60 \text{ seconds}}{1 \text{ minute}} = 40 \text{ seconds}$$

Tim and Sue will meet each other after 1 minute and 40 seconds.

378. **D. 4 years**

Because you know that Ed needs to earn $10 in interest income, you can use the interest formula: $I = Prt$, where I is interest, P is principal, r is rate, and t is time.

Just plug in $I = 10$, $P = 50$, and $r = 0.05$, and solve for t:

$$10 = 50(0.05)t$$

$$10 = 2.5t$$

$$t = \frac{10}{2.5} = \frac{100}{25} = 4 \text{ years}$$

379. **C. 15**

Let s = student tickets and a = adult tickets. Because you sold three times as many student tickets as adult tickets, $s = 3a$.

Set up the following equation with the information given:

$8s + 12a = 540$.

Substitute for s:

$$8(3a) + 12a = 540$$
$$24a + 12a = 540$$
$$36a = 540$$
$$a = \frac{540}{36} = 15 \text{ adult tickets}$$

380. **D. 6**

Use the formula $0.25q + 0.10d = \$3.30$, where q stands for the number of quarters and d stands for the number of dimes. Because there are three times as many dimes, $d = 3q$.

Therefore,

$$0.25q + 0.10(3q) = 3.30$$
$$0.25q + 0.30q = 3.30$$
$$0.55q = 3.30$$
$$q = \frac{3.30}{0.55} = \frac{330}{55} = \frac{66}{11} = 6$$

To double-check your work, plug your answer back into the equation. If $q = 6$, then $d = 3(6) = 18$. Keep going:

$$6(\$0.25) = \$1.50$$
$$18(\$0.10) = \$1.80$$

Now add them together and you get $3.30. So the correct answer is (D).

381. **D. 4.8 hours**

Because you know it takes Bill 2 hours to travel 30 miles by boat and you want to know how much time it takes to travel 72 miles by boat, you can set up the following proportion to solve this problem:

$$\frac{2}{30} = \frac{x}{72}$$
$$30x = 144$$
$$x = 4.8$$

382. A. 328

Set up the following equation to solve this problem (x is the number):

$$\frac{1}{4}x + x = 410$$
$$0.25x + x = 410$$
$$1.25x = 410$$
$$x = 328$$

You can check your work by substituting:

$$0.25(328) + 328 = 410$$
$$82 + 328 = 410$$

Choice (A) is correct.

383. C. 136

Let x be the distance traveled to Larry's friend's house. The time it takes to drive to the house looks like this:

$$\frac{\text{distance}}{\text{speed}} = \frac{x}{60}$$

The time it takes to return looks like this:

$$\frac{\text{distance}}{\text{speed}} = \frac{x}{50}$$

The total time to travel and return is 5 hours. Therefore,

$$\frac{x}{50} + \frac{x}{60} = 5$$

Next, find the common denominator in order to add the fractions and solve for x:

$$\frac{6x}{300} + \frac{5x}{300} = 5$$
$$\frac{11x}{300} = 5$$
$$11x = 1{,}500$$
$$x = 136.36$$

The answer is 136 miles (rounded to the nearest mile), Choice (C).

384. C. 8

Set up the following equation for finding the average and then solve for x:

$$\frac{12 + 23 + 17 + x}{4} = 15$$
$$\frac{52 + x}{4} = 15$$
$$52 + x = 60$$
$$x = 8$$

385.   **C. 5 minutes**

First, you have to figure out how many square feet Louisa can paint in 45 minutes by using the formula for area:

A = length × width

A = 12 feet × 12 feet

A = 144 square feet

Now find the area of the square section:

A = 4 feet × 4 feet

A = 16 square feet

Finally, set up the following proportion to find the time, x, it'll take her to paint the small section:

$$\frac{144}{45} = \frac{16}{x}$$
$$144x = 720$$
$$x = 5$$

Easy enough! Choice (C) it is.

386.   **A. 110 pounds**

Set up the following equation and let x = Linda's weight:

$$3x = 2(165)$$
$$3x = 330$$
$$x = 110$$

Linda has done well! She weighs 110 pounds, or Choice (A).

387.   **C. $687.50**

Set up a proportion with $\frac{\text{yards}}{\text{cost}}$ and then solve for x:

$$\frac{10}{275} = \frac{25}{x}$$
$$10x = 6,875$$
$$x = 687.5$$

The answer is $687.50, Choice (C).

388. **D. $42,400**

The formula for interest is Interest = Principal × Rate × Time. Simply substitute what you know to solve this problem:

Interest = 32,000(0.065)(5)

Interest = 10,400

Now add the interest to the principal:

32,000 + 10,400 = 42,400

Martha is paying $42,400 for her new car.

389. **A. $272**

Let x = the amount Austin borrowed as you set up the following equation:

$$\$458 = 1.5x + 50$$
$$\$408 = 1.5x$$
$$\$272 = x$$

Choice (A) is correct, but let it be known that Wendell is a loan shark!

390. **C. $176,000**

Let x = the selling price of the house as you set up the following equation:

$$5\%(x) = 8,800$$
$$0.05x = 8,800$$
$$\frac{0.05x}{0.05} = \frac{8,800}{0.05}$$
$$x = 176,000$$

You have your answer — Choice (C).

391. **A. $150**

Let x = the price of one shirt.

Let y = the price of one pair of dress pants.

Let z = the price of one tie.

Here's what you know:

$$4x + 4y + 2z = 560$$

$9x + 9y + 6z = 1,290$, which you can reduce to $3x + 3y + 2z = 430$.

Now subtract the smaller equation from the larger one:

$$4x + 4y + 2z = 560$$
$$\underline{-3x - 3y - 2z = -430}$$
$$x + y = 130$$

Use that simplified equation to find the value of z:

$$3x + 3y + 2z = 430$$
$$3(x + y) + 2z = 430$$
$$3(130) + 2z = 430$$
$$2z = 40$$
$$z = 20$$

Finally, add the three prices together:

$$(x + y) + z = \$130 + \$20 = \$150$$

---

392.   **A. 33%**

Set up the following proportion to find out the percentage of laborers who work overtime (represented by x):

$$\frac{40}{120} = \frac{x}{100}$$
$$120x = 4{,}000$$
$$x = 33.3$$

The answer is Choice (A).

Alternatively, you can reduce $\frac{40}{120}$ to $\frac{1}{3}$, which is roughly 33%.

---

393.   **D. 6**

Let x = the number of books Sophia has as you set up the following equation:

$$x + 2x = 18$$
$$3x = 18$$
$$x = 6$$

Sophia has 6 books, Choice (D).

---

394.   **D. 4.75**

Let x = the number of miles to the camp and $x - 2.5$ = the number of miles on the return path. Then set up this equation and solve for x:

$$(x) + (x - 2.5) = 7$$
$$2x - 2.5 = 7$$
$$2x = 9.5$$
$$x = 4.75 \text{ miles}$$

395. B. 12

Let x = the number of shots fired.

Let $x - 11$ = the number missed.

$$\frac{3}{4}x = 9(x-11)$$
$$3x = 36(x-11)$$
$$3x = 36x - 396$$
$$-33x = -396$$
$$x = 12 \text{ shots}$$

Ted is a good shot!

396. B. 30

First, set up your equation to reflect the number of single desks and the number of double desks.

Let x = the number of single desks.

Let y = the number of double desks.

The total number of desks is:

$$x + y = 36$$

The number of seats in the room is the number of single desks, x, plus two times the number of double desks, or $2y$. So the equation for the total number of seats is:

$$x + 2y = 42$$

To figure out how many single desks are in the room, solve the first equation for y:

$$x + y = 36$$
$$y = 36 - x$$

Then plug $(36 - x)$ in for y in the equation for the total number of seats:

$$x + 2y = 42$$
$$x + 2(36 - x) = 42$$
$$x + 72 - 2x = 42$$
$$x = 30$$

There are 30 single desks, Choice (B).

397. **C. $81**

Let x = the cost of the program and $9x$ = the cost of the computer system without the program. Then set up this equation:

$$x + 9x = 810$$
$$10x = 810$$
$$x = 81$$

The program alone would cost $81, Choice (C).

398. **B. 21**

Let x = the first odd number. Here's what your equation looks like:

$$x + (x+2) + (x+4) + (x+6) = 88$$
$$4x + 12 = 88$$
$$4x = 76$$
$$x = 19$$

19 is the first number, so the next odd number would be 21.

To double-check your answer, add the four odd numbers:

$$19 + 21 + 23 + 25 = 88$$

Choice (B) is right.

399. **C. 11**

Let d = the number of dimes and $d + 3$ = the number of quarters. Set up the following equation:

$$(0.10d) + \left[0.25(d+3) \right] = 3.55$$
$$0.10d + 0.25d + 0.75 = 3.55$$
$$0.35d = 2.80$$
$$d = 8$$

Lenny has 8 dimes, so he has 8 + 3 = 11 quarters. Choice (C) is the winner here.

400. **C. 288**

Let r = the rate of the first train.

Let $r + 24$ = the rate of the second train.

Knowing that distance = rate times time, you can determine the following information:

	Rate	Time	Distance
First train	r	6	$6r$
Second train	$r + 24$	4	$4(r + 24)$

Now just set up the following equation and solve:

$$6r = 4(r + 24)$$
$$6r = 4r + 96$$
$$2r = 96$$
$$r = 48$$

The distance until they meet is $6r$, or $6(48)$, so the answer is Choice (C), 288.

401. **C. 19**

Let x = the number of rainy days.

Let $3x + 8$ = the number of clear days.

Then set up this equation (note that you multiply 12 by 7 to convert weeks to days):

$$x + (3x + 8) = 12 \cdot 7$$
$$4x + 8 = 84$$
$$4x = 76$$
$$x = 19$$

There were 19 rainy days and $84 - 19 = 65$ clear days, so Choice (C) is correct.

402. **D. 57**

Let x = the number of peanut butter cookies.

Let $x - 18$ = the number of oatmeal cookies.

Then set up this equation:

$$x + (x - 18) = 132$$
$$2x - 18 = 132$$
$$2x = 150$$
$$x = 75$$

Joe received 75 peanut butter cookies; therefore, he received $75 - 18 = 57$ oatmeal cookies. Let's hope he shared!

403.

A. 787.4 yards

To solve this problem, set up the following proportion and solve for x:

$$\frac{3{,}937}{3{,}600} = \frac{x}{720}$$
$$3{,}600x = 2{,}834{,}640$$
$$x = 787.4 \text{ yards}$$

Choice (A) is correct.

404.

C. $270

Let i = the interest earned in 1.5 years and convert 1.5 years to months ($12 \times 1.5 = 18$ months). Then set up a proportion that represents the ratios of interest earned to time invested:

$$\frac{60}{i} = \frac{4}{18}$$
$$\frac{60}{i} = \frac{2}{9}$$

Cross-multiply to solve:

$$2i = 540$$
$$i = \$270$$

Jerry will make $270. Choice (C).

405.

B. 2 mph

Let r = the speed of the current.

Let $9 + r$ = Robert's speed downstream.

Let $9 - r$ = Robert's speed upstream.

Here's what you know:

	Rate	Time	Distance
Downstream	$(9 + r)$ mph	t	44 mi
Upstream	$(9 - r)$ mph	t	28 mi

Since $rt = d$, then $t = \frac{d}{r}$. Therefore, the time it takes for Robert's boat to go downstream looks like this:

$$t = \frac{44}{9+r}$$

The time it takes for it to go upstream looks like this:

$$t = \frac{28}{9-r}$$

Set these two equations equal to each other and solve for r to find the rate of the river:

$$\frac{44}{9+r} = \frac{28}{9-r}$$
$$44(9-r) = 28(9+r)$$
$$396-44r = 252+28r$$
$$-72r = -144$$
$$r = 2$$

Therefore, the rate of the river's current is 2 mph, Choice (B).

406. D. $3\frac{3}{7}$ **hours**

Let h = the number of hours working together.

Here's what you know:

	Hours to Complete the Job Together	Portion of Job Completed in 1 Hour	Portion of Job Completed in h Hours
Machine 1	h	1/8	$h/8$
Machine 2	h	1/6	$h/6$

Set up the following equation and solve:

$$\frac{h}{8} + \frac{h}{6} = 1$$
$$24\left(\frac{h}{8} + \frac{h}{6}\right) = 24$$
$$3h + 4h = 24$$
$$7h = 24$$
$$h = 3\frac{3}{7}$$

It would take $3\frac{3}{7}$ hours for both machines working together to attach the parts.

407. A. 4

Let x = the number sold in the first week.

Let $2x$ = the number sold in the second week.

Let $4x$ = the number sold in the third week.

Let $8x$ = the number sold in the fourth week.

Set up the following equation and solve for x:

$$8x = 32$$
$$x = 4$$

Noah sold 4 subscriptions the first week.

408. **B. $8.65**

Here's what you know:

	Pounds	Price per Pound	Total Cost
Lima beans	15	$9.22	9.22(15)
Pinto beans	3	$5.80	5.80(3)
Bean soup mixture	15 + 3	x	$x(15 + 3)$

Set up the following equation and solve for x:

$$9.22(15) + 5.80(3) = x(15 + 3)$$
$$138.30 + 17.40 = 18x$$
$$155.70 = 18x$$
$$8.65 = x$$

Alice's new bean soup mixture costs $8.65 per pound, Choice (B).

409. **B. 10,000**

Let x = the number of board feet per tie.

Let $250x$ = the total number of ties.

$$250x(x) = 400,000$$
$$250x^2 = 400,000$$
$$x^2 = 1,600$$
$$x = \sqrt{1,600}$$
$$x = 40$$

Now that you know how many board feet are in a tie, multiply that number by the number of ties in each car to find the total number of ties:

$$250(40) = 10,000$$

There are 10,000 ties, Choice (B).

410. **D. 6 hours**

Let t = time and rewrite the distance formula like so:

$$\frac{distance}{time} = rate$$

The equation for how fast the two dogs actually hauled the freight looks like this:

$$\frac{20 \text{ miles}}{time} = rate$$

Set up the following equation to represent how fast the dogs would've traveled if they had taken 2 hours longer and then solve for t:

$$\frac{20}{t+2} + \frac{5}{6} = \frac{20}{t}$$

$$\left(\frac{20}{t+2}\right)\left(\frac{6}{6}\right) + \left(\frac{5}{6}\right)\left(\frac{t+2}{t+2}\right) = \frac{20}{t}$$

$$\frac{120}{6t+12} + \frac{5t+10}{6t+12} = \frac{20}{t}$$

$$\frac{120+5t+10}{6t+12} = \frac{20}{t}$$

In a ratio, $\frac{a}{b} = \frac{c}{d}$ and $ad = bc$; therefore,

$$120t + 5t^2 + 10t = 120t + 240$$

$$5t^2 + 10t - 240 = 0$$

$$5\left(t^2 + 2t - 48\right) = 0$$

$$5(t+8)(t-6) = 0$$

Because the question is talking about time, –8 can't be correct, so the answer is 6 hours, Choice (D).

411. **D. 40,000**

Set up the following proportion and solve for x:

$$\frac{80}{100} = \frac{x}{50,000}$$

$$100x = 4,000,000$$

$$x = 40,000$$

Or you could just figure that 10% of 50,000 is 5,000 and twice that is 10,000. Then subtract that from 50,000 to get 40,000. However you solve this problem, Choice (D) is your answer.

412. B. 52

Let w = the number of women.

Set up the following equation and solve for w:

$$78 = 2w + w$$
$$78 = 3w$$
$$26 = w$$

Then multiply the number of women by 2 to find the number of men:

$$26 \times 2 = 52$$

Choice (B) is your answer.

413. D. 9

Let x = the number of Dr. Green's patients.

Let $x + 2$ = the number of Dr. Owen's patients.

Set up the following equation and solve for x:

$$16 = x + (x + 2)$$
$$16 = 2x + 2$$
$$14 = 2x$$
$$x = 7$$

Then just add 2 to find out how many patients Dr. Owen sees: $7 + 2 = 9$.

414. B. $376.70

First, you must figure out how much George's gross earnings are.

Let x = gross earnings and set up the following equation:

$$\$425 = x - 0.12x$$
$$\$425 = 0.88x$$
$$\$482.95 = x$$

To find the amount he will give to charity, find 10% of $482.95, which is $48.30.

Now just subtract this from the net earnings:

$$\$425.00 - \$48.30 = \$376.70$$

Answers
401–500

415.   A. $70

Let c = the cost of goods. Set up the following equation and solve for c:

$$\frac{c}{100}(c) = c - 21$$

$$\frac{c^2}{100} = c - 21$$

$$\frac{c^2}{100} - c + 21 = 0$$

$$c^2 - 100c + 2{,}100 = 0$$

$$(c - 70)(c - 30) = 0$$

$$c = 70 \text{ or } 30$$

Because $30 isn't one of your choices, the answer is $70, or Choice (A).

416.   C. $\frac{12}{18}$

Let d = the denominator.

Let $\frac{1}{2}d + 3$ = the numerator.

So $\dfrac{\frac{1}{2}d + 3}{d}$ is the fraction you work with.

Set up the following equation and solve for d by cross-multiplying:

$$\frac{\frac{1}{2}d + 3}{d} = \frac{2}{3}$$

$$2d = \frac{3}{2}d + 9$$

$$4d = 3d + 18$$

$$d = 18$$

Therefore,

$$\frac{1}{2}(18) + 3 = 9 + 3 = 12$$

The answer is $\frac{12}{18}$, Choice (C).

417.   A. 64, 65

Set up the following equation to solve this problem:

$$x + (x + 1) = 129$$

$$2x + 1 = 129$$

$$2x = 128$$

$$x = 64$$

Therefore, the two numbers are 64 and 65.

Tip: You can also solve this problem simply by looking at each choice to find out which two consecutive numbers add up to 129.

418. **C. 30**

Let x = the percentage of profit. Set up the following proportion and solve for x by cross-multiplying:

$$\frac{x}{100} = \frac{6}{20}$$
$$20x = 600$$
$$x = 30$$

Mr. Cameron increased the price by 30% on the shirt he sold.

419. **B. 150 miles**

Here's what you know from the problem:

Distance = 200 + x, where x is the number of miles Asher drove before lunch

Time = 2 hours + 3 hours = 5 hours

Set up the following proportion and solve for x:

$$\frac{\text{distance}}{\text{time}} = \frac{70 \text{ miles}}{\text{hour}}$$
$$\frac{x + 200}{5} = 70$$
$$x + 200 = 350$$
$$x = 150 \text{ miles}$$

The answer is Choice (B).

420. **C. 129**

Let x, $x + 2$, and $x + 4$ represent the three integers. Set up the following equation and solve for x:

$$x + (x + 4) = 3(x + 2) - 131$$
$$2x + 4 = 3x + 6 - 131$$
$$129 = x$$

421. **C. 8**

Let x = the number of peanut butter cups Mason ate on day 1.

Set up the following equation and solve for x:

$$x + (x + 6) + (x + 12) + (x + 18) + (x + 24) = 100$$
$$5x + 60 = 100$$
$$5x = 40$$
$$x = 8$$

The first day he ate 8. That's a whole lot of peanut butter cups.

422. **A. $3.55**

Here's how you represent Nathanael's portion in equation form:

$$\frac{\$10.45 - \$1.25}{4} + \$1.25 = x$$

$$\frac{\$9.20}{4} + \$1.25 = x$$

$$\$2.30 + 1.25 = x$$

$$\$3.55 = x$$

Nathanael's share is $3.55, Choice (A).

423. **C. 1,389**

First, find out how many total calories are in 100% of the recipe:

$$4(310) = 1,240 \text{ calories}$$

To find how many are in 112% of the recipe, use this equation:

$$x = 1,240(1.12)$$

$$x = 1,388.8$$

Round to 1,389, Choice (C).

424. **C. 75 feet**

Use the formula for the perimeter of a rectangle, where w = width and l = length. The two short sides add up to 50, so replace $2w$ with 50 and solve for l:

$$\text{Perimeter} = 2w + 2l$$

$$200 = 50 + 2l$$

$$150 = 2l$$

$$75 = l$$

The answer is Choice (C), 75 feet.

425. **C. 20 feet**

You can express this problem as a simple ratio. Then just cross-multiply to solve for x.

$$\frac{5}{2} = \frac{x}{8}$$

$$2x = 40$$

$$x = 20$$

So the tree is 20 feet tall.

426. **B. 120 square feet**

The formula for area is length times width. So the area of the den is 12 feet × 10 feet = 120 square feet. Therefore, Choice (B) is correct.

427. **D. 1,536**

First, you have to find the area to be covered, using the formula length times width:

10 feet × 16 feet = 160 square feet

Because the bricks are measured in inches, you have to convert 160 square feet to square inches. There are 144 square inches in a square foot, so 160 × 144 = 23,040 square inches.

Next, you have to determine the area of one brick:

3 × 5 = 15 square inches

Divide this number into the area of the wall:

23,040 ÷ 15 – 1,536 bricks, Choice (D)

428. **D. 26,400 feet**

A pentagon has 5 sides. If each side measures 1,760 feet, the formula for finding the total feet Joe ran looks like this:

1,760(5)(3) = 8,800(3) = 26,400 feet

429. **B. 25 feet**

Use the formula for perimeter to find the answer; w = width and l = length:

$$\text{Perimeter} = 2w + 2l$$
$$150 = 2w + 2(50)$$
$$150 = 2w + 100$$
$$50 = 2w$$
$$25 \text{ feet} = w$$

430. **B. 30**

Set up this equation to represent the two parts of the line segment:

$$3x + 2x = 75$$
$$5x = 75$$
$$x = 15$$

Therefore, $2x$ (the length of the shortest side) is 30, Choice (B).

If you want to check your answer, just plug in the number:

$$3(15) + 2(15) = 75$$
$$45 + 30 = 75$$

431. **C. 11 feet**

Let A = area and S = the length of a side.

Given that A = 121, you can set up this equation:

$$A = S^2$$
$$121 = S^2$$
$$S = 11$$

Each side is 11 feet long, Choice (C).

432. **D. 10**

Let F = side F, S = side S, and H = hypotenuse.

Given that F = 6 and S = 8, you can use the Pythagorean theorem to solve for H:

$$F^2 + S^2 = H^2$$
$$6^2 + 8^2 = H^2$$
$$36 + 64 = H^2$$
$$100 = H^2$$
$$10 = H$$

Choice (D) is correct.

433. **A. 198 cubic inches**

To solve this problem, you have to know the formula for volume of a cylinder:

Volume = $\pi r^2 h$, where h is the height and r is the radius

Simply plug in the numbers from the question to solve:

$$V = 3^2(3.14)(7)$$
$$V = 9(3.14)(7)$$
$$V = 63(3.14)$$
$$V = 197.82$$

Round to the nearest whole number to get Choice (A).

434. **D. 18.36 feet**

A good first step in solving this problem is to draw a diagram:

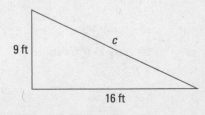

With the help of this diagram, you know you're looking for the hypotenuse of a right triangle. To find it, use the Pythagorean theorem:

$$a^2 + b^2 = c^2$$
$$9^2 + 16^2 = c^2$$
$$81 + 256 = c^2$$
$$337 = c^2$$

The answer choices are between 18.36 and 25, so $\sqrt{337}$ must be between those numbers. For reference, find the square of 20. You know that $20^2 = 400$, so $\sqrt{337}$ has to be less than 20. Therefore, Choice (D) is correct.

435. **C. 44 kilometers**

Use the formula Circumference = πd, where d is the diameter, to solve this problem:

$$C = \pi(14)$$
$$C = 43.96$$

Rounded to the nearest whole number, the sinkhole's circumference is 44 kilometers, Choice (C).

436. **C. 60 square inches**

The formula for the area of a rectangle is length times width. So just multiply 10×6 to get your answer — 60 square inches.

437. **A. 27 feet**

Let w = width and $2w + 24$ = length. Then set up this equation and solve for w:

$$2w + 2(2w + 24) = 210$$
$$2w + 4w + 48 = 210$$
$$6w = 162$$
$$w = 27 \text{ feet}$$

If you want to check your answer, plug it into the original equation:

$$2 \cdot 27 + 2(2 \cdot 27 + 24) = 210$$
$$54 + 2(54 + 24) = 210$$
$$54 + 108 + 48 = 210$$
$$210 = 210$$

Choice (A) is correct.

438. **D. 125 cubic inches**

The formula for volume of a cube is s^3, where s is the length of a side. Therefore, $5^3 = 125$ cubic inches.

Choice (D) is your answer.

Answers 401–500

439. B. 12 inches

Let p = the diameter of the pipe and c = the diameter of the casing. Then set up the following two equations:

$$p = \frac{2}{3}c$$

$$p = \frac{c}{2} + 2$$

Set them equal to each other to solve for c:

$$\frac{c}{2} + 2 = \frac{2}{3}c$$

$$6\left(\frac{c}{2} + 2\right) = 6\left(\frac{2}{3}c\right)$$

$$3c + 12 = 4c$$

$$12 = c$$

The diameter of the casing is 12 inches, Choice (B).

440. A. 252 feet $\times$ 151 feet

Let w = width.

Let $w + 101$ = length.

Let $w - 25$ = decreased width.

Then set up the following equation and solve for w:

$$w + 101 = 2(w - 25)$$

$$w + 101 = 2w - 50$$

$$-w = -151$$

$$w = 151$$

Now that you have the width, find the length:

$$151 + 101 = 252$$

Choice (A) is correct.

441. D. 370 feet

Set up the following equation to find the perimeter minus the doorway:

$$\text{Trim} = 2(130) + 20 + 20 + 70$$

$$\text{Trim} = 260 + 110 = 370$$

Joe has to paint 370 feet of trim, Choice (D).

442.

A. $166.80

The room measures $10 \times 12 = 120$ square feet.

Because there are 3 feet in a yard, 1 square yard = 9 square feet. Use this conversion factor to find out how many square yards you need to carpet:

$$\frac{120}{9} = 13\frac{1}{3} \text{ square yards}$$

Now just multiply to find the total price of the carpet:

$$13.333 \times \$12.51 = \$166.80$$

443.

A. 38 square yards

Surface area is the area of the six sides of the box. Simply put, it's twice the area of the three different sides. Here's what your equation looks like:

$$\text{Surface area} = 2\big[(4\cdot 1)+(1\cdot 3)+(3\cdot 4)\big]$$

$$\text{Surface area} = 2(4+3+12)$$

$$\text{Surface area} = 2\cdot 19$$

$$\text{Surface area} = 38$$

Choice (A) is the winner here.

444.

B. 50 feet × 30 feet

Let l = the length of the flag.

Let $\frac{3}{5}l$ = the width of the flag.

Set up the following equation:

$$\frac{3}{5}l(l) = 1,500$$

Combine like terms:

$$\frac{3}{5}l^2 = 1,500$$

Multiply both sides by 5 to get

$$3l^2 = 7,500$$

Divide both sides by 3 to get

$$l^2 = 2,500$$

Find the square root of 2,500:

$$l = \sqrt{2,500}$$

$$l = 50$$

218 Part II: The Answers

Now that you know the length, use it to find the width:

$$w = \frac{3}{5}(50)$$
$$w = 30$$

Therefore, the flag is 50 feet × 30 feet, Choice (B).

Tip: You can often solve this type of problem faster simply by running through the possible answers. Just multiply the lengths and widths in the answers until you find one that equals 1,500 (the area given in the question).

445. **A. 41 feet**

This is a simple perimeter problem. First, figure out the lengths of the three sides:

A = 12 feet

B = 12 + 2 = 14 feet

C = 14 + 1 = 15 feet

Now just add them all together:

12 + 14 + 15 = 41 feet

Choice (A) is your answer.

446. **A. $216.00**

The formula for the area of a rectangle is length times width.

To figure out the area of the bottom portion of the room, just take 4 yards × 8 yards = 32 square yards.

To find the area of the top portion, just divide the area of the bottom portion by 2 because the top portion is half the size of the bottom portion. Therefore, its area is 32 ÷ 2 = 16.

Add the two areas together to get the total amount of carpet Jeffrey needs:

32 + 16 = 48 square yards

Now find the price of the carpet:

48 square yards × $3.50 = $168

Then find the price of labor:

$12 × 4 hours = $48

Finally, add the two together:

$168 + $48 = $216.00

Answers
401–500

447. **D. 100 degrees**

The sum of the interior angles of a triangle is 180 degrees.

Let x = the missing angle. Set up the following equation and solve for x:

$$x = 180 - (50 + 30)$$
$$x = 180 - 80$$
$$x = 100$$

The angle is 100 degrees, Choice (D).

448. **A. 50.27**

To solve this problem, you need to know the formula for circumference (C):

$$C = 2\pi r$$

Plug in the radius (r) and solve:

$$C = 2\pi(8)$$
$$C = 16\pi$$
$$C = 50.265$$

Round to 50.27, Choice (A).

449. **D. 18,000**

The electric motor makes 3,000 360-degree rotations in one minute. To solve this problem, find out how many 360-degree rotations it makes per second:

$$3,000 \div 60 = 50$$

Then multiply the number of degrees by the number of rotations per second:

$$360 \times 50 = 18,000$$

450. **B. 24**

This is an easy one! Use the formula for diameter to solve for d:

$$d = 2r$$
$$d = 2(12)$$
$$d = 24$$

451. **B. 200**

First, change the question to an equation:

$$\frac{80}{x} = \frac{40}{100}$$

Next, cross-multiply:

$$40x = 8{,}000$$

Finally, divide both sides by 40:

$$\frac{40x}{40} = \frac{8{,}000}{40}$$
$$x = 200$$

452. **B. 2,160**

Ten percent of 2,400 is 240. Because you're looking for how many did NOT win a prize, you must subtract 240 from 2,400. The correct answer is Choice (B), 2,160.

453. **C. $27.60**

Ten percent of $23.00 is $2.30. Multiply that by 2 to find 20% — $4.60. Add that amount to $23.00 to get the total — $27.60, Choice (C).

454. **D. 43%**

To find the percent of vegetarians in the group, first reduce the ratio of vegetarians to the total group, like so:

$$\frac{30 \text{ vegetarians}}{70 \text{ total}} = \frac{3}{7}$$

Then set up the following proportion and solve to find the percent:

$$\frac{3}{7} = \frac{x}{100}$$
$$7x = 300$$
$$x = 42.8$$

You can round 42.8 up to 43, making Choice (D) the correct answer.

455. **C. $30,300**

Looking at the hundreds value in $30,303, you see 303, which rounds down to 300; therefore, Choice (C) is correct.

456. **A. $49.50**

The first year she lost 10%, giving her 50 – (0.1)50 = 50 – 5 = $45.

The second year she gained 10%, giving her 45 + (0.1)45 = $49.50, Choice (A).

457. **A. 2**

Four people are working on the fence for 7 hours a day; therefore, the family is spending (4)(7) = 28 person-hours on the job each day.

Divide the total number of hours needed to complete the job by the total number of person-hours to find the total number of days: 56 ÷ 28 = 2. It will take 2 days for the team to finish painting the fence.

458. **B. $336**

Find the sale price of the tablet first.

What is 20% of $400? If 10% is $40, then 20% of $400 is 2 × $40 or $80. Subtract to find the sale price:

$$\$400 - \$80 = \$320$$

Now find the tax.

What is 5% of $320? If 10% is $32, then 5% of $320 is $\frac{1}{2} \times \$32$ or $16.

So the final price is $320 + $16 = $336, Choice (B).

459. **A. 20%**

To solve this problem, all you have to do is set up the following proportion to find the percent (per 100) of responses to actual calls. Note that you can reduce the first ratio to make your cross-multiplication a little easier.

$$\frac{4,000}{20,000} = \frac{x}{100}$$
$$\frac{4}{20} = \frac{x}{100}$$
$$20x = 400$$
$$x = 20$$

460. **D. 166**

Don't let Jen's scores throw you off. They're completely irrelevant.

To solve this problem, first add up Mike's scores:

$$157 + 175 = 332$$

Then divide by 2:

$$332 \div 2 = 166$$

461. **A. 38**

First, find out how much Josiah makes per hour:

$368 ÷ 32 = $11.50

Josiah earns $11.50 per hour and must be being paid under the table because taxes aren't mentioned in the problem.

Use his hourly wage to find out how many hours he works to make $437:

$437 ÷ $11.50 = 38

Josiah worked 38 hours, Choice (A).

462. **C. 500.86**

First, subtract the monthly fee from the bill to find the total amount actually spent on electricity:

$90.12 − $20.00 = $70.12

Now divide your answer by the charge per kilowatt-hour:

$$\frac{70.12}{0.14} = 500.857$$

Choice (C) is the winner here.

463. **A. 28**

Let x = the first integer as you set up the following equation:

$$x + (x+1) + (x+2) = 87$$
$$3x + 3 = 87$$
$$3x = 84$$
$$x = 28$$

Now check your work:

28 + 29 + 30 = 87

(Of course, you could also just look at the choices and add the next two integers after each to see which answer is correct, but creating the preceding equation makes you look smarter.)

464. **D. 1,732.6**

Easy questions like this are included to throw you off. All you do is add:

1,293.1 + 439.5 = 1,732.6

465.   **A. $15,000**

If x = the value at the end of six years, then

$$x = \$30,000 - (\$2,500 \times 6)$$
$$x = \$30,000 - \$15,000$$
$$x = \$15,000$$

Choice (A) is the winner here.

466.   **A. $50,000**

Let x = the amount invested at 8% and y = the amount invested at 7%.

Here's what you know:

$$y = \$60,000 - x$$
$$0.08x = \text{interest received at } 8\%$$
$$0.07y = \text{interest received at } 7\%$$

Therefore, you can set up the following equation to find out how much Rod invested at 8%:

$$0.08x + 0.07y = 4,700$$
$$0.08x + 0.07(60,000 - x) = 4,700$$
$$0.08x + 4,200 - 0.07x = 4,700$$
$$0.01x + 4,200 = 4,700$$
$$0.01x = 500$$
$$x = 50,000$$

Rod was brave in these rough economic times, but it paid off. Choice (A) it is.

467.   **C. 60**

If Jack eats 3 hot dogs in one minute, you know he eats 3(12) = 36 in 12 minutes. If Jeff eats 2 per minute, he eats 2(12) = 24 in 12 minutes.

Add 36 + 24 = 60 and you have your answer. That's a lot of hot dogs.

468.   **B. 45 minutes**

The water is flowing into the sink at a rate of 6 – 2 ounces per minute, or 4 ounces per minute. Do the math to see how long it takes to get to 180 ounces:

$$\frac{180}{4} = 45$$

It takes 45 minutes to fill the sink.

469. **B. 1 in 3**

There are 6 chances in 10 that the first choice will be an orange. With 5 oranges and 4 apples left in the bowl, there are 5 chances in 9 that the second choice will be an orange. The product of the two choices is

$$\frac{6}{10} \cdot \frac{5}{9} = \frac{30}{90} = \frac{1}{3}$$

So there's a 1-in-3 chance that both pieces will be oranges, Choice (B).

470. **C. $153**

The item originally sold for $200. The first reduction was 10%, taking the item down to $180:

$$200 - 0.1(200)$$

$$= 200 - 20$$

$$= 180$$

The second reduction was 15%, taking the item down to $153:

$$180 - 0.15(180)$$

$$= 180 - 27$$

$$= 153$$

Choice (C) is your answer.

471. **D. 18**

First, find out how many person-hours are needed to produce 36 tons:

36 tons × 3 person-hours/ton = 108 total person-hours

Then find out how many people are needed to meet that person-hour requirement in 6 hours:

108 person-hours ÷ 6 hours = 18 people

472. **A. $47.68**

This is an easy one. Simply multiply:

$2.98 × 16 = $47.68

Choice (A) is your answer.

473. **B. 8°**

Solving this problem just requires a little addition and multiplication:

$$12° + 4(2°) + 4(-3°)$$
$$= 12° + 8° + (-12°)$$
$$= 8°$$

The temperature was 8° at 5 p.m.

That's one cold day.

474. **A. 31**

Let d = the age of the daughter now.

Let $d + 28$ = the age of the mother now.

Let $d + 11$ = the age of the daughter in 11 years.

Let $d + 39$ = the age of the mother in 11 years.

Now set up the following equation to determine the daughter's current age:

$$d + 39 = 3(d + 11)$$
$$d + 39 = 3d + 33$$
$$39 = 2d + 33$$
$$6 = 2d$$
$$3 = d$$

If her daughter is 3 now and Mrs. Jones is 28 years older than her daughter, she is 31 years old. Choice (A) is correct.

475. **A. 11**

To solve this problem, set up the following equation and solve for x:

$$x = 2.75(4)$$
$$x = 11$$

She needs 11 hours of music to fill up all four CDs, so Choice (A) is your answer.

476. **B. 10**

Use the formula for finding the nth term of an arithmetic sequence:

$$a_n = a_1 + (n - 1)d$$

Here's what the variables in this problem represent:

$$d = -10$$
$$a_1 = 200$$
$$n = 20$$

Solve for a_{20}:

$$a_{20} = 200 + (20-1)(-10)$$
$$a_{20} = 200 + (19)(-10)$$
$$a_{20} = 200 - 190$$
$$a_{20} = 10$$

The 20th term is 10, Choice (B).

477.   **C. 130**

Mean is another way to express "average." So just add up the scores and divide by 4:

$$120 + 125 + 135 + 140 = 520$$

$$520 \div 4 = 130$$

The mean or average is 130, Choice (C).

478.   **C. $118**

First, add all the prices together:

$$\$850 + \$1,155 + \$355 = \$2,360$$

Then multiply by 0.05:

$$\$2,360 \times 0.05 = \$118$$

The correct answer is (C).

479.   **C. 44 BC**

Here's how to solve this one:

$$-100 + 56 = -44$$

The answer is 44 BC, Choice (C).

480.   **B. $200 gain**

All you have to do is add the gains and losses together:

$$300 - 500 + 400 = \$200$$

Sometimes the test-makers throw in easy ones to make you wonder if they're trying to trick you!

481.   **C. $\frac{1}{8}$**

There were nine balls total before Jason removed the first purple ball. Because only **one** purple ball was left in the box after Jason picked the first one and the box contained **a total** of eight balls, the probability that Jason picked another purple ball was $\frac{1}{8}$, Choice (C).

482.   **C. $113.85**

First, find the number of gallons Jimmy needs to fill up:

42 − 9 = 33 gallons

Then multiply the number of gallons by the price per gallon:

$3.45 × 33 = $113.85

Choice (C) is the correct answer.

483.   **C. $893.75**

Amount of investment = $p + prt$, where p is the principal, r is the rate, and t is the time.

Here's what your equation looks like:

Amount = 650 + 650(0.075)(5)

Amount = 650 + 243.75

Amount = 893.75

Choice (C) is the winner here.

484.   **A. 4.5 hours**

To solve this problem, just divide the miles by the rate of travel:

$$\frac{250}{55} = 4.5454$$

It will take approximately 4.5 hours, Choice (A).

485.   **D. $3,650**

To find out how much Ralph can make in each scenario, multiply the two ticket prices by their corresponding amounts:

250 × $25 = $6,250

450 × $22 = $9,900

Then subtract to find the difference:

$9,900 − $6,250 = $3,650

People like a discount!

486.   **C. $\frac{4}{14}$**

If Nat had completed $\frac{5}{7}$ of the assignment, you know that Nat had $\frac{2}{7}$ or $\frac{4}{14}$ left to do. So Choice (C) is the correct answer.

487. **C. $0.95**

Add the change to see how much Billy has before he buys lunch:

15($0.25) + 15($0.10) + 22($0.05) + $0.12

= $3.75 + $1.50 + $1.10 + $0.12

= $6.47

Subtract the cost of the lunch:

$6.47 − $5.52 = $0.95

488. **B. 95**

First, find the average of the 3 tests:

97 + 88 + 90 = 275

275 ÷ 3 = 92 (rounded up)

Next, let x = the final exam score and set up the following equation to find out what score Bentley needs on the final test:

$$\frac{x + 2(92)}{3} = 93$$

$$\frac{x + 184}{3} = 93$$

$$x + 184 = 279$$

$$x = 95$$

Bentley has to get a 95 on the test to get the scholarship. Choice (B) is the answer.

Tip: You could also plug the given answers into the formula until you find the correct answer.

489. **A. 11, 15**

Let the two numbers be a and b.

Here's what you know: $a + b = 26$ and $ab = 165$. Therefore, $b = 26 - a$. Substitute this for b in second equation:

$$a(26 - a) = 165$$

$$-a^2 + 26a - 165 = 0$$

$$a^2 - 26a + 165 = 0$$

$$(a - 11)(a - 15) = 0$$

$$a = 11 \text{ and } a = 15$$

Use $b = 26 - a$ to find b.

When $a = 11$, $b = 15$ and when $a = 15$, $b = 11$.

Tip: If you don't know how to set up the algebraic formula, you can evaluate each answer group to determine if its product and sum are equal to the ones given in the question. For instance, $11 + 15 = 26$, and $11 \times 15 = 165$.

490.

C. 0.4

This is a simple multiplication problem:

$$2(0.20) = 0.40$$

Choice (C) is the answer.

491.

A. 10

Express each term as a decimal and then add them together:

$$1.75 + 3.75 + 4.5 = 10$$

Choice (A) is your answer.

492.

B. $720

First, find out how much Cooper would pay on the installment plan:

$$\$230(24) + \$1,000 = \$6,520$$

Then subtract the pay-in-full amount from the installment-plan amount:

$$\$6,520 - \$5,800 = \$720$$

Cooper would pay $720 more if he chose to use the installment plan.

493.

D. 12 days

First, find out how many pages Cole has left to read:

$$445 - 157 = 288$$

Then divide that by 24 to find out how many days he has to read:

$$288 \div 24 = 12$$

It will take Cole 12 more days to finish the book, or Choice (D).

494.

C. 11

First, convert 6 minutes to seconds. You know that 1 minute = 60 seconds, so 6 minutes = 360 seconds (6×60).

Each tweet takes 24 + 8 = 32 seconds to write and send, so just divide to see how many tweets you can send in 360 seconds:

$$\frac{360}{32} = 11.25$$

The most tweets that can be sent are 11, Choice (C).

495.

B. $30.05

The cost of apps = 5($1.99) or $9.95. The cost of the apps and the headphones = $9.95 + $10 = $19.95. Therefore, Justin still has $50 − $19.95 = $30.05 left on his gift card.

496. **A. 14.25**

The trip consists of 300 − 45 = 255 miles of city driving.

Therefore, the car will use the following amounts of gas:

$\frac{255}{20} = 12.75$ gallons for city driving

$\frac{45}{30} = 1.5$ gallons for highway driving

Add them together to get the total:

12.75 + 1.5 = 14.25

497. **C. $2,182**

Jasmine's gross earnings were

60($50) = $3,000

Her expenses were

$380 + $0.30(800) + $198

= $578 + $240

= $818

Therefore, her profit was

$3,000 − $818 = $2,182

498. **D. 11**

If 56% of the balloons are not red, then 44% are red, and 44% of 25 is

0.44(25) = 11

Eleven of the balloons are red.

499. **A. 3**

First, find out the rate at which one groomer grooms a dog:

2 groomers × 3 hours = 6 hours to groom 8 dogs

6 hours ÷ 8 dogs = 0.75 hour per dog

Now multiply that rate by the number of dogs the groomers have to groom:

12 dogs (0.75 hour) = 9 hours

Finally, divide that time by the number of groomers:

$\frac{9 \text{ hours}}{3 \text{ groomers}} = 3$ hours

500.   **C. 4**

For this problem, you need to know a variation of the distance formula:

$$\text{time} = \frac{\text{distance}}{\text{speed}}$$

Since the length of the train is 1 mile and the tunnel is 1 mile, the train has to travel 2 miles total, so the equation looks like this:

$$\text{time} = \frac{2 \text{ miles}}{30 \text{ mph}}$$

$$\text{time} = \frac{1}{15} \text{ hour}$$

You want to know the time in minutes, so you need to find what $\frac{1}{15}$ of an hour is.

There are 60 minutes in an hour, so set up the following proportion:

$$\frac{1}{15} = \frac{x}{60}$$
$$15x = 60$$
$$x = 4 \text{ minutes}$$

Therefore, the answer is (C).

501.   **C. theory**

A hypothesis becomes a theory after it holds up to repeated testing. It may then become a law, fact, or principle if it holds up consistently over time.

502.   **A. meter**

A *meter* is the fundamental unit of length in the metric system and in the International System of Units.

503.   **B. liter**

A *liter* is a special term used for a measurement of a cubic decimeter: 10 centimeters × 10 centimeters × 10 centimeters = 1 liter.

504.   **C. gram**

A *gram* is a unit of mass in the International System of Units; it represents one one-thousandth (0.001) of a kilogram.

505.   **C. deci-**

Deci- is a metric prefix that represents one-tenth.

506.   **B. mega-**

Mega- is a metric prefix that represents one million.

507. **B. one-thousandth of a gram**

Milli- is a metric prefix meaning one-thousandth, so a milligram is one-thousandth of a gram.

508. **B. the physical history of the Earth**

Geology is the study of the physical and dynamic history of the Earth.

509. **C. weather**

Meteorologists study the weather and attempt to predict it.

510. **D. dinosaurs**

A *paleontologist* studies fossils of plants and animals of prehistoric life, including dinosaurs.

511. **B. archeologist**

An *archeologist* studies past human life and cultures by recovering evidence and examining materials left in a given area.

512. **A. weight**

Weight exists because gravity exerts a force on mass.

513. **D. farming**

Although *agriculture* is, in part, the study of plants, animals, and soil, as a whole, it's the science of farming.

514. **A. the study of plants**

Botany is the study of plant life.

515. **D. the study of the environment**

Ecology is the study of the interactions of organisms with the environment.

516. **C. the study of bugs**

Entomologists study bugs, concentrating on six-legged insects.

517. **B. heredity**

Geneticists study genes, heredity, and the variation in living organisms.

518. **A. carnivores**

A *carnivore* is a flesh-eating mammal; examples include lions, tigers, and polar bears.

519. **C. taxonomy**

Taxonomy classifies groups of organisms in a ranking system according to the characteristics they share with each other.

520. **B. Many disagreements occur among scientists about where an organism belongs.**

Scientific groupings don't follow specific rules enough to completely shut out debate, so you find some experts who are yay and some who are nay about the classification groups.

521. **A. animals**

The animal kingdom contains more than one million species.

522. **B. plant**

The plant kingdom is characterized by unmoving living organisms with cell walls made of *cellulose,* an organic compound.

523. **B. moncrans**

The moneran kingdom includes bacteria and cyanobacteria.

524. **C. protists**

Amoebas belong to the kingdom of protists because they're one-celled organisms.

525. **D. fungi**

Fungi don't use light to make energy. Instead, they absorb energy and nutrients from their environment.

526. **D. central nervous system**

The brain receives, processes, and responds to physical stimuli in the body.

527. **A. circulatory system**

The heart receives blood from the body, sends it to the lungs to be oxygenated, and then returns it to the rest of the body.

528. **B. digestive system**

The rectum is part of the digestive system. It helps eliminate waste after the digestive system gets energy from food.

529. **B. musculoskeletal system**

Bones support the body, including the muscles and tendons, allowing the body to move effectively.

530. **B. carbon dioxide**

Humans inhale air, use oxygen, and exhale the carbon dioxide.

531. **A. a cell's nucleus**

The nucleus holds a cell's genetic material, like DNA.

532. **C. water**

Cytoplasm is a watery gel-like substance found in between the cell membrane and the outer membrane of the nucleus.

533. **A. cell membrane**

Think of the cell membrane as a sac that holds the cytoplasm and nucleus, protecting its structure.

534. **C. chlorophyll**

Plants contain *chlorophyll,* which is a chemical that helps them create food using sunlight. This process is known as *photosynthesis.*

535. **A. ribosome**

The *ribosome* is the part of a cell that combines amino acids into proteins.

536. **B. cellular respiration**

Cellular respiration is the process during which a cell produces energy by breaking down nutrients within the cell. Cellular respiration is more correct than Choice (A) because metabolism involves not only breaking down nutrients but also building molecules. Choice (B) is more specific.

537. **C. photosynthesis**

Photosynthesis occurs in plants when they use sunlight to make energy by converting carbon dioxide and water into glucose and oxygen.

538. **D. osmosis**

Osmosis occurs when a solvent, such as water, moves through the cell membrane in order to equal out the solvent concentrations on either side.

539. **B. mitosis**

Mitosis occurs when the nucleus of a cell divides to form two cells with identical chromosomes.

540. **A. meiosis**

Meiosis occurs when a cell divides to form egg or sperm cells. Each parent cell divides into four cells, also dividing up the chromosomes so that when an egg and sperm cell join at fertilization, they add up to the appropriate number of chromosomes (for humans, 46).

541. **C. whether the offspring is a boy or girl**

The mother's sex chromosomes contain only X chromosomes, while the father contributes either an X or a Y, which determines the sex of the offspring.

542. **C. recessive**

Genes come in pairs, and one gene is always more likely to express itself than the other. The stronger gene is known as the *dominant gene,* while the other is considered *recessive.*

543. **B. gene**

A gene is found in DNA and located on a chromosome, and it is responsible for controlling the inheritance of traits in the human body.

544. **D. vacuole**

A *vacuole* is more or less a storage area of fluid within the cytoplasm of a cell.

545. **C. mitochondria**

Mitochondria are found in the cytoplasm of a cell; they produce energy for the cell using stored fats, proteins, and enzymes.

546. **D. coronary sinus**

The *coronary sinus* is a collection of veins that forms a large vessel to collect blood from the heart muscle.

547. **B. cardiac skeleton**

Although the cardiac skeleton isn't real bone, it does separate and support the atria and general structure of the heart.

548. **B. from the heart to the abdomen**

The *aorta,* the largest artery in the body, originates at the left ventricle of the heart and extends down to the abdomen.

549. C. 212 degrees

Water reaches its boiling point at 212 degrees Fahrenheit.

550. B. 100 degrees

The Celsius scale is the metric standard worldwide, and the boiling point of water on that scale is 100 degrees.

551. D. 0 kelvin

The temperature 0 on the Kelvin scale is considered *absolute zero,* meaning nothing can get colder than that point. It's equivalent to –273.15 degrees Celsius or –459 degrees Fahrenheit.

552. B. $F = \frac{9}{5}C + 32$

The formula to convert Celsius to Fahrenheit is $F = \frac{9}{5}C + 32$.

553. A. $C = (F - 32)\frac{5}{9}$

The formula to convert Fahrenheit to Celsius is $C = (F - 32)\frac{5}{9}$.

554. B. element

Elements are the most basic form of chemical substances. The elements known to man are categorized as metals, nonmetals, and metalloids on the periodic table.

555. B. atom

An *atom* is the smallest recognizable part of an element.

556. A. the number of protons

The *atomic number* of an element is equal to the number of protons in its nucleus.

557. B. hydrogen

Hydrogen is the only element with just one proton in its nucleus, and thus, it's the only element with an atomic number of 1.

558. C. electrons

Electrons are negatively charged particles that float around the core of an atom's nucleus.

559. C. It classifies the elements.

The periodic table lists the atomic number, the abbreviation for each element, and its atomic weight. It also arranges the elements according to their atomic numbers and families of similar elements.

560.   C. 92

Every element is assigned an atomic number. The atomic number is determined by the number of protons in its nucleus, and a uranium atom contains 92 protons. Therefore, uranium's atomic number is 92.

561.   B. 11

Every element is assigned an atomic number. The atomic number is determined by the number of protons in its nucleus, and a sodium atom contains 11 protons. Therefore, sodium's atomic number is 11.

562.   B. 2

Every element is assigned an atomic number. The atomic number is determined by the number of protons in its nucleus, and a helium atom contains only 2 protons. Therefore, helium's atomic number is 2.

563.   **C. the energy of motion**

An object's kinetic energy depends on the object's mass and velocity. *Kinetic energy* is defined as the work necessary to accelerate a mass from a resting position to a certain speed, or velocity.

564.   **C. They don't change.**

When a physical change such as freezing or heating occurs to an element, the molecules themselves do not change.

565.   **B. a group of rare earth metals on the periodic table**

The periodic table classifies like elements. The lanthanide series is a group of rare earth metals with atomic numbers ranging from 57 to 71.

566.   **B. product**

A *product* is a new element or molecule that results from a chemical reaction.

567.   **B. It experiences only a physical change.**

When liquid water changes to a gas or solid, the molecules themselves still remain H_2O; therefore, only a physical change occurs.

568.   **A. plutonium**

Plutonium is a radioactive element chemically similar to uranium; both appear on the periodic table within the actinide series.

569. **A. magnesium**

Magnesium is responsible for more than 300 chemical reactions in the body, and it's essential for proper nerve and muscle function.

570. **B. osmium**

Osmium is a dark bluish, brittle, heavy metal that has a very high melting point.

571. **C. mercury**

Mercury is a poisonous metallic element that's in a liquid form at room temperature.

572. **A. outer space**

Astronomers study the existence, locations, orbits, energy, and compositions of planets and celestial matter (in other words, *outer space*).

573. **B. solar wind**

The solar wind consists of gases and particles that escape the sun's gravity and create a heliosphere around the solar system.

574. **C. 100 times**

The sun's diameter is approximately 109 times larger than the Earth's.

575. **A. celestial bodies**

A *celestial body* is a single structure bound by gravity with naturally occurring physical existence. Examples include planets, moons, stars, and asteroids.

576. **C. 67**

Jupiter has the most moons of all the planets.

577. **A. because the Earth rotates on a tilted axis**

Except for two days per year (known as the vernal and autumnal equinoxes), the hours of daylight and darkness are unequal because the Earth spins on its axis on a tilt (think about your friends in Alaska).

578. **B. iron and rock**

The four terrestrial planets (Mercury, Venus, Earth, and Mars) are mostly made of iron and rock.

579. **C. jovian planets**

Jovian planets are also known as *gas planets* because their entire outer mass is made up of gases like hydrogen and helium.

580. **D. Jupiter**

Since Jupiter is much larger than Mercury, Uranus, and Neptune, you can view it from the ground on Earth. You can also see Venus, Mars, and Saturn on a clear night.

581. **B. a dwarf planet**

In 2006, the International Astronomical Union determined a new definition of the word *planet;* at that time, Pluto became known as a *dwarf planet.* In order to receive the classification of a planet, according to the new definition, Pluto would have to orbit the sun, be a sphere, and have a clear pathway in its orbit. Pluto doesn't have a clear pathway in its orbit, as it is in the region of the Kuiper Belt, where large icy bodies also orbit the sun.

582. **B. 1/6**

Pluto's diameter is about 2,390 kilometers, or 1,485 miles. Earth's diameter is about 12,756 kilometers, or 7,926 miles; that makes Pluto's diameter about 1/6 the size of Earth's.

583. **B. the second planet**

The terrestrial planets go in this order from the sun: Mercury, Venus, Earth, and Mars. So Venus is the second planet.

584. **B. Jupiter's moon, Ganymede**

You may need a little more General Science practice if you chose Pluto's moon, because one of Jupiter's 67 moons, Ganymede, is larger than Pluto and even Mercury.

585. **B. Jupiter's moons**

Four of Jupiter's moons are known as the *Galilean satellites* because Galileo Galilei discovered them with his telescope in 1610.

586. **C. a shooting star**

A meteor is also known as a *shooting star* because you can see a streak of light when the rock heats up and burns off when it enters the atmosphere.

587. **B. a meteor that strikes the Earth**

A *meteoroid* is a piece of space debris that's on a collision course with Earth. When a meteoroid enters Earth's atmosphere, it becomes a *meteor;* it's called a *meteorite* if it strikes the Earth.

588. **A. Vapors from its nucleus are blown by solar winds.**

Even though a comet is made mostly of ice and rock, the ice in its center turns into gas as it approaches the sun and forms a cloud around it. Solar winds push the cloud back, forming what looks like a tail.

589. D. Halley

Halley's comet is a short-period comet visible to the naked eye. A short-period comet is one that has an orbital period of less than 200 years. People on Earth are able to see Halley every 75 or 76 years. This comet was last visible in 1986, and astronomers expect it to return in 2061.

590. C. between Mars and Jupiter

The asteroid belt is a thick band of orbiting asteroids located in between Mars and Jupiter.

591. D. Ceres

The asteroid belt consists of several hundred larger asteroids, several hundred thousand medium asteroids, and millions of tiny asteroids — even some as small as a dust particle. The largest asteroid, Ceres, makes up almost 25 percent of the mass of the entire belt.

592. A. minor planets

Scientists often call asteroids *minor planets* because they, like regular planets, are smaller bodies that orbit the sun.

593. A. crust

The Earth's crust is the top layer of the rocky part of the Earth. It varies in depth from a few miles to approximately 30 miles.

594. B. mantle

Found underneath the Earth's crust and above the core, the mantle makes up most of the mass of the Earth.

595. D. faults

When cracks appear in the Earth's crust, they're called *faults*.

596. B. iron

The Earth's core is made primarily of iron. It also contains nickel, and scientists are currently trying to determine whether there is any oxygen or sulfur in the core.

597. C. rock

The Earth's mantle is made of rock.

598. **A. tectonic plates**

As tectonic plates shift, magma can force its way through the cracks left behind. Magma can push through the weakened or cracked crust, causing a volcanic eruption.

599. **C. rock**

Lava is magma that has erupted onto the Earth's surface; it's comprised of molten rock.

600. **B. over tectonic plates**

Tectonic plates, which are rough-edged parts of the earth's crust, are constantly moving. Sometimes the rough edges get stuck together while the plates continue to move. When they break free, the Earth experiences earthquakes and volcanic activity, as well as the formation of trenches and rifts.

601. **B. exosphere**

Sometimes the exosphere is called *outer space* because there's no boundary between space and the exosphere, which extends about 62,000 miles into space.

602. **D. atmosphere**

The Earth's atmosphere consists of all the layers from the Earth's crust out to "outer space."

603. **B. thermosphere**

Of the layers listed, the *thermosphere* is closest to outer space. Its height varies with solar activity and may be between 220 and 500 miles from sea level. It meets the exosphere, above which lies the boundary to outer space.

604. **A. mesosphere**

The *mesosphere* is a layer of the atmosphere approximately 50 miles long that burns up millions of meteors daily as a result of the gases contained within it.

605. **A. troposphere**

The *troposphere* is the first layer of atmosphere over Earth. It extends about 4 miles up from the North and South Poles and about 12 miles up from the equator.

606. **C. jet streams**

Jet streams are narrow air currents that flow in between the troposphere and the stratosphere.

607. **B. air density**

Air density — how closely packed together air molecules are — is affected by the Earth's temperature and elevation.

608. **D. front**

A *front* is when two different air masses meet in the atmosphere, causing weather changes.

609. **A. barometer**

A barometer measures atmospheric pressure, an anemometer measures wind, and a manometer measures pressure of gases and vapor in the atmosphere.

610. **A. cirrus**

Cirrus clouds often appear higher in the sky and are thin and wispy.

611. **B. cumulus**

The big, white, puffy clouds you make out to look like angels or marshmallow men are called *cumulus clouds*.

612. **A. precipitation**

If you see nimbo- or -nimbus added to the name of a cloud, you know the cloud is producing or carrying precipitation.

613. **C. stratus**

Stratus clouds are low hanging, broad, and flat. They often look like heavy fog that doesn't quite hit the ground, oftentimes resembling a gray blanket.

614. **B. alto-**

Alto- is the prefix used to describe mid-level clouds, such as altocumulus or altostratus clouds.

615. **D. none of the above**

All clouds are capable of producing precipitation.

616. **D. 8**

A V8 engine is a V engine with eight cylinders mounted on the *crankcase* (the housing for the crankshaft) in two banks of four cylinders.

617. **B. piston rings**

A *piston ring* is a split ring that fits into a groove on the outer diameter of a piston in an engine. It regulates engine oil consumption.

618. **A. piston**

In an engine, a piston's purpose is to transfer force from expanding gas in the cylinder to the crankshaft by a piston rod and/or a connecting rod.

619. **A. the engine cooling system**

An internal combustion engine generates heat and must be cooled. The typical cooling system is based on pumping water around the hot engine block. The heated water is then pumped into the radiator, where it's cooled and then recirculated back to the engine block. The thermostat regulates the flow of water to keep the engine warm without letting it overheat.

620. **B. to lubricate engine parts**

Oil's main purpose is to lubricate engine parts to protect the working mechanisms.

621. **B. intake valve**

The intake valve, a component in a four-stroke engine, opens as the connecting rod pulls the piston down, drawing the gas and air mixture into the cylinder.

622. **B. zero emission vehicle**

A zero emission vehicle releases no pollutants from the tailpipe of the vehicle.

623. **A. a lighter load**

Every 500 pounds a vehicle carries can decrease the fuel efficiency by 2 to 5 miles per gallon. A heavier load burns more gas.

624. **C. constant velocity**

A constant velocity (CV) joint allows a drive shaft to transmit power without an increase in friction.

625. **D. All of the above.**

Poorly functioning spark plugs can cause a vehicle to misfire. Having bad spark plugs can also decrease gas mileage by about 25 percent and can cause the vehicle to eventually break down.

626. **D. a spray used to prevent rust**

Undercoating is a rust inhibitor spray that is useful on older vehicles or metal surfaces.

627. **B. One of the vehicles has a digital ignition system.**

Capacitive discharge ignitions, like digital ignition systems, store charged energy for the spark in a capacitor within the vehicle, releasing it to the spark plug on demand. Because all the energy is stored in the capacitor for the vehicle to release the energy, using the battery doesn't help give or receive power and could result in an overload.

628. **D. all of the above**

While hot weather can also attribute to the overheating of a vehicle, you'd first want to check the coolant level in the radiator, then any leaks in the system, followed by the thermostat.

629. **D. all of the above**

Internal combustion engines (ICEs) can be fueled by gasoline, diesel fuel, natural gas, and other combustible fossil fuels.

630. **B. crankshaft**

The function of the *crankshaft* is to change the up-and-down motion of the pistons to a rotating motion.

631. **D. all of the above**

The purpose of *push rods* is to actuate rocker arms above the cylinder head in order to actuate the valves.

632. **B. It could misfire.**

A spark plug that has too wide of a gap may not fire at all, or it may misfire at high speeds.

633. **B. engine block**

In order for coolant to lower the temperature in an engine, it must absorb heat by passing through the engine block, where it absorbs the heat, and then return to the radiator to cool down again.

634. **C. antifreeze**

Antifreeze is a chemical additive that lowers the freezing point of a water-based liquid.

635. **A. crankshaft**

The oil pump circulates oil to the crankshaft and then to the connecting rods, lubricating the parts to reduce heat and friction.

636. **C. exhaust valve**

The *exhaust valve* opens as the connecting rod moves the piston back up, pushing out the exploded gases.

637. **C. carburetor**

A *carburetor* is an assembly used in an engine (mostly used in older cars and machines) that mixes fuel and air to an appropriate amount in order for the engine to run properly.

638. **D. muffler**

An internal combustion engine uses a *muffler* to reduce noise created by the exhaust system.

639. **A. filter**

The emissions control system uses filters to keep pollutants from traveling out of a vehicle with the exhaust (or at least reduce them).

640. **B. calipers**

Brake calipers squeeze brake pads against the surface of the brake rotor to slow or stop a vehicle.

641. **B. redline**

Gears shift within an engine in order to keep a vehicle's rpm value from reaching dangerous levels.

642. **A. clutch**

A manual engine has a clutch located in between the engine and the transmission.

643. **C. rpm value**

The value of a vehicle's revolutions per minute, or rpm, changes when a vehicle changes gears.

644. **A. differential**

When a vehicle turns, a wheel that's traveling around the outside of the curve has to roll farther and faster than one on the inside of the curve. The *differential* transmits power to the wheels while allowing them to rotate at varying different speeds.

645. **B. differential**

The *differential* has three jobs: to aim the engine power at the wheels; to reduce the gear, slowing the rotational speed of the transmission one last time before it hits the wheels; and to transmit the power to the wheels while allowing them to rotate at different speeds.

646. **C. 12**

The standard battery voltage in a vehicle is 12 volts.

647. **B. alternator**

The electromechanical device that converts mechanical energy to electrical energy in the form of alternating current is called an _alternator_.

648. **B. starter**

Modern electronic ignition vehicles still use a starter.

649. **A. distributor**

A _distributor_ routes high voltage in a vehicle from the ignition coil in an internal combustion engine to the spark plugs in the correct firing order.

650. **B. to distribute the air/fuel mixture**

The primary purpose of an _intake manifold_ is to evenly distribute the air/fuel mixture to the cylinders in an internal combustion engine.

651. **C. starter**

A _starter_ is an electric motor powered by a battery that starts the engine when you turn the key.

652. **B. hydraulic motor**

A _hydraulic motor_ converts pressure and flow into angular displacement and torque.

653. **B. torque**

There is consistent rotation in an automobile during ignition, and accurately measuring torque allows all the parts to run safely and smoothly.

654. **C. Engine Control Unit**

The _Engine Control Unit_ (ECU) is the most powerful computer in modern vehicles, using a variety of sensors to monitor and control the functions of a running vehicle.

655. **C. It could crack the engine block.**

Adding cold water to a vehicle when it has been running can crack the block of the engine. There is no reason to remove the cap until the temperature drops to safer levels.

656. **C. 50/50**

The standard proportion for a coolant and water mixture is 50/50.

657. **B. air conditioning**

While you should always be cautious when working on a vehicle, you should leave replacing air conditioning hoses to the experts. Air conditioning hoses contain refrigerant under pressure and could blind you.

658. **A. CFC-12**

Freon (or CFC-12) was the refrigerant of choice prior to 1992, but it was replaced with R-134a because Freon was so damaging to the ozone layer.

659. **C. oil**

When an engine is running, oil pressure forms a cushion that keeps the crankshaft and connecting rod bearings trom touching.

660. **D. winter**

The multi-viscosity rating for oil is used to rate the oil's ability to flow in cold weather. The *W* stands for *winter*, meaning the oil is approved to be used during the winter months.

661. **A. water pump**

A *water pump* is a device that circulates the liquid through the cooling system by pumping it from the engine water jackets to the radiator.

662. **C. oil pump**

An *oil pump* is a small pump located in the crankcase that circulates the oil from the oil pan to the moving parts of the engine.

663. **B. jack**

A *jack* is used mostly to facilitate repairs by lifting a vehicle off the ground.

664. **B. hydrometer**

A *hydrometer* is used in a vehicle to test the coolant and battery. *Tip:* Knowing that *hydro* means liquid (water, to be exact) can help you get this one right!

665. **C. gasket**

A *gasket* is used in between two parts to prevent leakage from or into the joined parts under compression.

666. **B. overdrive**

Overdrive is the highest gear of the transmission. It allows the drive wheels to turn faster without increasing the rpm, resulting in better fuel efficiency at high speeds.

667. **A. pounds per square inch**

The *psi* is a measurement of pressure and is mostly used in vehicles to test the pressure in tires and the combustion chamber.

668. **B. shock absorber**

A *shock absorber* is a device that reduces the vehicle's vertical movement for comfort of passengers and helps with handling rough roads.

669. **B. throttle**

A *throttle* regulates the amount of gasoline going into the cylinders, ultimately controlling the power of the engine.

670. **B. to indicate the amount of fuel**

A *fuel gauge* is located in the dashboard and indicates how much fuel is in the vehicle.

671. **A. tie rod**

A *tie rod* connects the rack and pinion to the steering arm.

672. **B. bearings**

Excessive play on an installed tire may indicate that the bearings are worn and need to be replaced or repaired.

673. **A. Spark plugs are not used in a diesel engine to ignite the fuel.**

In a diesel engine, the fuel is injected directly into the combustion chamber, where it is compressed heavily to cause ignition. Spark plugs aren't used.

674. **D. 4**

Choice (D) is a ball-peen hammer. You use it to cut gaskets and expand and shape the free end of copper, roves, light rivets, and set rivets (which complete joints).

675. **B. internal shake-proof washer**

An *internal shake-proof washer* holds the screw or bolt more firmly to the assembly.

676. **B. to drill holes in wood**

This tool is a hand brace; you use it to drill holes, usually in wood.

677. **B. a winch**

A level, a compass, and a chisel are all carpenter's hand tools.

678. **B. a hacksaw**

A hacksaw's teeth are very small and close together.

679. **C. a crescent wrench**

You use a crescent wrench to loosen and tighten different sized bolts and nuts.

680. **B. a plane**

You use a plane to smooth or level a piece of wood.

681. **D. torque wrench**

A *torque wrench* precisely applies a specific torque to a nut or bolt in order to prevent over-tightening. This special wrench measures the amount of twisting force needed to apply the appropriate amount of force on the nut or bolt. It's safe to say that the reading isn't always accurate, as changes in friction can change the torque reading.

682. **B. Sand the area with medium-grain sandpaper.**

After the filler dries completely, the next step is to sand the area to create a smooth surface for painting.

683. **A. to tighten a bolt in a tight space**

You use a *ratchet handle* to increase your stability and strength when tightening nuts and bolts or to reach into tight spaces where your hand can't fit.

684. **B. to cut against the grain of wood**

A *crosscut saw* is a type of handsaw that cuts against the grain of wood, using uniquely shaped, angled teeth.

685. **C. coping saw**

A *coping saw* is used to cut curved shapes and lines.

686. **A. to cut with the grain of wood**

A *ripsaw* is a type of handsaw that cuts with the grain of wood, using uniquely shaped, angled teeth.

687. **B. snips**

Tin snips have two cutting blades that scissor together when the handles close. They're strong enough to cut thin metal sheets and rods.

688. **A. to adjust the range of the jaw to fit different bolt shapes**

Slip-joint pliers allow you to pull apart or loosen parts, like nuts and bolts. You can adjust the pivot point to increase the range of the gripping jaw.

689. **C. finishing tools**

You use *finishing tools* to sharpen the blades of other tools and smooth the edges of cut metal.

690. **B. offset screwdriver**

Offset screwdrivers work well in tight spaces where access is limited.

691. **B. punch**

Punches have a sharp end that you place against a work piece; you strike the other side with a hammer in order to leave an impression, puncture a hole, or drive in other objects (such as nails).

692. **C. large**

Auger bits are large, uniquely shaped drill bits that you use to make larger holes, usually in wood.

693. **D. mortise and tenon joint**

You use a *mortise and tenon joint* when you need it to withstand weight and movement, such as in a piece of furniture.

694. **A. overlap joint**

Obviously, the *overlap joint* gets its name from the fact that it joins two pieces together by overlapping them.

695. **C. lap joint**

Lap joints consist of two pieces that are notched so that one fits on top of the other, forming a double layer that provides strength.

696. **B. butt joint**

A *butt joint* is the simplest form of joint, but it's also the least secure in construction.

697. **B. dovetail joint**

The fan-shaped segments create a strong but decorative look in the *dovetail joint*.

698. **A. It gives more leverage.**

A cross-shaft wrench (shaped like a cross) is better than the single-shaft wrench (one long handle) because you can push down and pull up at the same time, resulting in more leverage.

699. **D. washer**

When you use a washer with a nut, the washer distributes the pressure, and the nut will stay fixed longer.

700. **B. rivets**

Rivets fasten metal parts together with a bucking bar and come in a variety of lengths, diameters, and head shapes.

701. **C. hexagonal**

Lag screws have square- or hexagon-shaped heads.

702. **B. winding**

There are many bolt and screw head styles, but winding isn't one of them!

703. **C. machine screws**

Screws used to fasten wood are called *wood screws,* but screws used to fasten metal aren't called *metal screws;* rather, they're *machine screws.* The name *machine screw* probably has to do with industrial machinery because the machines are usually made of metal and use machine screws for fastening.

704. **D. double-headed nail**

It's easy to understand how this nail got its name. The *double-headed nail* is useful with temporary construction because you can drive the nail in to the lower head and then pull it out using the higher head.

705. **C. Make a groove cut into the surface.**

When you score a pipe or other material, you're cutting a groove into the surface, usually to make it easier to cut off completely.

706. **A. needle-nosed pliers**

Needle-nosed pliers are also called *long-nosed pliers,* and they have tapered jaws that fit into snug areas or hold small objects.

707. **B. wire**

For the most part, you use *cutting pliers* to cut wire.

708. **B. serrated jaws**

Vise-grip pliers, or *wrench pliers,* have serrated jaws that are easier to clamp onto various objects.

709. **C. hexagonal**

You use an Allen wrench on hexagonal screws.

710. **B. open-end wrench**

Open-end wrenches have open jaws on either side.

711. **A. socket wrench**

A *socket wrench* has box-type sockets of different sizes; you use it to tighten and loosen nuts and bolts.

712. **B. c clamp**

This clamp gets its name from the C shape. You use clamps to secure objects you're working on so they don't move.

713. **C. ratchet handle**

A *ratchet handle* has a connector that you use to attach different sized sockets.

714. **A. metalwork**

This is a ball-peen hammer used mostly for metalwork.

715. **C. stop nut**

A *stop nut* is used to prevent the bolt or nut from coming loose.

716. **A. animal hide**

For many centuries, animal hide was used to make wood glue.

717. **D. all of the above**

Resin can be used to make many things, including lacquers, varnishes, inks, adhesives, and synthetic plastics.

718. **B. viscosity**

The *viscosity* of a fluid is a measure of its thickness.

719. **B. hinges**

This small wood screw works best for small hardware assembly, including hinges.

720. **B. pipe vise**

Pipe vises hold round trim or pipes.

721. **B. brads**

Brads have heads that are made to fit flush with or slightly below the fastening material.

722. **A. spikes**

Nails larger than 20 penny are called *spikes* and are measured in inches.

723. **B. nail size**

Nail length is measured by the penny system, which is abbreviated with a *d*.

724. **C. level**

A *level* is used to make sure things are level horizontally and vertically.

725. **C. square**

A *square* is used to measure horizontally and vertically.

726. **C. for small measurements**

Calipers are used to make small and exact measurements.

727. **B. depth of holes**

Depth gauges measure the depth of holes.

728. **C. edger**

An *edger* breaks off sharp concrete edges when concrete is firm but still moist.

729. **A. claw hammer**

A *claw hammer* is most commonly used to drive nails into timber.

730. **B. per 50 mm**

Saw teeth are measured by counting the number of teeth per 50 mm.

731. **B. 60 joules**

Work is the amount of energy transferred by a force. To calculate how much work is done, use this formula:

work = force × distance

work = (50 newtons)(1.2 meters)

work = 60 joules

732. **B. Output force requires input force to exist.**

Output force can be smaller or larger than input force. Input force can be equal to output force, but output force requires input force to exist.

733. **C. 5**

The mechanical advantage (MA) of a machine is equal to the ratio of the output force to the input force. Therefore,

$$MA = \frac{\text{output force}}{\text{input force}}$$

$$MA = \frac{250}{50}$$

$$MA = 5$$

734. **C. 2**

The mechanical advantage (MA) of a machine is equal to the ratio of the load to the effort, so

$$MA = \frac{60}{30}$$

$$MA = 2$$

735. **D. 3**

You need to use the formula for mechanical advantage to solve this one:

$$MA = \frac{\text{output force}}{\text{input force}}$$

$$MA = \frac{90}{30} = 3$$

736.

A. 6

The mechanical advantage of this system is equal to the ratio of the resistance force (F_R) to the effort force (F_E):

$$MA = \frac{F_R}{F_E}$$
$$MA = \frac{300}{50}$$
$$MA = 6$$

737.

A. output force divided by input force

Mechanical advantage measures the output force divided by the input force.

738.

C. They are acted upon by an unbalanced force.

Newton's first law of motion states that an object at rest tends to stay at rest (just as an object in motion tends to stay in motion) unless it's acted upon by an unbalanced force.

739.

B. 60 pounds

Let x = the force used. Convert 5 feet into 60 inches. (***Note:*** The remaining 9 inches of the length of the crowbar is on the opposite side of the fulcrum.) Sketch the lever:

Use the following lever equation, where F_1 is the force (weight) of the motor, d_1 is the motor's distance from the fulcrum, F_2 is the force Aaron applies, and d_2 is Aaron's distance from the fulcrum:

$$F_1 d_1 = F_2 d_2$$
$$400(9) = x(60)$$
$$3{,}600 = 60x$$
$$x = 60 \text{ pounds}$$

740.

C. Heavy objects have a greater amount of inertia.

Mass is a measure of inertia, which is how difficult it is to accelerate (change the speed and direction of) an object. A heavy object has more mass than a lighter object. Force = mass × acceleration, so the more mass an object has, the more force you need to get the object moving.

741.

C. 36 pounds

The force (F) required to stretch a spring is equal to its force constant (k) multiplied by the distance stretched (x):

$$F = kx$$
$$F = 3 \times 12$$
$$F = 36 \text{ pounds}$$

742. **A. gravity**

One kind of force is *gravity,* an attractive force between objects.

743. **C. 14**

The question gives you the force of 210 pounds and the area of 15 square inches. You have to find the pressure, which is measured in pounds per square inch (psi). Pressure is force divided by area, so plug in what you know:

$$p = \frac{F}{A} = \frac{210 \text{ lb}}{15 \text{ in}^2} = 14 \text{ psi}$$

744. **A. 200**

The formula for force on a spring is $F = -kx$, with F representing force, k representing the spring constant, and x representing the displacement of the spring. The spring is compressed so the displacement, 3 inches, is negative. Just plug in the values from the question and solve:

$$600 = -k(-3)$$
$$600 = 3k$$
$$\frac{600}{3} = \frac{3k}{3}$$
$$200 = k$$

745. **B. force**

In physics, *force* is defined as a push or pull.

746. **D. 135 pounds**

This question asks you how much force Jose must apply to lift a 405-pound block. Using the property of levers to solve this problem, set up the following equation, where F_1 is the force (weight) of the block, d_1 is the distance of the block from the fulcrum, F_2 is Jose's force, and d_2 is the distance of Jose from the fulcrum:

$$F_1 d_1 = F_2 d_2$$
$$405 \cdot 3 = F_2 \cdot 9$$
$$1,215 = 9F_2$$
$$135 = F_2$$

747.   **C. 40 pounds**

The question asks how much force is required to lift the weights. Because this question involves two weights, you have to work out the force required to lift each weight and then add them together to get the total force required. Set up the following equation:

$$F_1 d_1 + F_2 d_2 = F_3 d_3$$

On the left side of the equation, F_1 is the first weight (force), d_1 is the distance of the first weight from the fulcrum, F_2 is the second weight, and d_2 is the distance of the second weight from the fulcrum. On the right side of the equation, F_3 is the force used to lift the weights, and d_3 is the distance from the force to the fulcrum.

When you plug in the numbers, you get the following:

$$(25 \cdot 10) + (30 \cdot 5) = F_3(10)$$
$$\frac{(25 \cdot 10) + (30 \cdot 5)}{10} = F_3$$
$$\frac{250 + 150}{10} = F_3$$
$$40 \text{ pounds} = F_3$$

748.   **B. 395.2 joules**

The equation for work is

work = force × distance.

Substitute Mrs. Nelson's force and the distance she moves the cart into the equation to find out how much work she does. Remember that work is measured in joules.

$$W = 26 \cdot 15.2$$
$$W = 395.2 \text{ joules}$$

749.   **C. 245 newtons**

For this problem, you're given the mechanical advantage of 3.5 and the input force of 70, and you have to find the output force. Set up the following equation for mechanical advantage and solve for x:

$$MA = \frac{\text{output force}}{\text{input force}}$$
$$3.5 = \frac{x}{70}$$
$$x = 70 \times 3.5$$
$$x = 245 \text{ newtons}$$

750. **D. 5 N**

In tug of war, the teams are applying force against each other. So you simply subtract the smaller of the forces from the larger to find the net force:

force = 90 N – 85 N

force = 5 N

751. **D. 20 newtons**

Work equals force times distance. The question gives you the amount of work done as 70 joules and the distance as 3.5 meters. Using the equation, substitute these values and solve for force:

$$W = Fd$$

$$70 = F(3.5)$$

$$\frac{70}{3.5} = \frac{F(3.5)}{3.5}$$

$$F = 20 \text{ newtons}$$

752. **B. gravity**

The force of gravity pulls objects back to Earth.

753. **A. 2,200 newtons**

To find the force applied in this situation, use the equation for work, where W = work, F = force, and d = distance. Then solve for F:

$$W = Fd$$

$$F = \frac{W}{d}$$

$$F = \frac{55,000}{25}$$

$$F = 2,200 \text{ newtons}$$

754. **C. 1,250 newtons**

Use the formula for work to solve this problem, where W is work, F is force, and d is distance:

$$W = Fd$$

$$F = \frac{W}{d}$$

$$F = \frac{25,000}{20}$$

$$F = 1,250 \text{ newtons}$$

755. **D. Five times as large**

A hydraulic jack uses an incompressible fluid, so the pressure has to be the same everywhere ($P_1 = P_2$). *Pressure* is force divided by area ($P = F/A$), so set up a proportion that represents the equal pressures:

$$P_1 = P_2$$

$$\frac{F_1}{A_1} = \frac{F_2}{A_2}$$

If the area at the output end of the jack is five times the area where James is applying the force, then the exerted force is five times the applied force:

$$\frac{F_1}{A_1} = \frac{5F_1}{5A_1}$$

Force is greater where the area is greater.

756. **B. 560 newtons**

To find the output force, simply rearrange the formula for mechanical advantage, plug in the given values, and solve:

$$MA = \frac{\text{output force}}{\text{input force}}$$

output force $= MA \cdot$ input force

output force $= (7)(80)$

output force $= 560$

Force is measured in newtons; therefore, the answer is 560 newtons, Choice (B).

757. **C. 6 feet**

The equation for a lever is weight$_1$ × distance$_1$ = weight$_2$ × distance$_2$. Let x = the distance of Jimmy from the fulcrum and $10 - x$ = the distance of Jolene from the fulcrum.

Set up and solve the following equation for x and then plug that number into the equation for Jolene's distance from the fulcrum ($10 - x$) to find the answer:

$$90(x) = 60(10 - x)$$

$$90x = 600 - 60x$$

$$150x = 600$$

$$x = 4$$

Jolene $= 10 - x$

Jolene $= 10 - 4$

Jolene $= 6$ feet

758. **B. 480 kilograms**

The question states that James was using "effort" to lift 80 kilograms without any mechanical advantage.

James is going to use a simple six-pulley system, which has a total of seven ropes — six within the pulley system supporting the load and the one James is applying downward force to. James's mechanical advantage will equal the number of supporting rope sections, and the effort force he is applying is still 80 kilograms. Let x = the maximum load that James can lift.

$$MA = \frac{load}{effort}$$

$$6 = \frac{x}{80}$$

$$6 \cdot 80 = x$$

$$480 = x$$

759. **A. 23.99**

To find the mechanical advantage of the block and tackle, use the following formula:

$$MA = \frac{output\ force}{input\ force}$$

$$MA = \frac{7,406}{308.6} = 23.99$$

760. **B. energy**

Motion is simply a movement, and *pressurization* refers to the process by which atmospheric pressure is maintained in an isolated or semi-isolated atmospheric environment. *Heat* is a form of energy, and it's measured in *calories*.

761. **B. oil is less dense than water.**

When two *immiscible* liquids (liquids that don't mix together) of different densities combine, the one that's less dense always floats to the top.

762. **B. Ball B will reach the bottom first.**

The steeper the ramp, the greater the acceleration of the ball. Because the rise is larger for ball B, it'll take less time to roll down the slope.

763. **C. pushing a couch across the room**

All the other examples involve using objects to gain a mechanical advantage.

764. **C. kilograms**

A *kilogram* is a unit that measures mass.

765.   **C. 405**

Two-thirds of the weight of the block (400 pounds) is supported by the left scale because the block is 2/3 closer to the left than to the right. The board is evenly placed, so each scale supports 1/2 of its weight (5 pounds). So the total weight being supported by the left scale is 400 pounds + 5 pounds = 405 pounds.

766.   **A. 20**

To find out how many revolutions Gear B makes, multiply the number of teeth and the number of revolutions for Gear A. This equals the number of teeth times the number of revolutions for Gear B. Then just plug in the values from the question:

$$\text{Teeth A}(\text{Rev A}) = \text{Teeth B}(\text{Rev B})$$
$$12 \cdot 10 = 6(\text{Rev B})$$
$$120 = 6(\text{Rev B})$$
$$20 = \text{Rev B}$$

767.   **B. also decreased his speed of travel.**

The smaller gear has to turn more revolutions than a larger gear to cover the same distance, so the bike's speed also decreases.

768.   **A. 4.2 feet**

Let x = Mr. Roth's distance from the fulcrum.

$$200 \cdot x = (80 \cdot 3) + (60 \cdot 5) + (50 \cdot 6)$$
$$200x = 240 + 300 + 300$$
$$200x = 840$$
$$x = 4.2 \text{ feet}$$

769.   **A. 30 newtons**

You determine the mechanical advantage of a ramp by dividing the output force by the effort or input force. Set up the equation like this and solve for x:

$$\text{MA} = \frac{\text{output force}}{\text{input force}}$$
$$6 = \frac{180}{x}$$
$$6x = 180$$
$$x = 30 \text{ newtons}$$

770. C. 11.2

The construction crew is lifting, or has an output force of, 560 pounds. The block and tackle requires an input force of 50 pounds. To find the mechanical advantage, set up the following equation and solve:

$$MA = \frac{\text{output force}}{\text{input force}}$$

$$MA = \frac{560}{50}$$

$$MA = 11.2$$

771. D. 147.27 pounds

The question tells you that the load is placed 12 feet from the fulcrum and the effort arm is 11 feet long. Assign x to Kenneth's force and use the following property of levers equation to solve this problem:

$$F_1 \bullet d_1 = F_2 \bullet d_2$$

$$x \bullet 11 = 135 \bullet 12$$

$$11x = 1,620$$

$$x = 147.2727...$$

Round the answer to 147.27. Therefore, the answer is 147.27 pounds.

772. B. 70 pounds

Find the mechanical advantage of an inclined plane by dividing the length of the slope by the height. In this case,

$$MA = \frac{9 \text{ feet}}{3 \text{ feet}} = 3$$

To find the effort required to move the 210-pound object, you simply divide the weight by the mechanical advantage:

$$\frac{210}{3} = 70 \text{ pounds}$$

Therefore, you need 70 pounds of effort.

773. C. 2 newtons right

The girls are applying force on the doll in opposite directions. To find the net force, subtract the force toward Sandy from the force toward Sara:

force = 7 newtons – 5 newtons = 2 newtons

Sara is pulling harder, so the net force is 2 newtons right.

774. B. The steel beam will deflect less than the wood beam.

Beams bend under force, which is known as *deflection*. Concrete is stiffer than wood, so it'll deflect less than wood. Steel is stiffer than wood and concrete, so it'll deflect less than concrete and wood.

775. B. B

Mechanical advantage of a ramp is determined by its length divided by its height. Ramp B is much longer (and the slope is much shallower), so it provides a greater mechanical advantage and requires less force to raise the barrel.

776. C. the same amount of work as Devon

Work equals force times distance. A simple machine can make work easier by allowing you to use less force, but the amount of work you do doesn't change. When Elliot uses the ramp, he uses less force but has to travel a greater distance than Devon, so the amount of work is the same.

777. A. The volume of the balloon would decrease.

The pressure of the water would press inward on the balloon and cause it to decrease in volume.

778. C. 3.6 meters

You know that Albert and his friends applied 489.5 newtons of force and did 1,762.2 joules of work. Set up the equation for work like so and solve for d, or distance (W stands for work and F stands for force):

$$W = Fd$$
$$d = \frac{W}{F}$$
$$d = \frac{1,762.2 \text{ joules}}{489.5 \text{ newtons}}$$
$$d = 3.6 \text{ meters}$$

779. D. 35,350 joules

Use the formula for work to answer this question:

$$\text{work} = \text{force} \times \text{distance}$$
$$\text{work} = 1,010 \text{ newtons} \times 35 \text{ meters}$$
$$\text{work} = 35,350 \text{ joules}$$

780. C. 5

To find the mechanical advantage of the lever, simply substitute the given values into the following formula:

$$\text{MA} = \frac{\text{length of input arm}}{\text{length of output arm}}$$
$$\text{MA} = \frac{5}{1}$$
$$\text{MA} = 5$$

781. **C. Both A and B.**

Two key concepts in hydraulics are that liquids are incompressible and that they maintain the same pressure in a closed system.

782. **D. 4**

Simply substitute the given values into the formula for mechanical advantage:

$$MA = \frac{\text{input arm}}{\text{output arm}}$$

$$MA = \frac{3}{0.75}$$

$$MA = 4$$

783. **D. All three cubes will either float or sink.**

Each block may have a different size and weight, but because all of them are made from the same material, they will have the same density. An object's density determines whether it will float or sink.

784. **D. 425.25 joules**

To find out how much work Paul does, use the following formula, where W = work, P = power, and t = time:

$$W = Pt$$

$$W = (40.5 \text{ watts})(10.5 \text{ seconds})$$

$$W = 425.25$$

Work is measured in joules; therefore, your answer is 425.25 joules.

785. **A. equilibrium**

When an object is at equilibrium, it has equal forces acting on it. When both people on a seesaw weigh the same, the seesaw is in equilibrium.

786. **A. a pogo stick**

Of the items listed, only a pogo stick uses springs.

787. **D. a temperature gauge**

This gauge shows degrees in Fahrenheit and in Celsius, so you can see that it measures temperature.

788. **C. 6,000 joules**

Use substitution and the formula for work to find the answer:

$$\text{work} = \text{force} \times \text{distance}$$

$$\text{work} = 30 \text{ newtons} \times 200 \text{ meters}$$

$$\text{work} = 6{,}000 \text{ joules}$$

789. **C. elasticity**

Shock absorbers have springs that can stretch but then return to their original shape, just like elastic-waist pants. This property is known as *elasticity*.

790. **B. 1 meter**

You are asked to find the length of the broom's output arm. You are given that the input arm has a length of 0.5 meters and that the broom is providing a mechanical advantage of 0.5. Use the formula for mechanical advantage and substitute the given information to find the answer.

$$MA = \frac{input\ arm\ length}{output\ arm\ length}$$

$$0.5 = \frac{0.5}{x}$$

$$0.5x = 0.5$$

$$x = 1\ meter$$

791. **B. work**

The formula for work is $W = Fd$, where W = work, F = force, and d = distance. When you apply force to an object, making it move from point A to point B, you're doing work on that object.

792. **D. 0.255 meters**

Set up the formula for mechanical advantage and solve for the input arm length:

$$MA = \frac{input\ arm\ length}{output\ arm\ length}$$

$$0.3 = \frac{input\ arm\ length}{0.85}$$

$$(0.3)(0.85) = input\ arm\ length$$

$$0.255 = input\ arm\ length$$

793. **B. 0 joules**

You know the force Bobby applies and the distance the dog moved (which was 0). Plug these numbers into the equation for work, where W = work, F = force, and d = distance and solve for w:

$$W = F \cdot d$$

$$W = 2,500 \cdot 0$$

$$W = 0$$

Because Bobby was unable to move the dog (the distance was 0), he didn't do any measureable work.

794. **B. 225,000 joules**

Substitute the given values into the equation for work and solve:

work = force × distance

work = (3,000)(75)

work = 225,000 joules

795. **A. 1,100 feet per second**

Although the speed of sound is 1,100 feet per second at sea level with static conditions, it varies with altitude, air density, and temperature.

796. **C. It will continue forward.**

Since both balls are moving at the same speed, the ball with more mass (the larger one in this case, because both balls have the same density) will have more momentum. Upon impact, the heavier ball will slow down but continue in the same direction and knock the smaller, lighter ball backward.

797. **D. 2.5 meters**

It really doesn't matter how many people were involved in moving the furniture because the question gives you the combined force of 425 newtons and the total work of 1,062.5 joules. To find the distance, simply plug these numbers into the following formula:

$$\text{work} = \text{force} \times \text{distance}$$

$$\text{distance} = \frac{\text{work}}{\text{force}}$$

$$\text{distance} = \frac{1,062.5}{425}$$

$$\text{distance} = 2.5 \text{ meters}$$

798. **A. A**

Two magnets are attracted by their opposite poles, and each magnet will repel the like pole of the other magnet.

799. **D. deceleration**

Deceleration means the act of slowing down.

800. **D. all of the above**

You consider acceleration to design the maximum rise of the first hill, momentum to ensure the train gets back to the starting point (since it has no motor), and friction to design the braking system.

801.   **A. to move liquids uphill**

Pumps aren't used to move liquids downhill because liquids flow downhill by gravity. Also, pumps don't separate or clarify liquids; instead, they agitate and mix them. By process of elimination, Choice (A) is your answer.

802.   **B. 20**

If a pulley is fixed (not moving), then the force required to pull the cord is equal to the weight of the object being pulled. A fixed pulley has a mechanical advantage of 1, which means it doesn't provide a mechanical advantage. The advantage of a fixed pulley is that it changes the direction of the force.

803.   **B. It stays the same.**

Using a machine doesn't change the work; it just makes the work easier to do.

804.   **A. Pulley 2 would spin faster than Pulley 4.**

In a series of pulleys, the larger the pulley, the slower it will turn.

805.   **C. Tank C**

Tank C has an inflow greater than its outflow, so it will eventually overfill.

806.   **B. 2**

In this problem, you're pulling the rope 4 meters and moving the weight 2 meters. Simply substitute these values into the mechanical advantage formula and solve:

$$MA = \frac{\text{input distance}}{\text{output distance}}$$
$$MA = \frac{4}{2}$$
$$MA = 2$$

807.   **B. 15 centimeters**

You find the mechanical advantage of a lever by dividing the length of the input arm (the arm you exert effort on) by the length of the output arm (the part of the lever holding the load). Therefore, you can set up the following equation and solve for x:

$$MA = \frac{\text{length of input arm}}{\text{length of output arm}}$$
$$4 = \frac{60}{x}$$
$$4x = 60$$
$$x = 15$$

808. **D. 150 newtons**

You determine the mechanical advantage by dividing the output force by the input force. In this case, you know the mechanical advantage and have to find the input force, so set up the following equation and solve for x:

$$MA = \frac{\text{output force}}{\text{input force}}$$
$$4 = \frac{600}{x}$$
$$4x = 600$$
$$x = 150 \text{ newtons}$$

809. **C. 20 pounds**

You can tell from the figure that the pulley is movable (not fixed), so each side of the rope is pulling half the weight. (That's why you can count both sections of rope in your calculations.) Unlike a fixed pulley, which simply changes the direction of the force, a movable pulley like this one provides a mechanical advantage. To solve this problem, divide the weight of Y by the number of supporting ropes:

$$\frac{40}{2} = 20 \text{ pounds}$$

810. **A. counterclockwise 5 rotations**

Gear A has 20 teeth. Gear B has 10 teeth. Therefore, Gear A will turn half as fast as Gear B. Because Gear A is rotating counterclockwise and there's a gear between them rotating clockwise, Gear B will also rotate counterclockwise.

811. **B. 6**

Set up the following mechanical advantage formula with the values from the question:

$$MA = \frac{\text{output force}}{\text{input force}}$$
$$MA = \frac{24}{4}$$
$$MA = 6$$

812. **B. 50 pounds**

To find the force or tension needed to hold the weight in equilibrium, you divide the weight of the weight by the number of supporting rope sections in the pulley system. The pulley shown has 4 rope sections supporting the 200-pound weight (the section you pull doesn't count because you pull it downward, so it doesn't help hold up the weight). Therefore, the equation looks like this:

$$\frac{200}{4} = 50 \text{ pounds}$$

813. **D. bearings**

A set of bearings is typically a set of small metal balls packed in a groove and lubricated with grease or oil. The wheel rubs against one side of each ball, and the axle rubs against the other side. The effect is that the wheel rolls much more easily.

814. **B. a crane**

An elevator is a crane that raises and lowers people.

815. **B. Gear A turns in a counterclockwise direction at a slower speed.**

Gears are used to reverse the direction of rotation, so the two gears turn in opposite directions. The smaller the gear, the faster it rotates. Therefore, the only answer that can be correct is Choice (B) — that Gear A turns in a counterclockwise direction at a slower speed.

816. **B. 450 kilograms**

The mechanical advantage of a pulley system is equal to the number of supporting ropes present at the weight end. A five-pulley system has a mechanical advantage of 5 and makes the work five times easier. To find the maximum load that David could lift with a mechanical advantage of 5, you simply multiply 5 times his effort of 90 kilograms to get the correct answer of 450 kilograms.

817. **D. It changes the direction in which Pulley Y turns.**

Crossbelts change the direction of the objects they connect.

818. **B. 320 rpm**

Each full turn of the pedals turns the rear wheel $48 \div 12 = 4$ revolutions.

If the pedals were to turn at 80 rpm, the rear wheel would rotate at 4×80 rpm = 320 rpm.

819. **D. 6 pounds**

You pull downward on the rope, so that rope section doesn't help support the weight. For this reason, you count only four of the ropes in your calculations; you don't count the rope on which you exert the force. Here's what your equation looks like:

$$\text{force} = \frac{\text{load}}{\text{number of ropes}}$$
$$\text{force} = \frac{24}{4}$$
$$\text{force} = 6$$

820. **C. friction**

When the brakes are applied, the brake pads rub on the wheel, and the frictional force of this rubbing slows down the vehicle.

821. B. B

To find the mechanical advantage of a lever, divide the length of the effort arm (the one you apply a force to) by the length of the resistance arm (the one carrying the weight):

$$MA = \frac{\text{length of effort arm}}{\text{length of resistance arm}}$$

The effort arms are the same length, but you get a greater mechanical advantage with handle B because the resistance arm is shorter (the weight is closer to the fulcrum). Therefore, lifting handle B requires less force.

822. A. gear

A bicycle sprocket is a *gear,* which is a toothed wheel or cylinder that meshes with a chain or with another toothed element to transfer energy or motion.

823. D. Liquid flows out of Pipe B four times as fast.

The area of a circle is π times the radius squared. Pipe A has a radius of 1 inch, and Pipe B has a radius of 2 inches, so the areas of the pipe openings are as follows:

Pipe A = $\pi(1)^2 = \pi$

Pipe B = $\pi(2)^2 = 4\pi$

The rates at which liquid flows out of the pipes is equal to the ratio of the areas of their openings:

$$\frac{B}{A} = \frac{4\pi}{\pi} = 4$$

Water flows out of Pipe B four times faster than Pipe A.

824. D. 120 rpm

To solve for revolutions per minute, set up the given information in a chart like so:

	Gear A	Gear B	Gear C
Teeth	20	60	10
Revolutions per minute	60		

In this system, the number of revolutions per minute multiplied by the number of teeth is equal for all gears. Therefore,

$$(\text{rpm}_A)(\text{teeth}_A) = (\text{rpm}_C)(\text{teeth}_C)$$
$$60(20) = (\text{rpm}_C)10$$
$$1{,}200 = (\text{rpm}_C)10$$
$$\text{rpm}_C = 120$$

825.

C. It changes the direction of the effort.

You change the direction of the applied force. With a fixed pulley, you can raise a load by pulling downward.

826.

D. 4

In this pulley system, you count only the four cables that support the load — not the cable on which the force is exerted — to find the mechanical advantage.

Because the weight of the load is spread over four cables, the mechanical advantage is 4.

827.

C. 1,200 pounds

You have to figure out how much force the 12-foot cable must apply to lift an 800-pound object. To solve this problem, set up the following properties of levers equation, where W_1 is the weight of the object, d_1 is the distance of the object from the crane, W_2 is the force the cable needs to apply, and d_2 is the distance of the cable from the object:

$$W_1 \cdot d_1 = W_2 \cdot d_2$$
$$800 \cdot 18 = W_2 \cdot 12$$
$$14,400 = 12W_2$$
$$1,200 = W_2$$

828.

D. 20 rpm

The circumference of Pulley A is three times that of Pulley B, so Pulley B has to complete 3 revolutions per 1 revolution of Pulley A. Therefore, Pulley A has to complete $\frac{60}{3} = 20$ revolutions.

829.

A. 9 inches

The 12-pound weight compresses the first spring like so:

12 pounds ÷ 2 pounds per inch = 6 inches

It compresses the second spring like so:

12 pounds ÷ 6 pounds per inch = 2 inches

Finally, it compresses the third spring like so:

12 pounds ÷ 12 pounds per inch = 1 inch

The total amount the platform compresses is 6 + 2 + 1 = 9 inches.

830.

C. metal

Metal would make the best boat anchor because it's both dense and strong.

831. **B. 6 feet**

Every foot that Block A is lowered raises Block B by the same amount. To equalize the 12-foot difference, Block A must be lowered 6 feet:

12 feet ÷ 2 = 6 feet

832. **A. 300**

You can find the mechanical advantage of a movable pulley by counting the number of ropes that lift the load. The mechanical advantage of the movable pulley shown is 2. Therefore, you simply multiply Susan's maximum force by 2 to get the answer:

150 pounds × 2 = 300 pounds

833. **D. all of the above**

Any of these sources can provide mechanical energy to a pump.

834. **A. 51,200 joules**

To find out how much work the crane did, substitute the given values into the equation for work, like so:

work = force × distance

work = (1,024 newtons)(50 meters)

work = 51,200 joules

835. **C. 4 feet**

First, determine the mechanical advantage of the ramp by using this formula:

$$MA = \frac{\text{output force}}{\text{input force}} = \frac{320}{80} = 4$$

The mechanical advantage of the ramp is also equal to the length of the ramp (16 feet) divided by the height of the ramp (x feet). Thus, the height of the ramp is 4 feet.

836. **B. 5 rpm**

Gear C is four times the diameter of Gear A. Therefore, Gear C must be turning four times slower than Gear A:

20 ÷ 4 = 5 rpm

837.   A. 6

To solve this problem, use the formula for mechanical advantage:

$$MA = \frac{\text{output force}}{\text{input force}}$$

$$MA = \frac{480}{80}$$

$$MA = 6$$

In this case, the mechanical advantage equals the number of pulleys you need.

838.   A. 2 meters

Use the formula for mechanical advantage to solve this problem. Simply rearrange the formula so you're solving for the output arm's length, like so:

$$MA = \frac{\text{input arm length}}{\text{output arm length}}$$

$$4 = \frac{8}{x}$$

$$4x = 8$$

$$x = 2$$

839.   A. 20

To solve this problem, set up a ratio of the gear teeth:

$$\frac{\text{teeth on Gear A}}{\text{teeth on Gear B}} = \frac{20}{10} = 2$$

This means that for each revolution of Gear A, Gear B makes 2 revolutions. Multiply Gear A's 10 revolutions by 2, and you get 20 revolutions for Gear B.

840.   A. potential

The swing stores energy as the result of its position, or height above the ground. This stored energy of position is referred to as *potential energy*. The swing isn't moving at the top of its arc, so it doesn't have any kinetic energy.

841.   B. pulley

Gene raises a flag up a flagpole by using a single fixed pulley, which changes the direction of the force Gene applies.

842.   D. hydrostatic

Hydrostatic pressure is the pressure exerted by a fluid at equilibrium due to the force of gravity.

843. **B. B**

The fluid leaving the can must be replaced by air. The fluid trying to leave the can with only one hole is fighting a vacuum that's being created at the highest point in the can when you tilt it to pour. Putting a second hole in the can allows air to be sucked into the can to replace the volume of liquid being poured out, allowing the liquid to pour more easily.

844. **B. Use two gears of different sizes.**

When a gear with more teeth is connected to a gear with fewer teeth, the one with fewer teeth turns faster but with less force. As a result, the machine that contains the gears increases speed because the gear with fewer teeth is turning faster.

Changing gears on a bicycle is a good example of using different sized gears to change your speed.

845. **A. to control the flow of a liquid**

Valves are placed in piping systems and can be opened or closed to control the flow of liquids or gasses.

846. **C. volts**

The amount of work done per unit charge when electrons move between two points is measured in *volts*.

847. **A. resistance**

The *ohm* measures resistance, including anything that could limit the flow of electrons.

848. **B. transistor**

A *transistor* is a semiconductor device used to amplify electronic signals.

849. **A. hertz**

The number of *hertz* equals the number of cycles per second of frequency.

850. **D. all of the above**

An *amplifier* is a complex circuit used to magnify current, voltage, and power.

851. **A. doorbell**

A doorbell is a transducer that converts electrical energy to sound.

852. **C. 30 microfarads**

µF is the symbol for microfarad, which is used to rate capacitors.

853.   **A. variable resistor**

A variable resistor, such as a radio tuner, has an *element* that provides resistance and a movable component called a *wiper* that sets the resistance.

854.   **B. voltage rating**

The standard set by a voltage rating greatly reduces the risk of damage and fire.

855.   **A. conductor**

A *conductor* is a substance that conducts an electrical charge; a wire is just one example.

856.   **D. transformer**

A *transformer* transfers electrical voltage from one place to another in increasing or decreasing amounts, as needed.

857.   **D. all of the above**

Any metal can be a conductor of heat and electricity. All of the ones listed are silvery and highly reactive conductors.

858.   **D. watts**

Power is measured in watts.

859.   **B. kilowatt-hours**

Electrical energy is usually measured in kilowatt-hours.

860.   **C. voltage**

Voltage is another word for electromotive force.

861.   **A. One opposes changes in voltage, and the other opposes changes in current.**

Capacitive reactance is an opposition to the change in voltage across an element. *Inductive reactance* is an opposition to the change in current on an inductive element.

862.   **A. chemical effect**

Current produces this effect when it passes through a chemical compound and breaks it down.

863.   **B. heat effect**

Heat develops when conducting electricity because the current must overcome the resistance of the wire.

864. **C. magnetic effect**

When a wire is wrapped around an iron core and a current is sent through the wire, the iron becomes magnetized.

865. **D. physiological effect**

Current produces this effect when it passes through a muscle and causes it to contract.

866. **B. a transistor**

A *transistor* controls the flow of electricity in a circuit by using an emitter (voltage output), a base (the control), and the collector (voltage input).

867. **C. Ohm's law**

Ohm's law says $I = \dfrac{V}{R}$, where I is current, V is voltage, and R is resistance.

According to this law, the current in a circuit is directly proportional to the applied voltage and inversely proportional to the circuit resistance.

868. **D. motor**

If you know kinetic energy is linked to motion, you can correctly choose Choice (D), motor.

869. **D. 1,000,000 hertz**

Most electronic devices operate at high frequencies, measured in hertz. A *megahertz* (MHz) is a measurement of 1,000,000 hertz.

870. **A. Yes.**

The illustration shows a correct connection of two batteries and a light bulb.

871. **D. semiconductor**

A *semiconductor* is a complex device, usually made of silicon, that is often found in small electronics, such as cellphones. A semiconductor conducts more electricity than an insulator but less than aluminum and copper.

872. **B. a storage compartment for electricity in a battery**

The cells in a battery hold equal amounts of voltage; just how much depends on their size and construction.

873. **D. lamp**

A *filament* is the fine wire heated electrically to incandescence in an electric lamp.

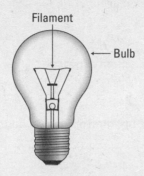

874. **B. ohms**

The amount of resistance that interferes with the flow is measured in *ohms*. The symbol used is the Greek letter omega, Ω.

875. **C. 120**

Watt-hours are measured by multiplying the amount of wattage by the hours used, so $40 \times 3 = 120$.

876. **B. magnetic flux**

Magnetic flux is the magnetic strength on a plane, like on one side of a magnet.

877. **C. lines of force**

In a wire, magnetic lines of force are perpendicular to the conductor and parallel to each other.

878. **D. all of the above**

You can increase magnetic field strength in a coil by increasing the number of coils, the number of turns, and the amount of current.

879. **A. static**

A *static* electrical charge is created whenever two surfaces come together and then separate, trapping electrical charges on the surface of the object.

880. C. comparator

Comparators compare voltage or current so a device can determine how much more (or less) is needed to perform a particular function.

881. C. germanium

Transistors are usually made of germanium or silicon.

882. A. air or iron

Most coils are either classified as air or soft iron, based on their cores.

883. C. a variable resistor

A *potentiometer* is a variable resistor with three contacts that are used to control voltage.

884. B. thermistors

A *thermistor* is a type of resistor that varies resistance significantly based on surrounding, fluctuating temperatures.

885. A. a resistor

A *flex sensor* is a resistor that changes its resistance based on being bent or flexed.

886. B. the path of a current

A *circuit* is the path of an electrical current.

887. B. short circuit

A *short circuit* occurs when electricity bypasses the circuit instead of following the intended path.

888. C. circuit breaker

A *circuit breaker* automatically interrupts electrical current.

889. D. circuit

A *circuit* is a closed path followed or capable of being followed by an electric current.

890. B. load

A *load* consumes the electricity from a circuit and converts it into work.

891.   **B. series**

A *series circuit* (perhaps the simplest type of circuit) can follow only one possible path.

892.   **C. The current running through the circuit generates too much heat.**

Although a circuit breaker can trip for many reasons, ultimately it does so for protection against generated heat from the electrical current.

893.   **C. Circuit B has brighter bulbs than Circuit A.**

When the bulbs are connected in parallel rather than in series, the total resistance in the circuit is lower. Therefore, each bulb in Circuit B receives more current and consumes more power, leading to brighter bulbs.

894.   **B. The flashbulb is turned off.**

When the switch is in contact with point A (as shown), the charges are being stored. When the switch moves to point B, the flashbulb turns on.

895.   **A. diode**

A *diode* was once called a *valve,* and it allows electricity to flow in one direction.

896.   **B. fuse**

This symbol represents a fuse; the circuit doesn't contain a fuse.

897.   **C. 3**

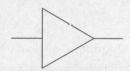

This symbol represents an amplifier. The simple differential amplifier circuit contains 3 amplifiers.

898.   **A. lamp**

The circuit diagram shows symbols for a battery, a switch, and a light source, consistent with a lamp circuit.

899. **B. transformer**

This symbol represents a transformer. According to the diagram, there are two circuits connected by one transformer. There are three resistors and many joined wires used to assemble this fluorescent lamp.

900. **C. ground**

Ground is any part of a circuit that measures 0 volts.

901. **A. resistance**

Resistance is set up in a circuit to regulate the electricity so the device isn't destroyed by electrical heat.

902. **A. It absorbs the electrical current.**

A *rheostat* can vary the resistance without opening the circuit by absorbing some of the electrical current flowing through it. (Think of a dimming light switch.)

903. **C. ammeter**

Current meters, called *ammeters,* measure the flow of current through a circuit.

904. **C. 100**

There are 100 ohms in this simple circuit. The symbol for ohms is Ω, and ohms measure resistance.

905. **B. voltmeter**

A *voltmeter* is an instrument used for measuring electrical potential difference between two points in an electrical circuit.

906. **C. voltmeter, ammeter, resistor, and cell**

The circuit consists of a voltmeter, an ammeter, a resistor, and a cell.

907. **D. lighting system**

This schematic is a closed circuit that includes a battery and three indicator lamps.

908. **B. It produces sound.**

You can conclude that the device produces sound because there's a speaker on the circuit:

909. **B. an intercom**

The schematic shown is for a two-way intercom. A close look reveals two speakers, one at the beginning and one at the end of the circuit.

910. **D. 0 volts**

Each component in the circuit offers resistance, lowering the amount of voltage as it passes. After the current makes one loop around the circuit, there's no voltage left.

911. **C. circuit analysis**

Circuit analysis is the process of finding the current and voltage of every component in an electrical circuit.

912. **B. The voltage is applied evenly to each branch.**

In a parallel circuit, the current is divided unevenly to each branch, and the voltage is applied evenly.

913. **A. The series completely breaks.**

In a series, all the components must function in order for the circuit to work. A good way to remember a series circuit is to think of Christmas lights. When one bulb comes out, the circuit becomes open and can't provide current to the other lights.

914. **B. The remaining components still work.**

In a parallel circuit, each light has its own circuit, so if a bulb blows, the remaining components are still able to function. A good way to remember a parallel circuit is to think of a light switch in your home that turns on multiple lights. If one bulb goes out, the other lights will still function.

915. D. electric current

An *electric current* occurs when electrons move from one place to another.

916. B. current

The *ampere,* or *amp,* is a unit of electric current.

917. B. rheostat

A *rheostat* is a type of variable resistor with two contacts usually used to control current.

918. B. magnetic field

When a magnetic field is near a wire, activating the field's repelling and attracting qualities, it causes the electrons to flow in a direct current.

919. B. rectification

Rectification occurs in certain electronic circuits that need to change incoming AC to DC in order to run properly.

920. C. fuse

A *fuse* is a safety device that "blows" if the current is too much for the components.

921. B. frequency

Frequency, measured in hertz (Hz), is the number of times an alternating current changes direction per second.

922. C. wood

Wood is a type of insulator that discourages electrons from moving freely.

923. C. electrical current

Coulombs are units of electrical charge, and a *battery cell* produces a certain electrical voltage. *Electrical current* is the term used for the rate of flow of electrons in a conductor. *Amperes* (amps) are the units you use to measure current; an amp equals 1 coulomb per second.

924. B. ampere

Amperes (amps) measure the number of electrons that move past a specific point in one second.

925. D. ammeters

Ammeters, or *current meters,* measure the flow of current through a circuit.

926. B. insulator

An *insulator* (like wood, rubber, or air) doesn't conduct electric current and, in many cases, prevents the flow of electrons.

927. C. converts AC to DC

The purpose of a rectifier is to change alternating current (AC) to direct current (DC).

928. A. impedance

Impedance is an opposition to the flow of electrons in an AC circuit. It's a combination of resistance, capacitive reactance, and inductive reactance. You can express impedance as the ratio of electromotive force (voltage) to current.

929. B. alternating current

Higher voltages are easier to transport and create using alternating current, so most electricity is created using this method.

930. B. capacitor

A *capacitor* is a passive two-terminal electrical component used to store energy in an electric field. When a capacitor is faced with an increasing voltage, it acts as a load by drawing current as it absorbs energy.

931. A. Voltage Alternating Current

VAC is an acronym for *Voltage Alternating Current* and is usually abbreviated next to a measurement of volts, indicating the power of battery in a household product.

932. A. from negative to positive

In conventional flow notation, the motion of charge is shown according to the (technically incorrect) labels of + and –, with the electric charge moving from positive to negative. But in electron flow notation, the actual motion of electrons in the circuit is followed. Negative electrons are always searching for positive charges, so current flows from a negative pole to a positive pole.

933. B. allows the current to flow in one direction

A *diode* is a two-terminal electric component that allows electricity to flow in one direction or changes alternating current to direct current.

934. C. total current

Voltage is equal between two resistors in parallel, but the current is divided between them. The divided current is equal to the total current.

935. **C. ground**

The symbol represents ground, which provides a good return path for electrons.

936. **A. resistor**

The symbol represents a resistor. This device provides *resistance,* which opposes electrical current.

937. **B. direct current**

The symbol represents direct current (DC), which is the unidirectional flow of electrical charge.

938. **B. relay**

The symbol represents a relay switch, which is an electrically operated switch that can operate multiple switches at one time.

939. **C. joined wires**

The symbol represents joined wires, which are used to pass current from one part of the circuit to another.

940. **D. all of the above**

The first two colors indicate the first two digits of the value, while the third represents the number of zeros. A gold or silver indicates tolerance, while anything following would represent quality.

941. **B. unjoined wires**

The symbol represents unjoined wires in a circuit.

942. **C. black is 0, white is 9**

The band code lists black at 0 value and white at 9 value.

943. **A. transistor**

The symbol represents a transistor, which controls the flow of electricity in a circuit.

944. **C. amplifier**

The symbol represents an amplifier, which is a complex circuit used to magnify power, current, or voltage.

945. **C. buzzer**

The symbol represents a buzzer, which is a transducer that converts electrical energy to sound.

946. **D. green**

A green-colored wire signifies that it's a protective ground wire.

947. **C. gray**

Red, black, and blue wires are always "hot" and should never be tampered with unless the power is off. The gray wire is a neutral, earth-connected wire.

948. **A. white**

Blue, yellow, and orange wires are used as three- and four-way switch applications; they become hot when turned on.

949. **C. It may conduct electricity.**

In some cases, a neutral wire may be used as a live wire, so black tape is wrapped around the end to alert electricians that it may be conducting electricity.

950. **B. lamps**

The symbol with the X represents an indicator lamp, while the symbol with a half-circle represents a lighting lamp.

951. **C. variable**

A variable resistor is a potentiometer with two connecting wires instead of three; it allows for finer control over the current by changing the amount of resistance.

952. **B. push-to-break switch**

The symbol represents a push-to-break switch, which, when activated, will power off the circuit.

953. **B. cell**

The symbol represents a cell, which supplies voltage.

954. **D. antenna**

The symbol represents an antenna, which is a device designed to receive or transmit radio signals.

955. **B. capacitors**

A *capacitor* is a passive two-terminal electrical component used to store energy in an electric field.

956. **B. neutral and ground wires only**

The U.S. National Electrical Code mandates only the neutral wire (white or gray) and the ground (green, green with a yellow stripe, or bare copper). The other wires tend to have common-knowledge use (such as red and black for "hot" wires).

957. **C. outlet**

The symbol represents an electrical outlet, which indicates where electronics can be plugged into a circuit.

958. **B. cathode**

The symbol represents a cathode — an electrode through which electrical current exits a polarized electrical device.

959. **B. capacitors**

Capacitors store electrical charge. A capacitor is polarized when charge can flow through the capacitor in only one direction.

960. **C. rheostat**

The symbol represents a rheostat, which is a type of variable resistor that restricts the amount of electrical current.

961. **C.** Mentally rotate the shapes in your mind, keeping track of the points. You find the correct assembly in Choice (C).

962. **A.** Don't be fooled by the mirror image in Choice (B). The correct assembly is in Choice (A).

963. **B.** Take note of the point of intersection in the heart in the question; then match it up with the correct answer, Choice (B).

964. **B.** Be careful not to confuse the correct answer, Choice (B), with the similar but mirrored objects in Choice (A).

965. **C.** Don't let the mirrored objects and placement of points in the other choices confuse you. Choice (C) is the only one with everything in the right place.

966. **C.**  Choice (C) is the only one that shows the correct intersection point for point B.

967. **A.** Awkward shapes plus mirrored images make this one a little tricky, but when you look at the points and the positions of the images, you can see that Choice (A) is right.

968. **A.** In order to correctly identify Choice (A), you must make sure to assemble the objects with the correct points of intersection.

969. C. The only answer with the correct intersection points is Choice (C). Watch out for mirrored images in this one!

970. A. Choice (A) correctly assembles the objects because the line from point B intersects the tip of the triangle and connects to point A.

971. C. 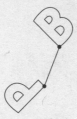 Familiar shapes can make choosing the correct assembly easy, as long as you avoid the mirrored images and incorrect points.

972. A. 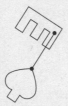 The connecting line must intersect correctly with the E shape to meet point B. Choice (A) is the only one that assembles the objects accordingly.

973. D. This one can get confusing if you don't carefully observe the mirrored images and points of contact, but Choice (D) reflects the correct assembly.

974. C. Keep in mind the points of contact and the locations of the small circles, and Choice (C) will stand out as the correct answer.

975. D.  Choice (D) is the only answer that shows the right intersection between the circle and *L*-shaped object.

976. B.  Choice (B) shows the only assembly in which the objects aren't mirrored and are connected at the appropriate points.

977. C. 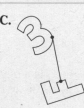 To avoid the mirrored images, you have to direct your attention to the correct answer, Choice (C).

978. C. Locate and connect the correct points for accurate assembly.

979. B. 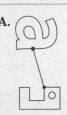 The objects resembling *2* and *N* can be confusing when mirrored. Choice (B) reflects the correct assembly.

980. A. Keeping your eye on the points of assembly and staying clear of any mirrored images, you can see that Choice (A) is connected appropriately.

981. C. 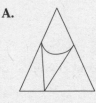 Because the shapes in all the answer choices are similar, figuring out that Choice (C) is correct is hard to do at first glance. But it's the only one with the same exact figures shown in the question.

982. A. Some choices imply that there could be a fourth shape; however, the supposed fourth shape is really just negative space. Studying the shapes closely, you can see that Choice (A) fills the bill.

983. A. 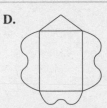 With so many triangles in the first box, you may have a hard time assembling the correct shapes with just your eyes, but if you look for the drawing that has two seemingly *right triangles* (triangles that have 90-degree angles), you see that Choice (A) is right.

984. D. The rectangle in the middle of Choices (C) and (D) is a negative space. You can tell (D) is correct by sizing up the proportions of the three curvy shapes and the triangle.

985. B.   Assemble the quadrilaterals and triangles into the octagon in Choice (B), and you're good to go!

986. D.   At first glance, you may wonder how the three shapes could make a circle. But when you size up the proportions of each individual shape, you see that Choice (D) fills the bill.

987. B.   Counting out the shapes and identifying the right proportions help you see Choice (B) as your shining star.

988. C.   Two overlapping triangles, as shown in Choice (C), are made up of three shapes — two triangles and one quadrilateral.

989. A.   Awkward shapes can make it difficult to mentally piece together multiple objects with the correct proportions. Don't be distracted by the shapes. Notice the proportions and lines in relation to one another. Make sure each element in the question appears in your answer.

990. B.   The three quadrilaterals and one triangle are correctly assembled in Choice (B).

991. B. The rectangle that looks like a door is a negative shape in each of the drawings, but the shapes are correct only in Choice (B).

992. D. The shapes in Choice (D) are assembled to reflect the shapes in the first box. You can tell by noticing the two right angles and the proportions of each curve.

993. B. 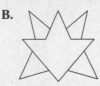 Unusual shapes can be awkward to dissect, but Choice (B) reflects the correct assembly. It has the right number of shapes in the right proportions.

994. A. By mentally piecing the shapes together, you can see that Choice (A) is the real deal here. The other options don't reflect the shapes shown in the first window.

995. A. The two triangles and two rectangular bars are proportionately accurate in Choice (A).

996. B. You may have incorrectly dismissed Choice (B) as correct because it seems to contain five shapes, but the large, center triangle is really just negative space.

997. D. The correct shape is the heart image in Choice (D); the space in the center is negative.

998. B. The three triangles and one quadrilateral are correctly assembled in Choice (B), because the shapes are the same size and proportion as those shown in the question.

999. A. Choice (A) is the only answer with one square and two equal quadrilaterals.

1,000. B. 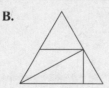 The rectangle in the center of Choice (B) is a negative shape, and the surrounding shapes accurately portray the correct assembly.

1,001. B. The four triangles are correctly assembled only in Choice (B).

Index

About the Author

Rod Powers joined the Air Force in 1975, fully intending to become a spy. He was devastated to learn that he should've joined the CIA instead because the military services don't have that particular enlisted job. Regardless, he fell in love with the military and made it both a passion and a career, retiring with 23 years of service. Rod spent 11 of those years as an Air Force first sergeant, helping to solve the problems of the enlisted corps.

Since his retirement from the military in 1998, Rod has become a world-renowned military careers expert. Through his highly popular U.S. Military Information website on About.com (http://usmilitary.about.com), Rod has advised thousands of troops about all aspects of U.S. armed forces career information. *1,001 ASVAB Practice Questions For Dummies* is Rod's sixth military book. Some of Rod's previous books — *ASVAB For Dummies, Veterans Benefits For Dummies, ASVAB AFQT For Dummies,* and *Basic Training For Dummies* — were also published by Wiley.

Rod is the proud father of twin girls, both of whom are enjoying successful careers in the Air Force while also being amazing wives and mothers. Rod is enjoying his role of grandpa to two new grandsons and one beautiful granddaughter. He currently resides in Daytona Beach, Florida, where he is attempting to prove that there's no such thing as too much sunshine.

Even today, Rod tries to run his life according to long-lived military ideals and standards, but he gets a bit confused as to why nobody will obey his orders anymore.

Dedication

This book is dedicated to my new grandsons! Welcome to the world, Marco and Connor! Of course, I can't go without mentioning my granddaughter, Princess Milani! Grandpa loves you all! A special shout-out to Charisa Raine. You can support the efforts of the Angelman Syndrome Foundation by visiting www.angelman.org.

Author's Acknowledgments

First and foremost, I offer my most sincere gratitude, appreciation, and respect to our nation's veterans and those currently serving in our armed forces. Without your sacrifices, dedication, and loyalty to our country, this book, and any freedom of expression, would not be possible.

Many thanks to my local United States Army, Navy, Marine Corps, Air Force, and Coast Guard Recruiting Command for their invaluable information and assistance and for keeping this ol' veteran in the loop!

I am grateful to Autumn McLeod, my right hand (personal assistant), who dotted many of my i's and crossed many of my t's. Thank you for your beautiful work on this book, Autumn!

I am so appreciative of Linda Parker, who provided her expertise in the areas of physics and mathematics.

I am continually grateful to my loyal editor, Barb Doyen, for her consistent encouragement, support, and hard work as my agent and for getting this project off the ground so that it can affect millions of American civilians. Thank you for your experience, wisdom, and service.

I cannot speak of a more amazing editor than Vicki Adang, who has led this project effortlessly with impressive precision and knowledge, and her technical assistants, Angie Papple Johnston and Suzanne Langebartels. Their contributions to this book cannot be overstated.

To Tracy Boggier, I appreciate your consistency, accuracy, and commitment to Wiley.

Overall, this team is dedicated to preparing millions to do well on the ASVAB, and I applaud the efforts of each individual involved as they are consistently dedicated to providing every individual the best possible outcome in joining our armed services.

Publisher's Acknowledgments

Senior Acquisitions Editor: Tracy Boggier

Senior Project Editor: Victoria M. Adang

Copy Editor: Amanda M. Langferman

Senior Copy Editor: Danielle Voirol

Technical Editors: Angie Papple Johnston, Suzanne Langebartels, Patrick Long

Art Coordinator: Alicia B. South

Project Coordinator: Katherine Crocker

Project Manager: Laura Moss-Hollister

Media Developer: ACT360

Illustrator: Precision Graphics

Cover Design: LeAndra Young

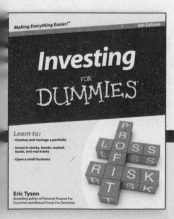

Math & Science

Algebra I For Dummies,
2nd Edition
978-0-470-55964-2

Anatomy and Physiology
For Dummies,
2nd Edition
978-0-470-92326-9

Astronomy For Dummies,
3rd Edition
978-1-118-37697-3

Biology For Dummies,
2nd Edition
978-0-470-59875-7

Chemistry For Dummies,
2nd Edition
978-1-1180-0730-3

Pre-Algebra Essentials
For Dummies
978-0-470-61838-7

Microsoft Office

Excel 2013 For Dummies
978-1-118-51012-4

Office 2013 All-in-One
For Dummies
978-1-118-51636-2

PowerPoint 2013
For Dummies
978-1-118-50253-2

Word 2013 For Dummies
978-1-118-49123-2

Music

Blues Harmonica
For Dummies
978-1-118-25269-7

Guitar For Dummies,
3rd Edition
978-1-118-11554-1

iPod & iTunes
For Dummies,
10th Edition
978-1-118-50864-0

Programming

Android Application
Development For Dummies,
2nd Edition
978-1-118-38710-8

iOS 6 Application
Development For Dummies
978-1-118-50880-0

Java For Dummies,
5th Edition
978-0-470-37173-2

Religion & Inspiration

The Bible For Dummies
978-0-7645-5296-0

Buddhism For Dummies,
2nd Edition
978-1-118-02379-2

Catholicism For Dummies,
2nd Edition
978-1-118-07778-8

Self-Help & Relationships

Bipolar Disorder
For Dummies,
2nd Edition
978-1-118-33882-7

Meditation For Dummies,
3rd Edition
978-1-118-29144-3

Seniors

Computers For Seniors
For Dummies,
3rd Edition
978-1-118-11553-4

iPad For Seniors
For Dummies,
5th Edition
978-1-118-49708-1

Social Security
For Dummies
978-1-118-20573-0

Smartphones & Tablets

Android Phones
For Dummies
978-1-118-16952-0

Kindle Fire HD
For Dummies
978-1-118-42223-6

NOOK HD For Dummies,
Portable Edition
978-1-118-39498-4

Surface For Dummies
978-1-118-49634-3

Test Prep

ACT For Dummies,
5th Edition
978-1-118-01259-8

ASVAB For Dummies,
3rd Edition
978-0-470-63760-9

GRE For Dummies,
7th Edition
978-0-470-88921-3

Officer Candidate Tests,
For Dummies
978-0-470-59876-4

Physician's Assistant Exam
For Dummies
978-1-118-11556-5

Series 7 Exam
For Dummies
978-0-470-09932-2

Windows 8

Windows 8 For Dummies
978-1-118-13461-0

Windows 8 For Dummies,
Book + DVD Bundle
978-1-118-27167-4

Windows 8 All-in-One
For Dummies
978-1-118-11920-4

ⓔ Available in print and e-book formats.

Take Dummies with you everywhere you go!

Whether you're excited about e-books, want more from the web, must have your mobile apps, or swept up in social media, Dummies makes everything easier .

Dummies products make life easier

- DIY
- Consumer Electronics
- Crafts

- Software
- Cookware
- Hobbies

- Videos
- Music
- Games
- and More!

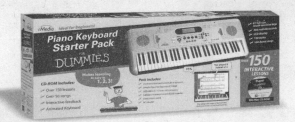

For more information, go to **Dummies.com**® and search the store by category.

FOR
DUMMIES®

A Wiley Brand